Thomas Dunlop

John Tamson's Bairns and other Poems

Thomas Dunlop

John Tamson's Bairns and other Poems

ISBN/EAN: 9783744711425

Printed in Europe, USA, Canada, Australia, Japan

Cover: Foto ©Thomas Meinert / pixelio.de

More available books at **www.hansebooks.com**

JOHN TAMSON'S BAIRNS

AND OTHER POEMS

BY

THOMAS DUNLOP

Edinburgh
ANDREW ELLIOT, PRINCES STREET
1897

IN MEMORY OF

MY FATHER AND MOTHER.

"IN MY FATHER'S HOUSE."

To Life's low bourne they brought me—left me there ;
   They entered in ; I linger on and wait
   In shadow of the cold side of the gate ;
They were a Home to me beyond compare,
Sober, and blissful, and exceeding fair,
   Tho' stained with toil, and shorn of earthly state,
   A House of God for me laid desolate,
Whose ruin'd walls, alas ! find no repair ;
But hope, on him who, leaving childhood's years,
   Learns to be not too wise, but filial more,
Bestows her smiles and intermingled tears,
   And leads him to the Father's open door,
Where things of God unshakable remain,
Whose fitful shadows erstwhile mock'd his pain.

CONTENTS.

JOHN TAMSON'S BAIRNS,	1
THE DIAMOND JUBILEE,	19
RETROSPECT,	22
JOHN BULL AT HIS DEVOTIONS, 1896,	24
THE CENTENARY OF LIFE—NOT DEATH— ROBERT BURNS, JULY 21ST, 1896,	28
ROBIN REDIVIVUS—AN INTERVIEW WITH BURNS,	31
A TWA-HANDED CRACK IN HADES,	35
THE CRAIKIN' CRAW,	38
THE AULD THORN TREE,	42
THE WEE BURN,	46
SYMPATHY,	49
SOUTER WILLIE—AN EPISODE,	50
SAIR HEART,	57
FATHER'S OLD CLOCK,	58
OURISK'S AWA',	65
DISCONSOLATE,	69
TRIUMPHANT,	70
THE AULD WIFE AT THE WHEEL,	72
MOEL FAMMA,	74
GRANDFATHER'S FLUTE,	75
LOVE AND WAR,	76
A VISIT TO CRAIGENDUNTON,	78
EPISTLE—IN CELEBRATION OF THE HALF-JUBILEE OF MINISTERIAL LIFE,	80

CONTENTS.

OLD IMMORTALITY,	87
THE ENDRICK,	101
ODE—ADDRESS TO AN OLD SHOE,	103
DID I DREAM?-	106
AN AUTUMNAL MONODY,	108
JOHN HOWIE, LOCHGOIN,	112
THE UNKNOWN,	113
COMFORT FOR THE BEREAVED—IN MEMORY OF JOHN WEBSTER SMITH,	114
FROM THE GREEK—PRIDE,	115
FROM THE GREEK—ENVY,	116
CHORUS, FROM EURIPIDES,	118
AN AYRSHIRE TRAGEDY,	121
IN MEMORIAM: W. P. PATON,	123
AN OLD BALFRON WORTHY—MICHAEL ROBERTSON, BANKER,	124
DR. JOHN BROWN,	128
GEORGE ELIOT,	130
ALEXANDER MACLEOD, D.D.,	131
WILLIAM HOWIE WYLIE,	132
ISAAC OLIVER JONES,	133
I. O. J.,	135
BISHOP MOULE,	136
WILLIAM PEDDIE, D.D.,	138
A FULL-GROWN MAN—IN MEMORIAM: REV. HUGH STOWELL BROWN,	139
TOO LATE FOR MARTYRDOM: OR TOO SOON,	140
SILVER WEDDING,	141
IN WEST KILBRIDE U.P. CHURCH,	142
A THOUGHT OF SYMPATHY,	145

BREEZE HILL, BOOTLE,	146
RETROSPECT,	156
A REMINISCENCE OF CONTINENTAL TRAVEL,	157
A BIRTHDAY ODE,	161
MEMORABILIA ROMANA :	
THE COLOSSEUM,	162
THE MAMERTINE PRISON,	163
THE EUCALYPTUS,	164
THE CATACOMBS AND ST. PETER'S,	164
THE PANTHEON,	165
THE CARICATURE,	166
THE CRUCIFIXION,	166
THE COMMUNION,	167
THE PILGRIMS,	168
AT SHELLEY'S GRAVE,	168
AT KEATS'S GRAVE,	179
PROVIDENCE,	170
A MEMORABLE DAY,	172
THE LANGUAGE OF FLOWERS — A ROADSIDE ROMANCE,	173
MY FRIEND. MY RESTING-PLACE,	174
AT WORDSWORTH'S GRAVE,	175
A BIRTHDAY IDYL,	176
A BIRTHDAY OFFERING,	177
TEMPUS FUGIT,	178
A NEW-YEAR MEDITATION,	179
AULD YEAR AND NEW,	180
BEN HARDY'S BAIRN,	182
LITTLE NELLY NOBODY,	195
TODDLIN' TAMMIE,	203

CONTENTS.

GAVIN'S BIRTHDAY,	206
INNOCENCE,	210
A GOOD FIGHTER,	211
A MAN OF WEIGHT,	212
MOTHERHOOD,	213
BE STILL,	215
VICTORY,	216
A REVERIE OF THE BEREAVED,	218
HOME-GOING,	220
THE GRACES,	222
A CHILD'S PRAYER,	224
A VISION OF FINAL JUDGMENT,	227
EPHPHATHA,	229
THE VICTORY OF LOVE,	231
SONG OF THE HEBREW MAID,	234
THE SUNBEAM,	237
MAJORITY,	239
FAINTHEARTED,	240
WISDOM FROM BELOW,	242
WAR,	245
THE FLOWERS, AND WHAT THE FLOWERS BEAR WITNESS TO,	246
HYMN OF DEDICATION,	252
LUX IN TENEBRIS,	257
"I WILL NOT LET THEE GO,"	258
PATIENCE,	260
THE WILDERNESS MADE GLAD,	262
THE MYSTERY OF MYSTERIES,	263
MISERERE!	265
NIGHTFALL,	267

DAYBREAK,	269
GRACE,	271
AT THE CHURCH DOOR—ENTERING,	272
AT THE CHURCH DOOR—LEAVING,	273
AT THE THRESHOLD,	274
AT THE COMMUNION,	276
PROPHECY,	278
TRANSFIGURED,	279
PRESENT NEEDS AND PATRIARCHAL MEMORIES,	282
DIVINE SERVICE,	284
SALVATION FOR THE SAVIOUR,	288
THE SMOKING FLAX,	290
LOVE'S ONLY CHOICE,	292
ALLELUIA,	294
A LYRIC OF CHRISTIAN LIBERTY,	296
THE SECRET OF STRENGTH,	298
A LADY'S ADDRESS,	290

JOHN TAMSON'S BAIRNS.

DEDICATION.

To Her who of her palaces hath made
 A Home wherein the lowly Christ might dwell;
And oft, in simple guise, beneath the shade
 Of cottage roof hath found, and loved it well,
A palace richer than her own, arrayed
 With heavenly peace and joy unspeakable—
To Her would I, far off, on bended knees,
Devotion's unskill'd offering, offer these.

I.

Edenic Toil! who would not hope to share
 Thy silken yoke and uncomplaining breast?
No groan from lungs of brass then vex'd the air,
 Nor beads of grime dropt from the brow oppress'd,
Mingling with bread of tears, life's daily fare,—
 More sweet thy labour was than is our rest
When in the calm of Sabbath morn embower'd,
And with the breath of dewy roses dower'd.

II.

John Tamson dwelt in Eden ;—not that place
  Where no sharp weeds bestrewed the velvet floor ;
Where never taint of sorrow marr'd the face ;
  Nor cripple vagrant limped from door to door ;
Nor mossy fields were stoned in deep disgrace ;
  Nor naked feet by frosts were bitten sore ;
It stood—still stands—apart from Scripture story,
Somewhere not far from Fife, or Tobermory.

III.

On lawful days a cobbler's craft he plied
  At open door, close by the babbling street ;
With cunning art well-spent on brutish hide
  He gave heroic help to human feet,—
Thence well prepared, whatever might betide,
  To wade thro' bloody fields, or blustering sleet,
To tread the snow-drift, leap the moorland hag,
Or tempt the frowning brows of mountain crag.

IV.

He was not old, but he had crossed the line
  Which bounds the middle stream from farther shore ;
Neighbours could see his "croon" begin to shine,
  And how the sable hair was tinged with hoar ;
He thumped his knee, and rax'd the resinous twine
  (Himself well knew) less bravely than before ;
And oft would pause and gaze on passers-by
With weary, wistful, unperceiving eye.

V.

Yet was he blessed sevenfold in gentle wife,
  Of stature small, but with enshrinéd soul
Just large enough to grace a lowly life,
  And clasp the earth in love from pole to pole ;—
If Thought means Power and tears can hinder strife,
  Kings felt but did not know her sweet control ;
Not less from cottage than Cathedral chair
God hears the wrestling spirit's inwrought prayer.

VI.

These two were mated years past three times ten,
  Each to the other's changeless full content ;
Blithesome they took their little " but and ben,"
  And there in frugal peace their days were spent,
Near by the echoing murmurs of the glen
  Where once their lover's troth to heaven was sent,
And carrier angels came with glad accord
To bless their honest toil, their bed and board.

VII.

Humble their cares and small their household stock,
  Simple and few, yet of substantial kind,—
Plain dresser, chest of drawers, the eight-day clock,
  Meal-kist and bookcase, food for frame and mind ;
Cupboard of curious wares, a dainty flock
  That shyly peep'd from crystal doors behind ;
Cat and canary—cage with muslin frill ;
Flower-pot with moss-rose on the window-sill.

VIII.

The Bible foremost, undisputed lord,
  To whom all else paid reverential due;
Not least, a rusty basket-hilted sword
  Which some brave hand for God and Covenant drew;
Next, the broad stool whereon the cobbler bored
  And beat the pliant leather old and new;—
And rocking-cradle, that need rock no more,
Not in dishonour laid behind the door.

IX.

Within a score of summers, one by one
  Nine bairns had come to fill that downy nest;
Three died ere yet their infant days had run;
  One at the Cape, two dwelt in the Far West;
A maid who saw her bridal year begun
  Had kirkyard gowan's growing on her breast
Before it closed; a sailor lad was drown'd;
Another lost and searched for—never found.

X.

In Israel's palmy age no godly seed
  Was ever rear'd with holier fear than they;
Was earlier taught that God was God indeed,
  Guardian of human frailty night and day,
Whence they might look for help in time of need,
  Whom only serve, on whom alone might stay;
And when the righteous cause was in the field
Might staunchly die, but neither spare nor yield.

XI.

The Sabbath came, for pleasure not their own ;
    Benignant angel from Jehovah sent,
To salve the eyes, and move the heart of stone
    With thankfulness, and love, and pure intent ;
That seed of life might not in vain be sown,—
    So to their Hill of Zion forth they went
In clean attire, and of the little band
Not one drew near to God with empty hand.

XII.

Not one sat listless in the House of Prayer,
    The high-back'd pew, familiar family nook ;
Mother, well-pleased, would smooth her lambkin's hair,
    And scent the fragrant leaf that mark'd her book ;
Nor would the boys, from love and reverence, dare
    To tempt the solemn father's side-long look ;
God spake, and all alike felt wholesome dread
What might befall to callous heart or head.

XIII.

Incense more free and holier still would rise
    When John and she, the priestess of the hearth,
Each day renewed their fireside sacrifice,
    And worshipp'd God with mingling fear and mirth ;—
Like Jacob's ladder lifted to the skies,
    So did the aspiring soul surmount the earth,
To drink unspoken joy at heavenly springs
Amid sweet odours waft by angels' wings.

XIV.

The floor swept clean, as tho' for Christ's own feet;
  No sloven attitude, nor thing mislaid;
Each child well knew, with face most gravely sweet,
  The very fly, if buzzing noise it made,
Would be rebuked when father took his seat
  And took the Book, and sang, and read, and prayed;
And so God's blessing caught them on their knees—
How strong the nation built of homes like these!

XV.

Alas! this pious home was vacant now
  Of chattering voices and of children's cares;
A silent sadness on the cobbler's brow
  Long since had settled almost unawares.
Most kind was she who shared his nuptial vow
  And proud parental joy that once was theirs;
But love will sooner stay the sunset sheen
Than brighten hope with bloom that might have been.

XVI.

At eve one day of wet and wintry breeze
  John sat demurely at the Book and read
"Whoso shall give to drink to one of these;"
  Just then a bairnly voice broke in and said,
"Help a puir wean the nicht, mem, if you please;"
  The pleading of a beggar boy for bread.
He tried the latch, by rarest chance not fast,
Peep'd in, his eyes with recent tears o'ercast.

XVII.

Up rose the cobbler's wife, his gentle Ann,
  Took in the boy and said, "What brings ye here
In sic a nicht sae late, my puir wee man?"
  "My mither's dead," said he with gathering tear;
"I'm cauld and hungry and my name is Dan;
  My mither's dead and gane this mony a year."
"But wha's your faither,—you're no left your lane?"
"My faither, mem! oh, please, I ne'er had nane."

XVIII.

"Nae faither!" and she eyed the little elf,
  The while her bosom heaved with strange desire.
With a shrewd glance at John, her other self,
  She set the boy to dry before the fire,
Syne rax'd a barley bannock from the shelf;
  "Hae, lad, nae better does a king require;"
So whilst the lad consumed this kingly fare
They spent the interrupted hour of prayer.

XIX.

Oh, saddest in a child! a worn, sad face
  Had Dan, but haply nothing to forbid;
No infant crimes had there their nursing-place,
  Nor crafty glance was lurking 'neath the lid;
His very rags had tongues to plead his case
  In such a home as this—and so they did.
John's voice groan'd deep, with burden'd soul oppress'd:
"God of the fatherless, Thou knowest best!"

XX.

The Book laid by, the cobbler then began
    To ask him whose he was and whence he came;
But this did sore perplex our little man—
    He did not know, and he was not to blame.
His memory could reach no further than
    A place beyond the sea he called his hame—
A darling mother who had clasped him there,
Patted his dimpled cheek and stroked his hair.

XXI.

That night, with no begrudging hand, they spread
    A woolly couch for weary Dan to sleep;
Kind sleep! the poor man's Paradise!—his bed
    Of roses balmed with slumbers soft and deep,
Where thorn is not, where never tear is shed—
    The gate whereat so many wail and weep;
But few of all the jewelled throng pass in
To ease them of their pleasures and their sin.

XXII.

Ye who by honest labour win your crust,
    And ye who beg it (now more seldom found
Honest as well), because, alas! ye must,—
    Know that your brows with golden peace are crown'd,
Whilst Kings are bare, tho' cringing in the dust—
    For you, sweet rills of sleep-provoking sound
Flow evermore in Nature's vale of rest,
And rise the dreamless mansions of the blest.

XXIII.

Dan dropt asleep; beside him lingered long
   The woman's wakeful eye and brooding heart;
His tartan breeks had suffer'd fearful wrong;
   No good Samaritan the healing art
Applied more deft to make the feeble strong
   Than she, with thread and needle, did her part
For that dear Master whom her task might please:
It may be done, thought she, to "one of these."

XXIV.

Beneath His guiding hand she clipped and sewed,
   Her house His home, her toil a sacrament;
The Christ had come into her mean abode—
   It was His garment's hem o'er which she bent,
And by the touch a healing virtue flowed,
   A saving health to heart and finger sent;
And through her spirit swept such wondrous thrill
As High Priest yearly felt on Zion's hill.

XXV.

By chance, some shred of crumpled paper fell;
   She looked, and turned away, and looked again;
What might it be, how dropp'd she could not tell;
   A while it lay, she eyed it now and then;
At last she took it up and searched it well,—
   A printed leaf, and scratched with ink and pen;
And lo! some hair within the inmost fold,
Two tiny locks, one black, and one like gold.

XXVI.

She gazed on these and on the slumbering child,—
  A stony gaze, as tho' her soul had fled ;
A long time gazed, whilst many a fancy wild
  Flew far and near, with living folk and dead ;
She frowned, she sighed, she all but wept, she smiled,
  A sudden start, she rose, and reached the bed
Where John a good hour since had lain and slept,—
She had a secret that might not be kept.

XXVII.

He woke ; he took the relics in his hand ;
  Viewed them with care, with wonderment not less
Than she ; anon the printed leaf he scann'd ;
  'Twas from the Bible, nor unlike the dress
That had concealed it, tatter'd, worn, and tann'd,—
  What might it mean, not he nor she could guess,
But words of God scarce absent from his mind
One waking hour, were there, and underlined.

XXVIII.

" I waited,"—long had served this patient man,
  Motto whereby he toiled, and hoped, and thrived ;
Thro' all his loss and lingering griefs it ran,
  From Holy Writ and jubilant Psalm derived,
Whence courage comes to hands that nothing can,
  And strength to hearts of every hope deprived ;—
The words were these : " I waited patiently,
And He to me inclined and heard my cry."

XXIX.

Swift as the clans by chieftain's clarion wake;
   As fluttering wings by crack of huntsman's gun;
As when a stone disturbs the placid lake;
   As rippling songsters greet the rising sun,—
So did old echoes of remembrance break
   On John afresh, with gladness full, or none,
When by the sacred word which marked this leaf
Past years rushed back; and one bright day in chief:

XXX.

It was the day when Rab, his youngest child,
   A clever lad, well-grown, sweet-natured, good,
And wise, left home, and every prospect smiled;—
   There was a spot within a wayside wood
Where sire and son the parting hour beguiled
   With blessings hardly breathed but understood;
Their words were few, that sacred word the last,--
Rab wept, and vowed that he would hold it fast.

XXXI.

So parted they; and many a look behind
   Each to the other gave, till lost to view;—
Ah me! the frequent letters soon declined;
   They could but murmur there was nothing new;
And then the lad slipp'd off where none could find;
   The old folks' joys thereafter had been few,
Save in the grace that by the Saviour's Cross
Might still prove more than victor over loss.

XXXII.

'Twas so this night; they both with chastened heart
  Quite melted o'er the old familiar name;
Their heads had long the grey that griefs impart,
  And now the cheek anew was flush'd with shame;
What crime can make a mother's love depart?
  "Puir Rab," said Ann, "he should hae stayed at hame."
"We'll wait," quoth John, "we'll trust the laddie's vow;
We kenna what God's will may bring, nor how."

XXXIII.

Faith sowed the seed, and Hope went forth to reap
  Harvests of joy from the well-watered lands:
But when she saw "wild oats" instead of wheat
  She strewed her head with dust and wrung her hands;
So did old Jacob leave, with fretful feet,
  The promised soil, and tread the alien sands,
Nor knew nor hoped his father's God would save
His hoary head from an unhallowed grave.

XXXIV.

Now when the kindly tear had soothed her grief
  Ann laid, with one more look, the slips of hair,
As on God's breast, within that guardian leaf;
  She had a secret drawer, she laid it there;
She turned to Dan: "Gude kens thou art nae thief;
  And in His ain braw time He'll mak' it bare."
"We've seen young hearts," quoth John, "made hard as airn."
"We'll dae our best, guidman—we'll keep the bairn!"

XXXV.

And at the cobbler's hearth from day to day
   This poor lost lamb was folded, nursed, and fed;
Ofttimes the minister was heard to say
   He was a wondrous boy for heart and head;
And when the "master" pursed his quarter's pay,
   "That lad will be a bishop yet," he said;
Ann too that vision had which brightest gleams
In every Scottish peasant's pious dreams.

XXXVI.

Ten times has Winter made the beech tree bare
   Whose stalwart form beside her cottage stood;
Ten times the throstle's young high-nested there
   Have raised their clamorous heads and gaped for food;
The kirk-bell rings, and to the House of Prayer
   Eden ascends devoutly, as it should;
The bell has ceased; the preacher takes his place;
An anxious awe broods in his pale young face.

XXXVII.

It was our Dan; and many strangers drew
   To hear his first "discoorse" for many a mile;
Among the rest, more obvious to the view,
   A kilted soldier strode along the aisle;
He sat him down in the old cobbler's pew,
   And in the good man's face he gazed awhile;
But at the wee auld wife—for she was there—
A glance he threw as tho' he hardly dare.

XXXVIII.

"I waited" was the text; when he began
    The preacher trembled, but he soon grew bold;
He spoke of hope in trickling rills that ran
    Thro' seer and psalmist in the days of old;
How patient Mercy waits on guilty man;
    How Grace can bring the lost sheep to the fold;
And home, long desolate, rings with joyful sound:
"My son was dead—was lost, and now is found!"

XXXIX.

In stillness rapt and reverential fear
    They heard; they gazed; they saw his visage glow;
Spell-bound, entranced; they felt that Presence near
    Who treads unseen the sacred courts below,
And salveth unused eyelids with the tear
    Of saintly joy or penitential woe;
Thankful, they drew a deep breath at the close;
Then, with the unction of his blessing, rose.

XL.

When now the murmuring throngs retook their way,
    And spoke in solemn speech their soul's delight,
The stranger said, "Gudeman, you aiblins may
    Give an old soldier quarters for the night;
I hoped to rest at home this Sabbath-day—
    The road was long, nor is my burden light."
"My cot is there," said John, "and nane e'er saw
The puir man or the stranger turned awa'."

XLI.

In twilight's lone sad hour he breathed the story
  That marr'd his fair young life with rueful strains;
And how he fought for Britain's gain or glory
  The turban'd tribes on Indian hills and plains;
What years had pass'd, unsmiling years and gory,
  Since first he followed to the bagpipe strains;
How often Scotia's onset swept the field,
And Sikh and Afghan like the drunkard reel'd.

XLII.

"But War's wild din," he cried, "to me was less
  Than Love's deep woes, for I had woo'd and wed—
My wife! my child! whom, if he lives, Heaven bless!
  We parted—met no more—I fought, I bled—
They knew not mine, nor I knew their distress;
  I was a captive long—they thought me dead—
God help! whose comfort is where needed most—
The mother pined and died—the child was lost!"

XLIII.

"The preacher's text 'I waited,'" murmured John;
  "'Tis in my heart," the soldier cried, "not here;"
He showed his Bible where the leaf had gone;
  Told how his wife once gave, for parting cheer,
Two locks—like jet, like yellow gold they shone—
  Her own hair and the child's; he held them dear,
Dear as the Scripture page he loved the best;
Enfolded there, she sewed them to his vest.

XLIV.

He bore them far, thro' many fields of strife;
　He lay a-dying long, nor knew what pass'd,
Nor where the trifles treasured more than life;
　And when from death-like wounds he woke at last—
But now, ere he had ceased, the cobbler's wife
　Drew from the secret place which held them fast
The leaf, the tufts of hair with silk entwin'd—
He looked, he stared on them like one stone-blind.

XLV.

She told how in his rags the little man
　Had brought them, as it seemed, across the sea;
"Your bairnie's name?" she asked him; "was it Dan?"
　To's feet he sprang and cried, "'Twas he! 'twas he!"
While down his hardy cheek the tear-drop ran;
　Living or dead, where might his darling be,
Thrice in one breath he pled with them to say.
"Patience," quoth John, "you heard him preach to-day."

XLVI.

Then Dan, for he was there and heard it all,
　Flew to his father's heart and firm embrace;
And oh! how sweetly then did love recall
　The sainted mother in the youth's pale face!
She knew that God, should hapless times befall,
　Would lead the shorn lamb to a sheltered place;
The vest, torn from her soldier's wounded side,
She found it, shaped it for his child—and died.

XLVII.

She died, nor did her last hope seem to fail;
   One friend—for friends not absent were, tho' few—
A kindly captain, heard the orphan's tale;
He thought the father's kindred once he knew
Whither his good ship soon was bound to sail.
   The ship went down, the home port full in view,
And he, the surly billows long had braved,
Was lost. His charge, the orphan child, was saved.

XLVIII.

And in that town, washed by the salt sea spray,
   The little stranger, friendless and alone,
A vagrant woman kept in such rude way
   As might by loose sobriety be shown;
From scanty store in wallet day by day
   His bread she doled, who mostly begged her own.
Poor wastrel boy! half-homeless, till at last
Blown to the cobbler's hearth by God's rough blast.

XLIX.

Then said the stranger to the aged pair:
   "Our God is just, and wonders He hath done;
The curse I brought, by His decree I bare;
   My sins of youth have found me one by one;
And now prevails the long parental prayer—
   My name is Rab, and I was once your son."
He tried, and tried again, but could no more;
Love could but speak with tears at Mercy's door.

L.

It might not be in human words to tell
　　The love that overflowed and would not cease;
Ann's joy ran from her eyelids like a well,
　　Crime could not crush, but made her love increase;
And when at worship on their knees they fell,
　　"Fain would I now," cried John, "depart in peace!
Wait on the Lord! I waited patiently,
And He to me inclined, and heard my cry!"

LI.

Not far had they, thro' mists of coming years,
　　This aged Simeon and his spouse, to go;—
In that still place where Love her tribute rears
　　To souls above and slumbering dust below,
Two often stand, and in their tranquil tears
　　The lingering rays of sunset sweetly glow;
Then drooping Night, and to their lifted eyes,
The jewell'd gates of opening Paradise!

THE DIAMOND JUBILEE.

I.

Our noble Queen!
Gentle and true
Lady, whose sceptred hand
Waves over sea and land;
None worthier to command
    The race of Man e'er knew;
    Nor Fame's keen eye hath seen
A happier lot betide
Monarch, more loved, more tried
Than thou, our Empire's pride—
        Our Queen!

II.

Our noble Queen!
In maidenhood
Sweetest and tenderest,
Truth-girt and Beauty-drest,
Brightest among the best
    Where all were pure and good,
    The tire of circling sheen
Came to bedeck thy brow,
Illustrious then, but now
Its rarest jewel thou—
        Our Queen

III.

Our noble Queen!
Full sixty years
Since then their work have done;
Countless the triumphs won;
Thy regal task, begun
    With trembling and with tears,
    Nobly achieved hath been;—
Hail! Diamond Jubilee!
God of the brave and free
Still bless and prosper thee—
        Our Queen!

IV.

Our noble Queen!
High, humble, wise,
Great-soul'd amongst the great;
The right Hand of the State;
At many a cottage-gate
    Bending to sympathise;
    A sister to the mean
On Grief's low sanded floor,
Wafted from shore to shore
The woman's heart she bore—
        Our Queen!

V.

Our noble Queen!
From East and West,
What symphonies are these
Borne on Atlantic breeze,
From Australasian seas,

From Himalayan crest,
From Tropic islands green,
Indian and Afric plains,—
Strong-voiced Imperial strains—
Belov'd, she lives, she reigns—
   Our Queen!

VI.

Our noble Queen!
With one accord
The far-off lands make haste
Over the billowy waste,
With welcome greetings graced!
 Men of the pen and sword,
 Of high or humble mien;
 All Arts their tribute send;
Hard Toil, high Thought attend—
Their sovereign and their friend—
   Our Queen!

VII.

Our noble Queen!
In noble deeds
Would we embalm her name,—
That flowers of sweetest fame,
Outvie'd, might sink for shame
 And rank with merest weeds;—
 Our God, on whom we lean!
Till endless years have flown
Bright be the spotless throne,
And she still proudly known—
   Our Queen!

RETROSPECT.

That day will no proud heart forget
    Who saw it rise and set ;
Clear dawn, bright noon, and blissful eve
    So loth to take her leave ;
The sky, the cloud, the sun's warm ray,
    Themselves kept holiday ;
Her regal bounty Nature sent
    In every element,
To bless with unexampled smiles
    Our gay green-mantled isles ;
June's loveliest waving on the trees,
    Her sweetest in the breeze ;
One voice, one mighty song it bore,
    Swelling from shore to shore ;
One prayer laid at the Throne unseen :
    God save our gracious Queen !

Herself to the high Temple came
    In her great Sovereign's name,
To own the ever-during Sway ;
    Her humble thanks to pay.

On, on thro' the tumultuous roar
    Which million voices pour ;
Amid the dinsome trumpet's blare ;
    Girt by the brave and fair ;
Led by the pride of prancing steeds
    In Honour's antique weeds ;

With tramp of men whose feet had trod
    Antipodean sod,
Cape veldt, the swamps where Niger flows,
    Hot plains and Indian snows;
Sons whom Canadian forests knew,
    Foremost amongst the true;
Homage by every kindred paid,
    Of every sunburnt shade;—
On, on she came with joyous peal,
    Thro' serried ranks of steel.

Soft jewell'd hands, wave after wave,
    Their myriad greeting gave;
The brighter flash from fair eyes given,
    Like stars new-dropt from heaven;
And those that wept whilst looking on
    With mellowed lustre shone.

She, welcome rest for every eye,
    Her own could not keep dry;—
Not now, when at His Temple gate
    She and her people wait,—
Praise rising to the King of Kings
    On far out-spreading wings.

Then had the sacred moment come;
    The murmuring hosts were dumb;
Stillness divine that moment reigned—
    Held every soul enchained;

The head bowed down, the drooping eyes,
　　Witnessed her sacrifice;
Thanks offered to the Sovereign Good,—
　　An Empire's gratitude;
The solemn vow, the meek request,
　　In her, for all the rest:
Thee, Lord of Love, Thy subjects bless,—
　　Thou King of Righteousness!
Long as Thou reignest Prince of Peace,
　　Our power thro' Thine increase!

JOHN BULL AT HIS DEVOTIONS, 1896.

I. From the Continental point of view.

Great Being, with supernal powers
More just and loftier still than ours,
Afar from Thy rose-mantled towers,
　　　　See'st Thou what's passin',
Where 'neath the waning crescent cowers
　　" The Great Assassin?"

For that most fit and gruesome name
We give him thanks who shares Thy claim,
And humbly owns Thy greater fame,
　　　　Our sainted Will'em;—
For slaughtered hosts, what hellish blame
　　When we don't kill 'em!

Badger the Turk! heed not his cries!
The meek Armenian bombs baptise,

Soft-swaddling them with Christian lies
        As with a garment,—
Should he the crafty Greek despise,
        Root out the varmint!

Once on a day, we must confess,
We clasp'd our Turk with fond caress;
In his behoof we bore the stress
        So grim and gory;
The butchery done, as Thou might'st guess,
        For England's glory!

Hang me this European pottle
Of heads, save ours, not worth a dottle,
Where each his neighbour fain would throttle,
        Tho' sweet as honey!
Give John his Bible and his bottle,
        And shoals of money!

With leave all else on earth to trample,
He shall Thee praise both loud and ample,
And lend Thee many a swatch and sample
        Out of his stores,—
If Thou but let him rowte and rample
        Like beast on fours!

Hear how Thy slumbering Zion wakes,
While shepherds ply their crooked stakes!
Thy chosen flock such bleating makes—
        Hast Thou not felt it?
The heart no high-swung hammer breaks,
        This plaint would melt it!

Make Russ and German fight and tumble;
Heed not the fiery Frenchman's grumble;
Let "Cock-a-doodle" funk and fumble,
    Our Yankee brothers,—
We are Thy people, meek and humble,
    Confound all others!

II. From the Patriotic point of view.

Oh Thou, to whom our thanks we raise,
More worthy than our worthiest praise,
Whose hand upholds the heavens, and sways
    Their dark mutations,—
Whom the whole suppliant world obeys,
    Thou God of Nations!

Gird us with Truth; our souls beguile
From every motive mean and vile;
Bless with the sunbeams of Thy smile,
    In mercy shed;
Let the proud waves that guard our isle
    Still keep Thy tread!

Our hearts with love, our homes with peace,
Our stores with righteousness increase,
Our haggard poor bless with release
    From want and grime;
The scowl of Discontentment cease,
    And rankling Crime!

Let lowly Worth, unshackled now,
Lift unabashed her modest brow,—

Let Freedom, loos'd from Mammon's vow,
        And sordid Ease,
Drive thro', with keen industrial plough,
        Waste lands and seas!

Guide Thou our guardians of the State;
Thy fear within our Temples wait;
With the pure aims that scoffers hate
        Our Press empower;
And should we perish—make us great
        In Ruin's hour!

Oh! keep us blameless in Thy sight;
Clothe us with honour and with might;
Quick to relieve and slow to smite,
        The wide world o'er—
A safeguard and a beacon light
        From shore to shore!

Our nation be the Friend in Need
When tyrants rage and subjects bleed,
For all who suffer by the greed
        Of lust or gold—
A Good Samaritan indeed,
        Like him of old!

From civil strife defend our sod;
Never by foreign foe be trod;
Our armour Thine, our feet well shod
        With peace always;
Our bulwark still the Book of God,
        As in past days!

THE CENTENARY OF LIFE—NOT DEATH.

Robert Burns, July 21st, 1896.

I.

Not thine, beloved Minstrel! foremost, best
   Of all whom Love holds captive at her feet,
   Nor ours, the doleful mood, when thee we meet
Where once thy mortal woes were laid to rest;—
With smiles we greet thee, a perennial guest
   In pure Affection's most familiar seat,
   Mellifluent Burns! Yet not too sweetly sweet,
Not over-coy thy Muse, nor over-dress'd;—
With smiles, with evermore transcendent mirth,
   Thee, happy Bard! most fortunate of men,
On this proud day that hail'd thy better birth,
   Unnumber'd souls whom thou hast charm'd since then
And all those hundred years, a choral throng,
Sing whilst they share thy heritage of song!

II.

I who, long since, and in my native air,
   While yet a child, thy witching wood-notes found;
Whose sires beside thee toil'd and till'd the ground,
And children to their children would declare
What bursts of human joy when Burns was there,
   As at the evening hearth we gathered round,
   Or where the loom shot forth its clickering sound,—
No breast so cold but would the rapture share,—
I knew thou would'st not scorn the little rill

With moist kiss making glad the moorland heath;
Nor would " wee modest flower " with crimson frill,
　　Thought I, be absent from thy floral wreath;
So this poor reed its tribute too would raise
While great ones yield their trumpet-blasts of praise!

III.

None else but thee could win the world's great heart;
　　Not Homer, nor the polished Mantuan swain;
　　Nor he who tuned his lyre to endless pain;
Nor high surmounting Shakespeare far apart;
Nor mighty organ-peal of Milton's art;
　　Nor those Lake-showers of soul-refreshing rain,
　　Sir Galahad, and all his silken train
Of lady-lords: in college, kirk, and mart
Thee have they crowned the worthiest of men
　　To draw all hearts as tho' they were but one;—
Like some frank maid in dewy hawthorn glen,
　　So shall the world, while countless ages run,
Clasp thee with fonder arms—not asking why—
With ever-smiling cheek and tearful eye.

IV.

Thy song a Benediction breathed on men
　　Who dare do right, and dare not but be free,—
　　That man to human-kind might human be;
Might spare the "timorous beastie's" lowly den,
And strike with truth-anointed sword or pen
　　Tyrant and rogue of mean or high degree,
　　And crook-knee'd hypocrite; oh! but for thee,

Thou fearless Voice, we soon had drooped again
Where only Flood might quench or fire consume ;—
   Well might False Faith revile thee, whilst the True
Thou summoned like a dead saint from the tomb,
   In light and love to walk the earth anew,
Nor vainly cast, where'er her altars rise,
Fresh incense on the pure heart's sacrifice !

V.

Thine was the martyr-soul, enrobed with flame
   As Hebrew Psalmist was, that fervid King
   On Ruin's verge who sat or could not sing,—
In depths of woe the ecstatic vision came,
While passion rent the heart and ruled the frame;
   Whose lyre, like thine, a sweeter note would bring
   When Pain compelled and Sorrow swept the string;
Thy kindred cross will ever link thy name
With his, who both beside the sheepfold grew ;—
' Take, then, the pledge a thankful world bestows,
The cup of "auld acquaintance" ever new,
   The same in Shepherd-Psalm that " overflows ;"
Long as thy laurels live, with his entwined,
Will Hope's great " haggis " reek for all mankind !

VI.

Lone shepherds far away in southern seas
   Enraptured are by Mailie's plaintive moan ;
   By light of whaler's fire in frigid zone
Rides "Tam o' Shanter " madly through the breeze ;
Behold, our " Holy Willie" on his knees
   In Syrian tent ; by sweet-voiced Mendelssohn
Wherever wind may blow is "cauld blast" blown ;

The "Jolly Beggars" in hilarious ease
Join "Holy Fair" beneath the Sphinx's nose ;
　The "ae fond kiss" renewed on every shore ;
More wide than Amazon "sweet Afton" flows ;
　The "banks and braes" are fresh for evermore ;
And strange new tongues the world has not yet heard
Shall sing thee "Auld Lang Syne," Immortal Bard !

ROBIN REDIVIVUS :

AN INTERVIEW WITH BURNS.

Oh ! for a waff o' that snell win'
On Robin's pow "blew hansel in ;"
Love's frolic wild and flustering din,
　　　Unheeded then,
But evermore to dirl and spin
　　　Thro' hearts o' men !

My rhyme it had nae further gane,
While sitting on a brook-side stane,
A busy bumble in my brain,
　　　When, sooth to tell,
There at my elbow, flesh and bane,
　　　Sat Rab himsel'.

He leugh to see me gape and glower,
To see me near-haun whummelt ower,
Wi' draps o' Terror's cauldrife shower
　　　Upon my broo,

To hear my tongue, dry as the stour,
          Click in my mou'.

"Tut, man," said he, "why fidge and reel?
Nae wisp o' strae or pock o' meal
Could harm ye less." Quoth I, "Braw chiel,
          I'm in a swither,
Ye're Robin Burns, or else the Deil,
          Tane or the tither."

"The Deil! and what for no?" cried he;
"If cups o' kindness, twa or three,
Lang syne hae passed 'tween him and me,
          'Twas no his blame;
Unbidden weet aye blins my e'e
          To hear his name.

"And up in yonder bonnie sphere,
They think mair o' the Deil than here;
His wark to keep the causeway clear
          Wi' subtle skill,—
Big souls are they wha can revere
          Baith guid and ill."

"Weel, Rab," quoth I, "ye've lent a haun'
To keep the Cart o' Progress gaun,
Whaur midden holes o' grace wad staun'
          At the kirk door;
And braw folk there, wi' faces thrawn,
          Thou skelpit sore."

"Nae doubt, I've been ower fierce and fell,
Forgetfu' I had fauts mysel',
But whether come frae Heaven or Hell,
   It had to be,
As needless try to curb or quell
    The rowin' sea.

"Seek ye in every neuk and hole
Where sorrows, like the worming mole,
Gnaw deep and rend the quivering soul
    Wi' tooth and claw—
A lowin' heart is sair to thole
    Abune them a'.

"Ere I could sing my wee bit sang,
Oh frien', it cost me mony a pang—
The agony that keepit thrang
    My rhyming noddle;
Nor, house and hainin' a' gaun wrang,
    Cared I a bodle!"

"D'ye mind the lasses?" whispered I.
"Brawly!" he groaned; "I winna lie;
Love's e'e is fain, and never dry;
    And mine, I ween,
Whiles roved for mony mae forbye
    My bonnie Jean."

I saw the blush his cheek displayed;
In glowing e'e a brightening shade;
The tremor on his lip that played—
    "Ha! come what will,

While Rob is Rob, and jade is jade—
  I lo'e them still!"

"Bravo! with a' my heart," I cried,
"The odious prude thou hast defied,
Hypocrisy and holy pride,
    Wi' a' their scunner;
That Lust would tremble at thy side,
    I'd stake a hunner!

"The modest e'e, affection pure,
The honest heart in king or boor,
The hamely sang, the dainty flower
    In yird or field,
The truth that's crushed amid the stour
    And winna yield;

"The cottar wi' his haffets bare
At ingleside in wrestling prayer,
His cattle housed, his bairnies there
    A' gathered roun';
His wee bit sowp o' halesome fare
    When sun gaes doun;

"'Twixt lad an' lass the tender pain,
The cruel rug when toil is vain,
The lingering hope in lover's grane
    That canna be,
The patriot's on the battle plain
    For Liberty;

"The hale braw world, baith but an' ben,
A snug wee house for weary men,
Wi' smiling board an' chimlie en'
      For each and ither,
And ilka chiel, contented then,
      Lo'ed like a brither!

"These, these are they thy sorrows bought,
When for us a' thy *facht* was fought;
What tho' the mead thy bosom sought
      It never cam'?
See! Love has brewed her peck o' maut—
      We'll hae a dram!

"Here's to thee, Rab! ye needna spier
Wha's King o' men, I'll pledge thee here;
A' ither cups are feckless cheer
      Match'd wi' thine ain!"
The tassie I began to rear,
      But—Rab was gane.

A TWA-HANDED CRACK IN HADES.

"Rax me the goblet, worthy crony,"
Quoth Shanter Tam to Souter Johnny,
"I seem na to hae tasted ony
      A towmond maist—
Tho' like yoursel' a skin-and-bony
      Yet drouthy ghaist."

"Weel, Tam, (for guidsake, steek the door!)
Havena we had twal' times galore
O' a' this centenary splore?
   Wha brocht it here,
For me, may let it sleep and snore
   Ten hunner year!

"Puir Rab! they didna mean to hurt,
But oh! they row'd him in the dirt;
Rosie, nae less, roused a' his art
   And did it gran',
As tho' upon a ragman's cart
   He took his stan'."

"Come, Johnny, weet your rusty thrapple;
Wi' higher powers ye needna grapple—
Thank goodness, they hae tint their tattle,
   And rack'd their tethers;
Let wind nae mair their inwards rattle—
   Peace to their blethers!"

"My couthie frien', it gars me grane
To hear them curse, wi' might and main,
Some chiels' apologetic vein
   Ower Rab's auld duddies,
And yet, ten waur, indulge their ain—
   The menseless cuddies!

"Some things there are that fain would dee
Would but the gowkies let them be—

I'm sure nae pleasure it can gie
    But sad mischievin'
To dirt-made chaps like you and me,
    To keep them leevin'.

"Damn'd be that deathless whisky-gill
That anti-moralistic pill,
That pride o' theirs in gabbling skill
    To rake and splutter—
Would you find Rab and comfort still?
    Go, search the gutter!

"Na, na, that airt we winna gang;
We a' a wee thing whiles gae wrang,
Nae doubt; but Virtue's clatterbang
    Will never mend it;
A swatch o' Robin's bonnie sang,
    Nocht else can end it."

"Johnnie, your haun', its rale weel spoken;
This cudgel let me rear in token—
Some heads are hale that should be broken
    Like cockle-shell;—
Come skyward, and our gabs we'll sloken
    Wi' Rab himsel'."

THE CRAIKIN' CRAW.

I.—RETRIBUTION.

A craw sat craikin' on a tree,
    Its leefu' lane, its leefu' lane;
    A callant strack it wi' a stane,—
It wadna flee, it wadna flee;—
    He clamb the tree, he claught the craw,
    An' syne its thrapple he wad thraw,
It wadna dee, it wadna dee;—
    He mauled it weel, he swung it roun'—
It wadna kill, it wadna kill;—
He took it to the miller's mill,
    He grew afeared an' wished it dead,
    He plunged it three times ower the head,
Wi' mony a wicked stroke an' stoun,—
It wadna droun, it wadna droun;—
    To send it hame he tried an' tried,
    " Awa', awa', black beast!" he cried,—
It wadna gang, it wadna gang,
But wi' a sudden skreigh it sprang
    Upon his croun, upon his croun.

Waes me, waes me! it settled there,
    An' naething wad it stir ava,—
    That craikin' craw, that craikin' craw;—
Lang years hae come an' fled since then,
The callant is threescore an' ten,—
    It craiks awa', it craiks awa';

The auld man's heart is unco sair,
    He fain wad hae the craw to flee,—
    That canna be, that canna be ;—
It sits upon his thin grey hair
For evermair, for evermair!

II.—REDEMPTION.

The callant was threescore an' ten,—
He wandered but, he wandered ben ;
    It was a waesome sight to see,
    He tried to live, he couldna dee.
Syne he gaed out, an' syne cam' in,—
O sic a din ! O sic a din !
Guid save us, that it should be sae,
The craw sat craikin' night an' day
    Upon his croun, upon his croun,—
    When he gat up, when he lay doun
It aye was there, it aye was there,
Upon the auld man's thin grey hair ;—
    He tried to greet, he tried to pray,
    But that (waes me !) he couldna dae ;
His tongue wad aye rin owre wi' lees
Whene'er he drappit on his knees,—
    His heart was toom as ony drum,—
He'd gi'en the warld wi' a' its gear
For ae saut tear, for ae saut tear,—
    It wadna come, it wadna come.

Quoth he, "O wad my heart but break !"
Na, na, the craw maun hae its craik ;

He tried to stap his ain auld breath,
Held oot a bluidy haun' to Death,—
   Wi' rape, or at the roarin' linn—
Nae harm was dune, nae harm was dune;
In slippery loops o' hempen tether
He swung as lightly as a feather;
He clamb the craig, an' ower he loupit,
But like a cork nae waur he coupit;
The rowin' flood frae bank to brae
Bore him as bravely as a strae;
Naething he ever met or saw
Could hurt him but that craikin' craw;
An' naewhere wad it haud its blether,
   Gang he into the dinsome street
   Whaur clatterin' beasts an' bodies meet,
Or 'mong the whaups on moorland heather.

Ae night the snaw was on the grun',
The Christmas revels had begun;
But nane had he o' joyous fare,
His heart was wae, his head was sair,
And on his grey pow, warst of a',
That craikin' craw, that craikin' craw.

A weary stranger passin' by,
   Cam' to the auld man's door an' chappit
(The craw it gie'd a gruesome cry,
   Twice ower its twa black wings it clappit).
The auld man shook wi' fear; quoth he,
" Whae'er ye be, whae'er ye be,

Gae wa', gae wa', an' come na here
For ony gude o' Christian cheer."
Then frae the drivin' snaws oot-bye
A voice cam' plaintive in reply :
"Hae mercy, mercy on the puir,—
    A wee bit lowe to dry my claes,
    A fender for my frozen taes,
I want nae mair, I want nae mair."

He rose to let the stranger in,—
The craw it made a desperate din ;
" Deil tak' ye, bletherin' beast ! " he cried,
The sneckit door then opened wide
To gi'e the stranger welcome true,
    But nane was there, but nane was there,
    Only an icy blast o' air
That thrill'd his auld banes thro' an' thro' ;—
    A fearfu' glamour o'er him fell,
    What happened syne he ne'er could tell,—
But something in his heart was new.

The weary craw had craik'd its last,
It flew forth on the bitter blast ;—
The auld man at his ain hearth-stane,
His leefu' lane, his leefu' lane,
Sat doun an' grat thro' a' that night,
Till baith his e'en near lost their sight,
Wi' joy that strack the angels dumb,—
The Christ had come ! the Christ had come !

THE AULD THORN TREE.

On Craigie knowes
An auld thorn grows,—
Lang has it been a frien' to me,
That auld thorn tree, that auld thorn tree,
On Craigie knowes.

Lang syne, lang syne,
I ca'd it mine,
When first that auld thorn tree I saw
Buskin' the green braes far awa',—
Lang syne, lang syne.

A bairn was I,
Thro' wat or dry
Chasin' the bum-bees an' the birdies,
Wearin' my first breeks on my hurdies,—
A bairn was I.

It strack my e'e
Sae winsomely,
I ne'er sin' syne hae seen anither;
I lo'e 't as it had been my mither,—
That auld thorn tree.

Wi' reverent air,
Would I repair
Like ither folk to bare my pow
In the auld kirk on Gallows-knowe,—
Wi' reverent air.

THE AULD THORN TREE.

Frae faither's pew,
The window thro'
On the far knowes that thorn I saw,
Like wee bird's feather faint an' sma',—
Frae faither's pew.

It grew to be
God's priest to me;
It telt me things I shouldna dae;
It made me glad, it made me wae,—
That auld thorn tree.

For its ain sake
I kept awake,
When ither folk sank doun an' sleepit;
My twa blest een aye gleg it keepit,—
For its ain sake.

I dinna ken
But souls o' men
Wad maybe gang the richt road hame,
If they wad keep their een the same, –
I dinna ken.

That auld thorn tree,
It follows me,—
In cities or on loupin' seas
I see it wavin' in the breeze,—
That auld thorn tree.

Absent for years,
I hae my fears,—

THE AULD THORN TREE.

My heart wi' very joy is sair
To find it there, to find it there,—
    Absent for years.

Could I but see
Hope smile on me,
As oft the daybreak on thy crest,
Or the warm crimson frae the west,
    O auld thorn tree!

Could I but trust!
As thou e'en must,
Head-bare in mony a bitter blast,
Shaken, but stronger when it passed,—
    Could I but trust!

Mine let it be,
Thy charity,—
The robins' refuge frae the snaws,
Their wee bit meal o' halesome haws—
    Thy charity.

My thorn, my thorn!
Ae winter morn
The farmer thocht he'd strike the blow,
An' lay thee low, an' lay thee low,—
    My thorn, my thorn!

Quoth I, gude faith!
Let be thy skaith;
Or else thy sapless life and brittle
Snaps like a thread! Lay doun thy whittle!
    Quoth I, gude faith!

THE AULD THORN TREE.

    The honest chiel
    Said, Weel-a-weel,
Syne be it sae, syne be it sae,
Thrive thou and it till Judgment-day!—
    The honest chiel !

    O must thou dee,
    My auld thorn tree?
I'm daunerin' to the hungry mouls,
Like ither fools, like ither fools,—
    O must thou dee?

    Upon my grave,
    Auld thorn, I crave
Some sprout o' thine may e'en let fa'
Thy scented blossoms like the snaw,—
    Upon my grave !

    Maybe, maybe,
    For thee and me,
There is a place in that fair Fauld
Whaur growin' things nae mair grow auld,—
    Maybe, maybe.

    Great Tree o' trees !
    If Thou but please,
Our life shall taintless be like Thine,
Plant of Renown, True Living Vine,—
    Great Tree o' trees !

THE WEE BURN.

Bonnie wee bit wimplin' burnie,
    Warstlin' thro' amang the stanes,
Whumlin' ower at ilka turnie,
    Nane the waur for a' thy pains;
Like a' young things fu' o' daffin',
    Loupin', rowin' doun the brae,—
Bouncin' brawly, greetin', laughin',
    Changefu' like sae mony mae.

How my heart rins doun beside thee,
    Brisk like thine, and fu' o' glee!
A' that ever may betide thee
    Like a trusty freen' to pree,—
Whiles wi' ready tongue gib-gabbin',
    Rantin' rowdily alang;
Whiles in secret slowly sabbin'
    Sorrow's langsyne lanely sang.

Braes a' white wi' saintly gowan,
    Lace o' bonnie birken tree,
Broom wi' yellow fire a' lowin',
    Haud their charms for thee and me,—
Linties wi' their rustic rhymin'
    Lead thee to the hawthorn dell,
Fairy-like the while are chimin'
    Hyacinth and heather-bell.

Whaur the buttercup sae glossy
    Keps the dew's fresh-fallen tears;

THE WEE BURN.

Whaur on dreepin' banks and mossy
    Grasses rise like swords and spears;
Whaur wee minnows, unco happy,
    On thy sunny bosom shine,—
And the laverock drinks its drappie
    O' the best o' heaven-brewn wine.

Ower the linn I see thee linkin'
    Like an arrow frae the bow,—
Yonder sits an auld man thinkin',
    On a muckle stane below :—
And a hare frae hunter fleein',
    'Mang the bracken hirples thro',
Stains thee wi' its bluid, and deein',
    For the last time weets its mou'.

Whan the slow wings o' the gloamin'
    Spread their saftness roun' an' roun',
Up the glen twa lovers roamin'
    Hear thy sang and settle doun ;—
On a tree stump sit thegither—
    He is strong, and she is fair;
O how fain wi' ane anither,—
    And it may be nevermair!

Blythe wee burnie! auld creation
    May nae aulder be than thou;
And the latest generation
    Still may see thee on this knowe!
Mony queer auld-fashioned bodies,
    Worshippin' the sun and mune,

THE WEE BURN.

Here hae met to wash their duddies,
   Or to paint their freckled skin.

Mony Hielan' raids for thievin'
   Back an' for' hae passed thee by :—
Thou their mou's and cloots relievin'—
   Puir wee lambs and muckle kye.
Aft the clans hae made thee muddy
   Wi' their fechtin' might an' main ;
Aften ran thy waters ruddy
   Wi' the life's bluid o' the slain !

Thou hast lang since left behind thee
   Thae unhappy graceless days,
And in thankfu' peace we find thee
   Bubblin' doun the same auld braes ;—
Bairn o' some heath-covered fountain,
   Nursling o' the cloud and breeze,
Fondled by the mist-clad mountain,
   Dandled on its rocky knees !

See ! how sturdy now thou boundest
   On by yonder mossy wheel,
Whaur wi' groanin' mill thou soundest
   Like a very thunder-peal,—
While the miller's daft wee doggie
   Rows upon the bank sae green,
And his wean wi' parritch coggie
   Keps thy jaups, wi' glowerin' een.

On thou flow'st for gentle, simple,
   Close by mony a house an' ha',—

By the clachan inn dost wimple,
   By the kirk-yard's broken wa';—
On till in the silent river
   (Death's cauld flood we a' maun feel)
Thy sweet sang is hushed for ever,—
   Blythe wee burnie, fare-thee-weel!

SYMPATHY.

I heard, amid a group of barefoot boys,
   One urchin say, "This is the lassie's grave;"
And in a moment their shrill-piping noise
   Was hushed. Puir lassie! by the clear crisp wave,
And the bright yestermorn, enticed to gain
   The rapture of a first plunge on the shore;
But ah! the fatal grip of sinewy pain
   Which made thy first the last for evermore!

No help nor witness to thy lingering throes,
   Spent, lonely one! from home and kindred far;
I love thee for thy young life's hapless close;
   To me thou shinest like a sweet sad star;—

With this wee flower, upon the new-laid sod
I drop a tear, and wish thee well with God!

SOUTER WILLIE:

AN EPISODE.

Dark was the night and keen the blast
That blew as it had blawn its last,
And sharply fell the blattering sleet,
Upon the auld man's naked feet,
While in his arms he press'd the bairn
And sought the shelter o' the cairn.

A queer auld carle was Souter Willie,
Clean daft, yet only skin-deep silly ;
O' common prudence he had nane ;
His sense could scarcely stan' its lane ;
Yet gumption had, nae doubt, in plenty
Hadna his neibors been sae scanty :
Denied of Heaven the grace o' thievin',
He made himsel' an honest livin'—
Darning auld bauchles, boots, an' shoon ;
Sair faught had he when a' was dune,
Thro' muckle sweat and weary swither,
To keep his skin an' banes thegither.

Fine shoon he made, but, sooth to tell,
He never wore a shoe himsel',
Close at his wark a' nicht he keepit,
And a' day lang he snor'd an' sleepit ;
'Mid thunder peals and lightning flame,

When ither folk would stay at hame,
Daft body! he would lea' his wark,
And, like a warlock in the dark,
Wi' shoonless feet an' dreepin' duds,
Gang arm in arm wi' rowin' floods;
Or cross the heath for mony a mile,
Croonin' a wee bit sang the while;
Or thro' the storm-struck forest rakin',
While trees like shanks o' pipes were breakin';
Or in some deep untrodden dell
Sit chatterin' to his lanesome sel'.

Auld Souter Willie's heart was guid,
But in an ill-faur'd frame was hid,—
His een were thrawn, his back was humpit,
His croon had never kenn'd a hair,
An auld red nightcap flappit there
While at his wark he rax'd an' thumpit.
His face had ae resplendent feature,
Worn by nae ither man or creature,—
A nose had he o' wondrous power
That micht hae served for three or four,
And wi' as mony hues upon it
As Joseph's coat or Aaron's bonnet.
Shrivell'd and lean, in stature scrimp,
Ae leg was bent, and ane was limp,—
Twa thoombs on ae haun', nane on tither,
His parts were a' reel-ral thegither;
As tho' Mischance, not over nice,
Had fixed them by the cast o' dice.

Dark was the night; the icy blast
Like vengeance on the wing flew past,
While o'er the moorland waste the Souter
Clasping his twa arms tight aboot her,
Fled swiftly with the slumbering bairn
For shelter at the whinstane cairn.

He reached the place, he gasped a prayer,
Stark deid—there was a woman there ;
Half on the stanes, half on the sod,
Her pallid face turned up to God,
As in the moonbeams' watery sheen
Her corse was for an instant seen.

Like timid hare press'd in the chase,
Auld Willie hurried from the place,
Doun the stey braeface o' the glen,
And thro' the " Deil's " ghost-haunted den,
Where midnight gloom and torrent's roar
Never had stirr'd one fear before.
Nor had he known these strange alarms
Save for the treasure in his arms,—
Wee bairn, sair fraucht in time o' need
Betwixt the living and the deid ;
For it, his full heart wished for hame ;
For it, he breathed the Saviour's name,
That the All-merciful and mild
Would yield His wrath and spare the child.

And now he nears the foaming tide,
Which spreads fell ruin far and wide,

On-rushing with a frightful leap
Into the depths, five fathoms deep.
With rolling thunder crowned with spray
The floods are forth on holiday ;
And scarce the Deil himsel' could ken
The wreckage o' his ain dark den.

The timber-brig whereto he sped
Stands firm beneath the auld man's tread.
Alas ! alas ! the hameward shore,
Oft yielding to his touch before,
Will print his living feet nae mair,—
Ae ither step, he had been there,
But sudden came a mighty blast,
And a great oak-tree groaned its last ;
Prone on the tender planks it fell,—
Then rose one weird and desperate yell ;
One moment rose, then all was hush'd,
Only the waters roar'd and gush'd;
O'er-awed by innocence and death,
It seemed the tempest held its breath !

The morning dawned : a dreadful tale
Was wafted over hill and dale ;
In a small nook of mossy ground
The Souter and the bairn were found ;
Among the tangled thorns they lay,—
The flood had washed their souls away ;—
A lifeless bairn on lifeless breast
In deathless agony was press'd.

Up on the moorland's breezy height,
All senseless to the day or night,
Hard whinstanes pillowing her head,
The mother of the babe lay dead.
While now the sun shone on her face,
A lad came whistling to the place,—
He ceased, he stood, he stared, he ran,
More like a greyhound than a man,
And scarcely a full breath he drew
Till the whole vale the tidings knew.

Poor soul ! her story ne'er was told,
Save this, she perished in the cold ;
With a few rags of raiment clad,
And it was all the wealth she had.
Beside her lay an infant's hood,
Oatcake, and ither scraps o' food ;
A few sticks gathered for a fire
Within the auld weed-mantled byre,
Where in sad poortith's lonely plight
She left her sleeping babe last night ;
No morsel lingered in her store
And forth she went to beg for more ;
"'Tis but a short run through the rain,"
Said she, " I'll soon be back again."

'Twas there the Souter chanced to stray,
And bore the innocent away,
In terror lest the bairn should waken,
Poor friendless thing, outcast, forsaken !

Next day a common grave was made,
And there the luckless three were laid;
The sexton with his shovel came,
And happ'd them in their last lang hame;
This done, he tapp'd his weel-worn mull,
And to himsel' said trade was dull;
"Let times," quoth he, "be bad enough,
There's comfort in a pinch o' snuff!"

Nane thocht that Willie e'er would dee;
He aye had been, and aye would be.
But ah! the finest form e'er cast
Maun fail, and reach the grun' at last;
And sooth! who came to break or bruise,
Not much the Souter had to lose.

They searched his house wi' curious eyes—
To find an angel in disguise;
One had been there, tho' all unknown,
Whose heart God fashioned like His own.
In scraps o' pictures on the wa's,
In daisy chains, in hips an' ha's,
In odds and ends in vast array
That little children use in play,
'Twas clear that he had seen full well
Beauty in a' things but himsel';—
The solace of his toils and pains
Were singing birds and silly weans,—
The green leaves on the summer trees,
The whispering music of the breeze;

The wee burns wimplin' doun the braes—
Nature in a' her simple ways;
Or when, confounding east and west,
The storms obeyed her stern behest,—
Spake from the heaven in thunder tones,
And shook the dead men in their bones.

Daft body! he could see right well
God's hand in a' things but himsel'.
How sad and lonely he had been,
Fit to see all, not to be seen!
And when at last the ransom came,
And his free spirit wandered hame,
How beautiful to such as he
The unveiled face of God would be!

SAIR HEART.

The day is wearin' to its fa',
The sky fu' o' unfallen snaw—
      Sae woefully, sae wearily;—
Dark is the pine tree on the hill,
The yew-tree shade is darker still—
      Sae dolefully, sae drearily.

Oh that my heart had greetin' een!
But nane will come whaur tears hae been,
      Sae woefully, sae wearily;—
A wee bird in the cauld keen air
Sits by as tho' its heart was sair—
      Sae dolefully, sae drearily.

Ae brown leaf quivers on the tree,
The wee bird sits and blinks at me,
      Sae woefully, sae wearily;—
The leaf is fa'en, the bird is gane,
The gloomy mirk and me alane,
      Sae dolefully, sae drearily.

The leaf lies doun on Nature's breast,
The wee bird in its sheltering nest,
      Not woefully, nor wearily;—
Oh, heart of mine! there's welcome there,—
Gang hame to God, and mourn nae mair
      Sae dolefully, sae drearily!

FATHER'S OLD CLOCK.

CANTO THE FIRST.

Father's old Clock ! I list with tears
  To that slow steady stroke of thine ;
What hast thou done with all his years ?
  And now what would'st thou do with mine ?

Full fourscore years he gave to thee,
  In patient hope and loving trust,
Nor knew how cruel thou could'st be
  To beat them into viewless dust.

Swing after swing, and stroke on stroke,
  A weary warfare thou did'st wage ;
His pride of budding youth it broke,
  And wore down his declining age.

Sometimes soft Mercy's tender feet
  Have safely trod the tiger's den ;
Eagles have spared the lambkin's bleat,
  And lions have been mild to men.

The fierce bear on his milk-white floor,
  Where bird ne'er sang, and grass ne'er grew,
Has torn the flesh and lapp'd the gore
  Of many a bold ship's gallant crew ;

FATHER'S OLD CLOCK.

Yet has he known a gentler mood,—
  With lazy jaws and languid eye;
Like a dull ox bewildered stood
  And left the rash youth room to fly,—

To fly where he a mother's pain
  Might soothe to see her sailor boy;
Or wandering in the greenwood lane
  Kindle some love-struck maiden's joy.

But thou, old pitiless imp of Time!
  Art more than any beast of prey,—
With cruel teeth and hungry chime,
  And measured stroke that will not stay.

Hard is thy heart, and hooped with steel;
  No dews of mercy dight thy face;
No tenderness thy hands reveal;
  And deadly slow thy hurrying pace.

Click, clack,—once, twice,—on, on, for ever,
  The giant years thou breakest small;
Let life be like a shoreless river,
  Drop, drop,—drop, drop,—thou drainest all!

Oh false, oh unsuspected friend,
  Why give my sire the secret blow?
Why to its mouldy prison send
  His honoured head of saintly snow?

FATHER'S OLD CLOCK.

His days are numbered past recall,
    And thou who told them still art there,
Stiff'ning thy straight back 'gainst the wall
    With mocking and defiant air!

Go, hide thy blear'd and shameless face!
    Sooner than thou should'st spill my life,
I would, Fate reave me from my place
    By hangman's rope or bandit's knife!

Vague skeleton of ghostly power!
    Let go thy hand, unhook thy tongue;
Thou strik'st thyself the fatal hour,—
    Thy doom is reached, thy knell is rung!—

Ah me! a lingering echo there
    That wafts within my fevered breast
A breath of cool and balmy air
    From spicy islands of the blest.

Father's old Clock! forgive, forgive!
    When filial love so wildly rages;
Yes, yes; fain would I let thee live,
    Live on unhurt a thousand ages!

I set me down close at thy feet;
    I see thy face begin to shine;
In love and peace our bosoms beat,
    As did my father's heart and mine.

I feel that kindly smile; I see
   A rim of glory round thy head;
My father's spirit lives in thee,—
   I know, I know he is not dead!

Thou shinest thro' the mist of tears;
   Old Clock! thou art a spirit too,
And heir to the eternal spheres
   Where old things are for ever new!

CANTO THE SECOND.

All things in the Almighty's hand
   Are dower'd with mystic eyes and ears,
A secret omnipresent band
   In earth and sky and rolling years

In the grey dawning's drowsy star,
   And in the evening's whispering breeze;
In gloomy hailstorm's rattling car,
   Or sunbeam shimmering thro' the trees:

God's witnesses,—how manifold!
   The linnet in the hawthorn bower,
When the sweet tale of love is told,
   Bears witness with the daisy flower;

And many a dead insensate thing
   For ever keeps the mournful token,
When years bear falsehood on their wing,
   And love is lost and vows are broken.

Father's old Clock ! bear witness thou,
How oft he fell, how oft he rose,—
No coward fear to cloud his brow,
No shame to rankle in his woes.

O bliss ! enriched by earthly care,
The envy of the angel host,
When in the home of wedded pair
God's fear is found, and never lost !

When father and his new-made bride
Wedded their praises for the Throne,
Heaven op'd its pearly windows wide
And lent a music all its own.

Old Clock ! thy finger mark'd the time
When kneeling at the fireside chair,
He mingled with thy softening chime
The tremor of his family prayer !

Blame not the great God over all
If life is hard, and toils are weary ;
If love should sometimes taste like gall,
And bliss itself grow dull and dreary.

We reach the waters of despair ;
We sit and shiver at the brink ;
Yet there is more that we can bear,—
We fain would, but we cannot sink !

Father's old Clock ! hast thou not seen
  The sweat fall trickling from his face ?
And Sorrow's arrow, swift and keen,
  Fly to the poor heart's wounded place ?

But soon as rest to nature came,
  Those lids that let the lightning thro'
Were gleaming with a kindlier flame,
  And wet with penitential dew.

Ye stolid children of repose !
  Who never have inflicted pain,—
In whom love neither ebbs nor flows
  Thro' lukewarm heart and stagnant brain,

Ye cannot pass the golden gates
  Where Pity keeps her gracious dower;
'Tis not for you sweet Mercy waits
  In worship's reverential hour ;

'Tis not for you this dear old Clock
  Records two souls well-knit together,
Who bore the brunt of many a shock,
  And grew more kind thro' stormy weather.

When the soft shades of evening laid
  Their folds upon the family altar,
How fervently the good man prayed !
  How tremblingly his tongue would falter !

While pardon flowed from breast to breast,—
    To those who gave 'twas richly given ;
Frets of the rough day sank to rest
    Well-pillowed on the peace of heaven

O kind old Clock ! I give thee thanks :—
    And witness thou my wayward will ;
Nor let me wander from their ranks
    Who in their falls are rising still !

Not faintly in thy stroke I hear
    The music of the Saviour's grace ;
His pitying love to me more dear
    Because I see it in thy face !

OURISK'S AWA'.

Grey mornin' lifts a wat'ry e'e
On gloomy ha' an' dreepin' tree,
She kindly grieves an' sabs wi' me—
                      Ourisk's awa'.

Wi' horny han' an' glancin' spade
A cauld, cauld clayey bed is made,
An' his wee banes to rest are laid—
                      Ourisk's awa'.

Maybe it's wrang to mourn a beast,
But he'd a lowin' heart at least,
An' holier hasna king or priest!—
                      Ourisk's awa'.

His e'e-flash, as on me it fell,
Spak what nae tongue o' man could tell,
An' nae dog but his bonnie sel'—
                      Ourisk's awa'.

He sat ance at a scholar's feet,
Where mony puppies used to meet,
An' few could brag mair profit be't—
                      Ourisk's awa'.

But for he hated college fetters
He wad hae been a pup o' letters;
Dog-Latin spak as weel's his betters—
                      Ourisk's awa'.

Forfaughten sair, he sought at Mains *
Sweet solace to his puppy brains,
Rangin' the fields, an' sheughs, an' drains—
     Ourisk's awa'.

By Endrick's brambly banks an' braes
Rattens an' rabbits he wad raise;
But now, alas! frae frien's an' faes,
     Ourisk's awa'.

He row'd an' rantit on the green,
Swaggin' his tail, o' tails the queen!
Mair brisk was never lambkin seen—
     Ourisk's awa'.

His wee face hid ahint a screen
O' shaggy locks, an' then his e'en,
Like lichtit lucifers between—
     Ourisk's awa'.

He keepit Nature's fechtin' laws,
An' gar'd the fae gie owre wi' jaws
An' settle it wi' legs an' paws,—
     Ourisk's awa'.

He lo'ed the chase, but fear'd the gun,
And for himsel' sought a' the fun,
Like ither folk that rive or run—
     Ourisk's awa'.

---

* A mansion-house on the Endrick, near Loch Lomond.

O had that day ne'er open'd e'e
That greetin' saw baith him an' me,
The Mains an' happiness to lea'e !—
      Ourisk's awa'.

On Embro's waukit hichts an' howes
Nae rabbit rins, nae bracken grows,
Nae grassy mead where Ourisk rows,
      Ourisk's awa'.

Foul fa' the first hard-hearted loon
That causey'd streets an' made a toun—
A gude rough cudgel to his croon—
      Ourisk's awa'.

Ourisk's auld banes, an' mony mair
O' martyr dogs that suffer'd sair,
Cry, " Hit him hard, an' dinna spare !"—
      Ourisk's awa'.

Nae mair the dear wee sonsie doggie,
Wi' waggin' tail an' liftit luggie,
Rins at my feet—poor little puggie !—
      Ourisk's awa'.

Like roses, loves grow auld an' wither,
An' seldom friendships haud thegither,
But Ourisk lo'ed me like a brither—
      Ourisk's awa'.

Ne'er thocht ane o' his puggy race
Could ever haud sic gifts an' grace,
Or in my heart sae large a place—
     Ourisk's awa'.

Ae rest remains for him an' me,
Ae Frien', a kinder couldna be,
Wha took him hame an' closed his e'e—
     Ourisk's awa'.

Man lives his day as weel's his dog,
Till, after mony a rive and rug,
Death breaks the tether wi' a tug—
     An' *he's* awa'.

DISCONSOLATE.

I bide nae earthly things ava;
The former freen's are dweened awa,—
Gude tak' me hame to meet them a'
        In yon braw Toun,
Where nae puir body's heid is sair,
Saut tears frae sair een drap nae mair,
And silver founts in sunny air
        Loup up and doun!

The howffs o' men are ragin' fu'
Wi' mony a yaffin' yelpin' crew,—
Gude send to me short days and few
        Till I arise
To greet lost frien's, where honest men
Meet in auld Abram's but-an'-ben,
Or sup at Job's ain chimlie en'
        In Paradise!

Waes me! I canna shed a tear;
My heart is dry o' hope or fear;
Nane but the big black Deil is near
        To comfort me,—
He hauds his luggie to my chin,
Puts in my haun his cutty spoon,
"You'll like it weel, ance ye begin,"
        Aye, aye, quoth he.

I gape, nor am I loth to try;
But wheesht! I hear my bairnie's cry,—
Couldna the wee wretch langer lie
    An' let me be?
Oh wecht o' grief! like iron lid
That presses doun on a' that's guid;
My wee bairn's worthy o' my bluid,—
    Kind Heaven, forgi'e!

TRIUMPHANT!

Oh blithe wee bird, wha best could please
The merry heart o' morning breeze
That soughed thro' Eden's bonnie trees,
    Wi' music fine,
Dark was the sun-glint on thy crest,
And cauld the love that warmed thy nest,
Nae rapture thrilled thy panting breast
    Like mine, like mine!

My heart is fu' and rowin' o'er,
Nane ever tholed the like before;
Baith at the tap and at the core
    It sings, it sings!
And ilka thocht that ance did crawl,
Or tied as nowte are in the stall,
Mounts cherub-like oot o' its thrall,
    With wings, with wings!

It isna that I lack nae gear,
It isna that I've nocht to fear,
It isna that a dribblin' tear
        Draps nae mair doun;
My daily bread is hard to win,
I'm scaur'd wi' cares baith oot and in,
Bent low beneath a wecht o' sin
        My croun, my croun.

But a' that dool, and muckle mair,
The dowie heart can crousely bear
While round it lies a Faither's care
        For waunert wean;—
Or Shepherd's love, whase bluid did dreep
For me, a daft-like doiter'd sheep,
Frae heavenly fountains large and deep—
        Like rain, like rain!

THE AULD WIFE AT THE WHEEL.

A coggie fu', a tidy cot,
    Wi' love and truth to spin the reel,
Blythe ever be the winding o't,
    My wee auld wifie at the wheel!

When heart is sick, and heid is sair,
    And stockings oot at tae and heel,
Ne'er fash my thoom, for thou art there,
    My wee auld wifie at the wheel!

My parritch ne'er will want for saut,
    Nor girnal e'er be scant o' meal,
Nor fail a drappie o' the maut,
    My wee auld wifie at the wheel!

Braw queans there are wi' scornfu' e'e,
    And some are slippery as an eel,
I carena them a broon bawbee,
    My wee auld wifie at the wheel!

Till drops o' rain forget to fa',
    Nor mice hae sense enough to squeal,
Trig be thy mutch and like the snaw,
    My wee auld wifie at the wheel!

We, ane and a', gang toddlin' hame,
    We, ane and a', maun coup the creel,
Syne leave thee a heroic name,
    My wee auld wifie at the wheel!

Life may be short, or may be lang,
　　The brae-tap unco sair to speil;
Aye breest it wi' a bonnie sang,
　　My wee auld wifie at the wheel!

When life like sawdust a' rins oot,
　　The e'e maun close, and then fareweel
To every mortal care and clout,
　　My wee auld wifie at the wheel!

Till Heaven itsel' can laugh nae mair,
　　And frowns on every canty chiel',
They'll need the likes o' thee up there,
　　My wee auld wifie at the wheel!

MOEL FAMMA.

(Welsh " Mother of Mountains," surmounted by Jubilee Tower in ruins.)

The scene from this high summit where I stand—
  So fair it seems to my enchanted eye—
Might be an angel's dream in fairyland,
  Drawn from the loveliest garden of the sky;
Yet one sad blot I see by man's weak hand,
  An unromantic ruin here doth lie,
Memorial tower, frail, formless at the best,
To tell that Royal George, by Heaven's behest,
  Had reigned full fifty years. So poor an aim
  Filled the old elements with wrathful shame;
Moel Famma, groaning to be dispossess'd,
Shook the vile structure from her ancient crest,
  And bade all Nature o'er the wreck declare—
  The eternal God and the eternal hills are there.

GRANDFATHER'S FLUTE.

My auld grandfaither left to me
   A guid auld flute to keep me cheerie;
"Blythe be thy whistle, lad," quoth he,
   "Tho' thou thysel' be wae and weary."
The auld flute, row'd wi' rozet strings,
   The ills o' life hae dunted sairly;
But sweet the warbling note it brings
   To dowie heart baith late and early.

Far, far ayont the rowin' sea
   Whaur Kaffirs roam wi' copper faces,
Ae nicht I laid me doun to dee
   In lanesomest o' lanely places;
Methocht my latest breath I drew,
   Nor kenn'd me near a Christian's dwelling,
When sudden rapture thrilled me thro'—
   The strains o' "Home, Sweet Home" were swelling.

He played his flute. Wi' a' my micht
   I played on mine the same auld ditty;
When forth there cam' a kindly licht
   Wi' hauns to help and heart to pity.
He wrapt me weel in woolly claes;
   He nursed me, fed me like a brither;
Thro' mony canty nichts and days
   We sang, we laughed, we grat thegither.

LOVE AND WAR.

" Love is strong as death."

Twa bonnie e'en beyond compare,
A ribbon in her coal-black hair ;
Upon her breast, well-suited there,
    A bursting rose;
Sweetest o' young love's honey dew
Lay ripening on her dainty mou' ;
And best of a', her heart was true—
    The bonnie lass o' Lockerbie !

A sodger laddie caught her e'e ;
A stalwart lad and brave was he,
Wi' nodding plumes and kilted knee —
    She lo'ed him weel.
His brave heart fluttered wi' surprise ;
Love's gentle touch bedewed his eyes ;
He wedded her 'neath smiling skies—
    The bonnie lass o' Lockerbie !

Then war-clouds gathered thick and fast,
Wi' lurid flame and thunder-blast ;
She trembled—it might be her last,
    Her last fond kiss !
He sickened by the ancient Nile,
No loving word for her the while ;
Fear stole the sunshine frae her smile—
    The bonnie lass o' Lockerbie !

The sickness and the warfare o'er,
Proud in the laurels that he bore,
He hastened to his ain ha' door—
    In Hope's blest hour!
Wae! for the beautiful and brave!
They met him there wi' funeral stave,
Bearing his true love to the grave—
    The bonnie lass o' Lockerbie!

There is ae Frien' for ever near,
Wha brings to man baith love and fear,
Wha kens weel hoo to dight the tear
    Frae Sorrow's e'e!
To Him gang a' things leal and fair;
Hope dawns in Him, and droops nae mair;
Her sodger lad is seeking there
    The bonnie lass o' Lockerbie!

A VISIT TO CRAIGENDUNTON:

TO A SICK CHILD.

My frail wee lass, like drooping flower,
In shelter of thy moorland bower,
At Hope's fair dawn and dewy hour
      Thy head laid low,
By sore Affliction's envious power
      And cruel blow.

The grey mists darkened on the hill,
The summer blast blew keen and chill,
The nodding daisy bore it still—
      Less frail than thee,
Nor felt the lingering woes that fill
      Thy wistfu' e'e.

Fain, fain would I, puir lassie, bring
Better than laverock's throat and wing,
That free thou mightest soar and sing
      From bed of pain,
And make the house of mourning ring
      With joy again!

No need to bring sweet-breathing rose,
Or scent that from the violet flows;
Here in this bower a floweret grows
      More sweet than they,
And sweet for ever—not like those,
      Born to decay.

The Rose of Sharon, too, was bruised,
And from His wounds the unction oozed
Which kind Omnipotence hath used
　　　　For human weal,—
Pale Sorrow's fragrance interfused
　　　　To help and heal.

Wee dainty flower! whate'er betide,
There is an angel at thy side,
Wafting the savour far and wide
　　　　Of tender grace,
That no dark hour of pain can hide
　　　　In thy meek face.

I saw the tear-drop stain the floor,
The deep, still grief thy parents bore;
Saw following, as I sought the door,
　　　　Thy plaintive e'e;
And still that look for evermore—
　　　　It follows me.

When kindlier skies shall crown our lot,
I see thee, sweet "Forget-me-not,"
By wimpling burn in some lown spot
　　　　On heavenly braes,
Where seeds of woe are all forgot
　　　　In flowers of praise!

EPISTLE

In Celebration of the Half-Jubilee of Ministerial Life.

Friends, comrades—for ye still are so—
Of five-and-twenty years ago,
Who stood in theologic row
      Like raw recruits,
Or stirks whom cribs no more shall know
      Nor Hebrew roots,—

Ye who in Sorrow's lonesome den
Have graned and warstled sair since then,
Or cooled your cloots in mossy glen
      'Mong pastures green ;
And ye whom Death has summoned ben
      Ahint the screen,—

I greet you a' wi' right good will
On this the bleak side of the hill ;
Tho' now not mine her bosom, still
      I keep one eye on
The friend who gave life's opening thrill
      Old Mother Zion.

Oh friends ! let saut tears drench this ditty—
The Deil has burnt his brumstane cootie :
A pious Deil (the mair's the pity !),
      Your holy function
He mocks in clachan, court, and city—
      With oil, not unction !

Ask him, auld rogue, the way to Hell ;
Na, na, the fient o' him can tell ;
Nor can his lips, love-slavor'd, spell
   The word *damnation* ;
His faith rings clear as ony bell
   In a' creation.

Strength to his red-hot ribs, I say ;
Saints frown and shudder as ye may !
The Church of God has had its day—
   Let us be civil :
Hail, Forward Movement ! rise and play,
   Church of the Devil !

Not so did Paul in ancient days
God's temples of the faithful raise ;
Our Churches,—oh ! the menseless craze,
   The modern problem,—
How best can we, in heathen ways,
   Patch up and cobble 'em ?

By good St. Simon and St. James !
The old sins walk with heavenly names ;
And loathsome vice—it seldom shames
   In gold's effulgence ;
Vile curse, more worthy of the flames
   Than Rome's indulgence.

Good cheer, my comrades ! gentle friends !
Who wield your crooks for nobler ends,
When fierce infernal wolf pretends,
   In woolly guise,

To be the meek lamb Mercy sends
  In sacrifice.

For ye have seen auld wrinkled faces,
Deep-furrowed with repentant traces,
When they sank doun to tak' their places
  In Promised Land,
Glow with the beatific graces
  At God's right hand.

Bravely the silver trump ye blew,
With all that joyful noise could do,—
Or piped it to a chosen few
  On slender reed,
With but one Gospel note or two
  To bless their need.

Oft have ye met the wanderer Cain,
Tainted, puir chiel, in bluid and bane;
And soothed sweet Rachael in her pain
  Of sore bereavement;
Found David with his chuckie-stane
  Of grand achievement.

And Judas, too, in gloomy shade,
Has crept behind with traitor's blade,
Then seemed to salve the wound he made
  With Christ-like kiss;—
'Twas no small boon to be betrayed
  On terms like this!

In many a poor man's moleskin guise
Your Lord has blessed your waiting eyes,
That thorn-crowned bleeding Sacrifice
   Upon the tree,
Whose voiceless whisperings would rise—
   Friend, lov'st thou Me?

Great critics, modern-wise and zealous,
Those ploddering puffy German fellows,
Winnow with philosophic bellows
   The Gospel grain,
And lo! no better mead, they tell us,
   Than husks remain.

But good or ill wind blaw its worst,
Blaw Learning till its haffets burst,
Blind Rage revile with lips accurst
   God's Word of grace,—
More pure, more vital than at first
   It holds its place!

So blustering tempests clear the sky,
And trodden seeds refuse to die;
So Word Incarnate, lifted high
   On Cross of shame,
Can capture all men, draw them nigh,
   And bring them hame!

Hail, Sacred Book! our fathers' pride,
Their children's comforter and guide,
Gang where they may to rest or ride
   On land or sea;

In cosy neuk at chimley side
          No friend like thee!

Ye Gospel mysteries, all hail!
Tho' Fantasy adorn the tale ;—
Was prophet Jonah swallowed hale?
          Or this the blether—
He drank the ocean and the whale?—
          I care not whether!

But sweet and sensible and true,
And ever fresh as morning dew,
The love and mercy shining thro'
          That Heaven ordains
For beasts, grown folk of every hue,
          And duddy weans!

The Church stands sure, and ever will,
Tho' she of skaith has had her fill,
And sometimes on the holy hill
          Is heard fierce wrangling ;
And clouts, not stainless, on her frill
          Hing dounwards dangling.

It was the Foreign Mission cause—
The rich men's gifts drew loud applause ;
The kirk was fu', and in their braws
          The gude folk crammed it,—
The widow's mite, not worth two straws—
          Their silence damned it!

Yet Zion noble children bears,
True hearts and cleanly hands are theirs,
Fruit of the Saviour's fervent prayers,
   For whom He died,—
He sees them throng the temple stairs,
   Well-satisfied.

My brothers, champions of the Faith!
Let no dishonour stain your claith,
Or stop your ministerial breath
   Till Time shall end it;
Then should the Judgment threaten skaith,
   May God defend it!

Alas! there are whom nevermore
We meet this side old Time's Hall-door,
Our loved, revered Professors four,
   Eadie, and Harper,
Lindsay of exegetic lore,—
   None could be sharper;

MacMichael, with the mobile face,
With kindly heart and queer grimace,—
"Noo state, p'raps, aye, the Deevil's case,
   P'raps, in his den;
Ower weel," quoth he, "ye ken the place,—
   Yes, aye, ye ken!"

Like shadows mirrored in a glass!
Yet lingering and loth to pass,—

EPISTLE.

Eadie still joined with Balaam's ass*
  In bonds fraternal ;
Lindsay's auld σαρξ *(sarks)* laid on the grass †
  Of fields supernal !

My gentle comrades, fare-ye-well !
What changes wait us who can tell ?
What tinklings of life's little bell
      There yet may be ?—
Gude grant us a' anither spell—
      Our jubilee !

---

* Periodical joke of the Professor at the expense of some dull scholar in Hebrew : "Tuts, man, the ass spoke better Hebrew than that !"

† Discussions of remarkable acuteness and great length on St. Paul's use of the term "flesh."

OLD IMMORTALITY.

I.

Once, on Egyptian soil, by chance I strayed
    Into a Waste, which I remember well;
Grim rocks rose high, and cast a dismal shade
    Upon the sand, where scorching sunbeams fell;
The languid air would not have kissed the blade
    Of dewy grass, had there been one to tell;—
It knew Old Nile, his swarthy sons and daughters,
Yet only near enough to mock his green-girt waters.

II.

I thought of past days when, on purple hills,
    Sweet Nature thrilled me with her notes of joy
From feather'd throats, and from the bubbling rills,
    While the free winds, in their unhired employ,
Brought me that odorous sense which life instils
    Into the love-struck and romantic boy—
All this came back with old-time fascination
In that lone place of dumb, weird, arid desolation.

III.

I crept aside from the fierce glare and heat,
    Whose shadow spread as tho' with blackest ink;
And there I found me at an old man's feet,
    Who stood upon a little bank, and on the brink
Of some low den or anchorite retreat;—
    He made my heart quake and my eyelids blink,
So filled seemed he with a strange, lucid whiteness,
As when a lamp doth shine with its own inward
    brightness.

IV.

He looked so old, then scarce looked old at all;
   From bright to brighter grew his lustrous eyes!
Over his brow I saw the forelock fall
   More gold than grey, and a more glad sunrise
Than ever loosed dark Night's defeated thrall
   Shone in his face, which glow'd like Paradise;
Yet fearful stood I, in forlorn condition,
Breathless and stony-still beside this apparation.

V.

"Why comest thou into this region bare?"
   Said he, in mellow tones and richly mild,
As when a silver bell rings through the air,—
   It cheered me like the laughter of a child.
To this I answered, why I wandered there,
   Or what strange fancy had my feet beguil'd,
I knew not; but at home had just been falling
The sacred oil that sealed me for the preacher's calling.

VI.

" Long years have gone since the first day that I,"
   Quoth he, " began that business; it was done—"
" Long time indeed," I hastened to reply,
   " If in thy youth the business was begun;
And if in this wild Waste was raised thy cry,
   The ample sphere could yield not more than one
For eager audience and a patient hearing!"
"Thy soul is dark," said he, "with mists of mere
   appearing!

VII.

"My field is large, nor are my hearers few,
  Tho' seldom apt to hear and to obey,
Or else the human family of two
  Who dwelt in Eden had been there to-day;
I saw the Flood rise—." "That thou could'st not do,"
  Cried I. My faithless ear then heard him say
That unexhausted years, forever mounting,
Made not one passing hour in *his* way of accounting!

VIII.

"My name is Immortality; I stand
  Where all the dreamy regions of the Past,
That are or shall be, yield at my command
  Whate'er the Destinies have said shall last;
A treasure-trove pluck'd from Destruction's hand,
  The flowers of life which Death would fain hold fast;
But if thou doubt this tale of my poor telling
Here is my humble door, and welcome to my dwelling."

IX.

He led, I followed; all else there was gloom
  Saving himself; the doorway rude and strait,
It seemed the unblest entrance to a tomb,
  The loneliest haunt and terminus of Fate,
Where souls, thrice dead already, meet their doom;
  Nor would I from the jaws of that grim gate
My steps have held from terrorised retreating
Had not my Guide looked back with a most kindly
    greeting.

X.

"Friend, keep thy faith; stay not, nor doubt, nor fear;
  With one step more thou hast the threshold cross'd;
The scene is changed which thou beholdest here,
  And all the earth's mortalities are lost—
Let me but make the cumber'd eyelids clear."
  He drew his hand across my brow and toss'd
Aside a somewhat which he called my blindness—
No better act I ever knew of human kindness.

XI.

For in a moment the dark doorway seemed
  A dome wherein Immensity might dwell;
The purest light of lights within it streamed,
  And at a glance I could distinguish well
A thousand charms where only I had deemed
  To find an anchorite's poor dingy cell—
Tier rose on tier of arch and gallery splendid,
And many a long-drawn aisle stretch'd far but never ended.

XII.

More than aught else it smote me with amaze
  To find the temple filled with shining ones,
Who flashed upon my sore-bewildered gaze
  With the strong radiance of unnumber'd suns;
I had been fifty times struck lifeless by the blaze
  Had not my brain been veil'd (as meek-eyed nuns
Are shielded from the world's attempted wiling)
From scenes that might have been too fatally beguiling.

XIII.

I stood entranced amid the ambient throngs;
    I watch'd their fervent flitting to and fro;
Their steps alone, it seemed, were yielding songs,
    So rhythmically did they come and go;
The music, too, was there for which one longs
    But never hears, persuasive, soft, and slow,
Like far-off many waters in its sweetness,
Nor bound to cease, out-wearied by its own completeness.

XIV.

At last to my companion at my side
    Enquiringly I turned—he met my sight
As a new star into the view might glide
    Of some surprised astronomer, so bright
Beyond himself in beauty stood my guide,
    He seemed the very soul of young delight,
Whose golden beams upon his forehead glancing,
No task of Life's eternal toil could be enhancing.

XV.

" Behold," said he, " the hosts who my commands
    Fulfil on joyful errands night and day;
They bring me welcome presents from all lands,
    And set them here in suitable array—
The secret things of faithful hearts and hands,
    Death may not touch, nor tooth of Time's decay;
Each in its order in my home protected,
By eyes of men and angels evermore inspected.

XVI.

"This you behold is but the vestibule
Of that unbuilt abode I call my own,
Whereof no niche, by measurement of rule,
　In all its untold vastness can be known;
Nor ever taught in any creature school
　Whereby its wealth in numbers may be shewn;—
But now, have done with needless sums and measures;
Put on thy humblest looks, and come, inspect my treasures!"

XVII.

Then showed he many curious things and rare,
　From Ruination's age-long Empire saved;
Elijah's mantle, Abel's crook, were there;
　The sling wherewith Goliath's wrath was brav'd;
The pot of manna, Israel's desert fare;
　The two stones with the Ten great Words engraved;
The silver trump the fiftieth year that sounded;
The cords and staves wherewith the awful mount was bounded.

XVIII.

With books, and arms, and pictured monument;
　With stands, and stalls, this House of Wonders teemed;
It held the veil, from top to bottom rent;
　The ladder-steps whereof the patriarch dreamed;
The shoe which Boas bought with pure intent;
　The sword which at the gate of Eden gleamed,
Before whose dread approach our Parents hasted;
The cruise of oil, meal-barrel too, that never wasted.

XIX.

A Peter's tear, still trembling, there was kept,
  And never would its bitterness be dried;
The sailor's bed whereon the Saviour slept;
  The spear which drank communion at His side;
Her broken box who kiss'd His feet and wept,—
  The very hairs with which the stains she dried;
Two pence whose worth can nevermore be counted,
The saddle whence the good Samaritan dismounted.

XX.

Unnumbered things not writ on sacred page
  Were there, with equal honours crown'd;
Her feathered helm and patriotic rage
  Who as the Maid of Orleans stands renown'd;
The cup our English knight did not assuage
  Until the wounded soldier's lips it found;
With Dorcas' thread and thimble close beside them;
Nor did Paul's winter cloak near by, and parchments,
    hide them.

XXI.

Tokens of King Melchisedec I saw;
  Joined with his sacramental bread and wine
Were martyr-bones pluck'd from the lion's jaw;
  The widow's mites were ranged in honour'd line
With gifts which did a nation's plaudits draw;
  And many a tarnished trifle saw I shine
More bright than polished gold, by Heaven's appointment,
When Penitence thereon and Pardon dropt their
    ointment.

XXII.

"Alas!" said I, to him who me had brought
   Into this wondrous place; "alas! not now
In all the earth are such achievements wrought;
   In the vile dust of Mammon's feet men bow;
Greatness is gone, the smile of God unsought;
   A wither'd chaplet sits on Honour's brow;
Idly thy hosts on the bleak earth are standing;
And nevermore thy crowded fane will need expanding!"

XXIII.

He answered with a smile: "Nay, friend, not so!
   Nobly the fruitful world supplies my store
With deeds which were not garner'd long ago;
   Men deeper feel each other's rankling sore;
More freely let their swift compassions flow
   Than ever they did let or feel before;—
With these the thronging angels fill my mansion,
Unwall'd, and unexplored, and vast beyond expansion!

XXIV.

"In chief they are the offerings of the poor,
   From sweat of brow and scanty wage," said he;
"The mead of woe love brings but cannot cure;
   The timid, weak, contemptible, who dree
Their hard life out in tasks and dens obscure;
   The fetter'd slave whose patient soul is free:—
But all ranks yield wherewith my sons are laden:
Priest, soldier, shepherd, clown, wife, widow, youth, and maiden."

XXV.

So spake my Guide, it made my poor heart melt;
  Long time I stood before him dazed and dumb;
I only half remember what I felt;
  Even now thought craves for speech that will not come;
I know that like a broken reed I knelt,
  Whilst life sank dwindling to a distant hum
Which in my faint ears still more faintly linger'd,
Before the brave things told of what the angels finger'd!

XXVI.

He touched me gently, raised me to my feet;
  He spoke of stranger things for eye and ear
A thousand-fold, which would my spirit greet
  Could I but safely see or bear to hear.
He drew a curtain —lo! a squalid street
  Which seemed both far away and yet quite near,
With reeking crowds and wet grime covered thickly,
And there a little maiden, ill-clad, lean, and sickly.

XXVII.

She carried in her arms a loaf of bread;
  And I could follow her, I knew not how,
Into her home, where, on a wretched bed,
  Her mother lay a-dying, on whose brow
The new Apocalyptic Name I read.
  "But whence," said I, for they were wafting now
Incessantly, "these gusts of choral singing
Which this poor scene, like Heaven's own Eolus, is bringing?"

XXVIII.

"No anthem this which voice or harp can raise;
  It comes," said he, "from being simply good;
Kind thoughts, on earth unheard, ascend like praise—
  In my domain they're Music's daily food:
List how that little maiden's thoughtful ways,
  And for her child what that poor mother would,
Compose a song, in humblest human dwelling,
Which round the crystal spheres is kept for ever swelling!"

XXIX.

One more and still another veil he drew:—
  A minister sat brooding in his chair;
Oh, that his not-too patient flock but knew
  What strong clear harmonies were rising there
From self-rebukes, from high thoughts pure and true,
  From agonies of inwrought secret prayer!
Him too I saw the pulpit steps ascending;
I heard his footfall sing, with angel anthems blending.

XXX.

A fair young wife of six months old or so,
  Richly attired, with softly-slippered feet,
Stood gazing on the flowery lawn below;
  What said her lips my pen may not repeat;
How ran her secret thoughts I do not know,
  But from her breast a music rose more sweet
Than ever came by proudest Art's achieving,
Nor did she know what strains her gentle soul were leaving.

XXXI.

What more, surpassing thought, to me disclosed,
  No language can, or else I dare not tell,
Lest Truth itself, to overstrain exposed,
  Might lose its placid temper and rebel.
But this I must: My guide at length proposed
  We two should tread a path not known so well;
Not far, he said, but yet beyond the portal
Where Time's dwarf tent is pitched beneath the Dome immortal.

XXXII.

I felt his hand touch mine—away we flew:
  More swift than lightning is to Arab steed
Did we outstrip what light itself could do,
  Or yet had done, since when it first gave heed
To God's command, and its own being knew;
  More swift by far we flew than Thought's own speed—
One moment, by I know not what assistance,
Brought us where yet no flash had reached of man's existence.

XXXIII.

Back thro' the dim Eternal did I look:
  I saw the earth a void and formless mass;
On lines of light, as in a printed book,
  I saw the story as it came to pass
Of man's brief bliss, in that green-mantled nook
  Girt by the four clear streams, until, alas!
Unblemished love broke up its dear duality;
Keenly I scann'd the bare, the unabridged reality.

XXXIV.

On, on, the tragic eras came and pass'd;
  I saw the dove's white wing across the dark
Gleaming, like hope on Ruin's visage cast,
  When she in fluttering fear re-sought the Ark;
The sparks of dying Sodom to the last;
  Sennacherib's host before me stiff and stark;
That day the Tempter once again dissembled;
And that wherein woe-stricken Nature moan'd and trembled.

XXXV.

I saw, but guided how I could not tell,
  The peopled earth ere History begins;
Long lines of unknown Empires rose and fell,
  'Mid well-known pleasures weltering, and sins;
The Roman galleys lifted on the swell
  Close by our shores where, in their painted skins,
Our fathers met proud Cæsar with defiance;
I saw the birth of Art, the growth of deep-brow'd Science.

XXXVI.

"But," said my Guide, "for things of marvel seen,
  List thou for equal marvels not yet heard."
I held my ear attent as eye had been;
  The treasured air pour'd out its meet reward;
I heard old Homer sing; the Egyptian Queen
  Bewail her Antony; the royal bard
Of Israel; the voice that cried repentance;
And His in whose mild tones false Judas heard his sentence.

XXXVII.

I heard Demosthenes upon the beach
    Meet undismayed the ocean's deafening roar ;
The soft low sigh of tremulous yearning speech
    Made by the Publican at Mercy's door ;
Our modern Abraham for the poor slave preach
    Straight words of simple strength unknown before ;
Horse-hoofs and chariot wheels of Pharoah clattering ;
Belshazzar's knees, his very teeth, I heard them chattering !

XXXVIII.

I marvelled that it did not sound more strange,
    All seemed so simple, natural and true ;
I learned that God, in human life's full range,
    Nought left unwitnessed by those faithful Two,
And in their store-house kept from loss or change
    Until the solemn Judgment's last review :
The nimble Air, the clear-eyed Light omniscient,--
These for the mighty task begot, and all-sufficient.

XXXIX.

Harsh noises clogg'd my ear and pierced my soul,
    But whence they rose I may not now reveal ;
Words came that burned me like a living coal,
    And some just warm enough to help and heal.
Oh, happy they in Truth's benign control
    Whose unveil'd hearts have nothing to conceal !
Not theirs to be by whispered things confounded,
When these on house-Tops of the Light and Wind are sounded !

XL.

I heard the wailing of my own birthday;
   I knew these sins of youth to be my own;
Along my life's whole melancholy way
   Were evils I had done, but had not known;
And one dread Voice of threatening heard I say:
   "No mercy give, for none himself hath shewn."
I sank like lead.—I woke up muttering "Saviour!"
Friends told how mark'd my sleep had been by strange behaviour.

THE ENDRICK.

The swallow's light wing lightly dips,
And willows cool their finger-tips,
Fresh lilies hang, with scented lips,
    In thy waters, winding lonely,
  Bonnie Endrick ! peaceful river,
  Winding in my soul for ever !

So fair beside no stream that flows
The birk waves and the hawthorn blows,
The rowan and the milk-white rose,—
    By thy waters, winding lonely,
  Bonnie Endrick ! peaceful river,
  Whispering in my soul for ever !

The music of my bridal day,
How soon in death it passed away !
Brief, bright as Eden was her stay
    Near thy waters, winding lonely,
  Bonnie Endrick ! peaceful river,
  Glimmering in my soul for ever !

Oh could'st thou backward flow, and bring
What happy moments heard her sing,
What rapture in her laugh would ring
    O'er thy waters, winding lonely,
  Bonnie Endrick ! peaceful river,
  Echoing in my soul for ever !

She trod thy banks, she cull'd the flower,
Charming the weary care-worn hour,
In many a dim green-mantled bower,
    By thy waters, winding lonely,
    Bonnie Endrick ! peaceful river,
    In my soul embower'd for ever !

Oh stay not, or his heart will break
That woos thee, yon impatient Lake !
Alas ! the salt rain, for her sake,
    In thy waters, winding lonely,
    Bonnie Endrick ! peaceful river,
    Rippling in my soul for ever !

Till thou shalt weep thy fountains dry,
Nor heave thine immemorial sigh,
Shall Sorrow's tide bedim the eye
    To thy waters, winding lonely,
    Bonnie Endrick ! peaceful river,
    Sorrowing in my soul for ever !

Thy flood shall cease ; yon ancient height
Its *Black Wing* fold from mortal sight ;
But the fair vision of delight
    By thy waters, winding lonely,
    Bonnie Endrick ! peaceful river,
    Still shall haunt my soul for ever !

ODE

Addressed to the Last Remnant of an Old Shoe in the Bottom of the River, near Auchencruive House.

In Ayr's deep rocky bed I found thee,
Snapt every tie erstwhile that bound thee,
And of thy kindred none stood round thee,
                Poor old sole!

By many a torrent sadly shaken,
Bare to the scorching sun and baken,
Outcast, unpitied, scorn'd, forsaken,
                Poor old sole!

This stream shall leave its ancient groove,
Rock Ailsa roll to Auchencruive,
Ere thou thy former comforts prove,
                Poor old sole!—

What palace floors have known thy tread,
On what far hills the beast was fed
In whose tough hide thy strength was bred,
                Poor old sole!

Christian or pagan, where is he
Who whack'd, and rack'd, and wallop'd thee
As in a vice, between each knee,
                Poor old sole?

Gone, gone long since to his account,
By sulphur pit and Dead Sea fount,
Or homeward bound by Pisgah's mount,
     Poor old sole!

Some lassie's fate on thee suspended,
Where mirth rose as it ne'er had ended;
What funerals hast thou attended,
     Poor old sole?

Worn to a shadow by the weather,
Come, slake thy thirst and rax thy leather;
Thou'st held what hero's toes together,
     Poor old sole?

Long since served thou the patriot's turn?
Perchance the Bruce of Bannockburn,
Or Wallace when the foe he'd spurn,
     Poor old sole?

Who knows, it was the rustic Muse
Wore thee in transport or "the blues?"—
Mayhap thou stood'st in Robin's shoes,
     Poor old sole!

Cast off to some auld tinker body,
Ramshackle, like thyself, and duddy,
On-draggling with a cart and cuddy,
     Poor old sole!

Whoever owned thee, saint or sinner,
At Life's scant feast he ate his dinner,
And then grew thin, like thee, and thinner,
Poor old sole !

Like thee, a patch of rag and rust,
We rise a wee bit from the dust,
Then to the dirt again we must,
Poor old sole !

So perish we,—no need for squallin'
E'en though the Doom's-day bell be callin',—
The scene is closed ; the mighty fallen,
Poor old sole !

DID I DREAM?

(Sequel to the song "O'er the moor I wandered lonely.")

Did I dream we wandered lonely?
    Ochon-a-rie, my heart is sore;
Favoured hour in frowning weather
When alone we walked together
    By the sad sea's murmuring shore;—
All I knew—thy presence only;
    Ochon-a-rie, my heart is sore;
Kindly thoughts, alas! unspoken,
Secrets of the heart unbroken,
    Sealed and silent evermore.

Brighter hour may Hope be sending—
    Ochon-a-rie, my heart is sore;
Fairer fields and fresh for ever
By the wimpling winding river,
    On some other happier shore;—
Loving eyes and voices blending,—
    Ochon-a-rie, my heart is sore;
Loving lips not now withholden,
Hearts unsealed and hands enfolden,
    And the parting—nevermore!

MISUNDERSTOOD.

Her heart had true love but it could not speak,
Except in tones of crimson on her cheek;
The beauty of a bright surprise there lay,
Like winter sunset,—cold, and far away.

He lost not faith, and yet was doubting still;
He knew the good, and yet suspected ill;
Dumb love he scourged with thunderbolts of blame,—
She sealed her lips more firmly by the flame.

With love's warm breath and golden mouth he pled,—
What spake she but a statue might have said?
A thousand were the voices in her brain,—
Oh had there been but one to sooth his pain!

It came not;—for she smothered all her sighs,
And marvelled at the deafness of his eyes;
The heart's best word of music could be seen,
Not heard, thought she. Ah then, what might have
    been!

AN AUTUMNAL MONODY.

"*Il Penseroso.*"

With tottering step he left the street,
 No friendly hand to guide him :
He sat down on the garden seat,
 I sat me down beside him ;
His bloodless lips were fain to speak,
And all a-down his withered cheek
 The tears would fain have wandered ;
I saw his eyes were all a-swim,
The drops kept quivering on the brim ;
 And thus he maundered :

My race is run, and I have miss'd the prize ;
 Belated hope may come, but brings no cheer ;
What boots the plainest path to blinded eyes ?
 Or loveliest music to the deafened ear ?

For me, grown old, there is the closing door
 Where friendship gave and found a resting-place ;
For me, alas ! the genial host no more
 Bids welcome with both hands and shining face.

Not thus they scorn'd me when, in days gone by,
 With all the pride a witless youth could yield,
I sowed, beneath bland showers and fervid sky,
 The promise of an unbless'd harvest field.

They loved me then ; and if, for one brief day,
    It chanced I did not warm me at their fire,
They thought me cold, and chid my long delay,
    Nor noon nor night would of my babblings tire.

For me the banquet blazed, the table groaned,
    The red wine flowed, the silver goblet rang,
The mirth flew round, while Music sat enthroned,
    And all Joy's flowery daughters danced and sang.

But now the heavy unrelenting years
    Lean hard upon me when I pant for peace ;
Love is an echoing sorrow in mine ears—
    Would that it might, but no ! it will not cease.

The friendships all are gone, when o'er my blame
    The grey beard Wisdom, like a mourner, stands ;
And when my Faults in misery and shame
    Sit in their lonely cells and wring their hands.

Whispers of hope, and dews of healing balm
    Might fall from me on hearts distraught with pain,
So dearly have I bought the heavenly calm
    Which comes, as on the mown grass gentle rain ;

Were I not old !—my sin of sins is this ;
    My venial trespass, not to be forgiven ;
And those who once were quarrelling for my kiss
    Draw off in fear, as from a leper driven.

Not yet was theirs the rude untender age
  When youth can break all pleasure but its own ;
Mocking the pain it sweetly might assuage,
  Trampling on life's gay flowers when overblown.

Whilst they were children, they and I were friends ;
  But now their own are prattling on their knees ;
Nor would I mourn what prudent Nature sends—
  The love withdrawn from me, and granted these.

The former days, perchance, may come once more—
  Affection come on Time's receding wave ;
Small hands grasp mine more kindly than before,
  And homeward lead me to a peaceful grave.

It may be so—as I have often read,
  God finds the fathers failing in His hand ;
With these no more contented, in their stead
  He makes "the children princes in the land."

It may be so ;—the children's children may
  A brighter hope and mellower music bring
Than that which in their sires has passed away,
  And left me here in silent sorrowing.

But Memory fails where Hope can bring no cure :
  As Alpine herds hear not their tinkling bell,
So had I ceased remembering I was poor,
  Because, alas ! I knew it all too well !

AN AUTUMNAL MONODY.

Poor, old, unsightly as a wasted wreath
    In winter-blown decay upon the tomb ;
Well-nigh as helpless as the bones beneath ;
    In woe rent-free, and bless'd with ample room.

No wealth is mine to draw the mourner's tear
    When I am dying, Fortune's favour'd child ;
To soothe my friends when they surround my bier,
    And make them to their sad fate reconciled.

But Heaven is kind, and there are richer stores
    Than that proud temple of the flesh can hold,
Where harsh unsleeping angels guard the doors,
    With gleaming wings of silver and of gold !

I am content, because my soul is free ;
    Fair-featured Nature fills my ravished eye ;
Kindly she speaks, and coyly smiles on me
    Like love-struck maid when her betroth'd is nigh.

So, not unpleased, would I unwind my strength,
    Devout and thankful, at the close of day :
Watching the autumn leaves, until, at length,
    Softly like them I fall, and pass away.

        Thus far he spoke, with many a sigh,
        A silvery brightness in his eye ;
        He rose e'er I could bid him stay,
        And like a spent ghost passed away.

That night in dreams I saw his face,
Asleep in its last resting-place—
  Two angels guarding head and feet ;
A pauper's coffin kept him hid,
One shining hand the screws undid,
I saw another lift the lid—
  His rest seemed sweet.

JOHN HOWIE, LOCHGOIN,

AUTHOR OF "SCOTS WORTHIES."

*(Inscribed to A. B. Todd, Esq.,
Secretary to the Howie Monument Committee.)*

Nobly he said what yet must needs be sung ;
  A Voice uplift in the lone wilderness,
  Whom ever we must proudly claim not less
Than they whose names dwelt dearly on his tongue,
And on his page are like the stars outhung
  In the all-during firmament : we bless
  Both him and them, who bore so well the stress,
Nor grudg'd that soul and sinew should be wrung
For God and Freedom. Well done, moorland scribe!
  Thou stout-brain'd son of a most strenuous race !
And, worthier still of thee, oh, may thy tribe
  Keep these ancestral moors, and guard the place
Where crumbling stone proclaims on shifting sod
Thy name indelible in heart of man and God !

THE UNKNOWN.

Here's to the lass, the bonnie lass,
    I ne'er may see again ;
She thrill'd me, as I saw her pass,
    With pleasure and with pain ;—
No smile, no word from her fair lips
    Was glinted or was spoken ;
The radiant face, the liquid eye,
    Were all I had for token.

Yet never sun the morn has cheer'd
    With more entrancing beams ;
A lovelier image ne'er appeared
    In any angel's dreams ;—
Love, Truth, and royal Peace were there,
    With meek-eyed Resignation ;
She came upon me like a breath
    Of holy inspiration !

One glance ; and had I ventured more
    I had been stricken blind,
So lustrous was the charm she wore
    To dazzled eye and mind ;—
And for the ear a rhythmic flow
    Mellifluent was blended,
As tho' an unseen seraph choir
    Upon her steps attended.

Sweet lass ! I know not what her name,
  Nor what her lot may be ;
But since I've seen her, not the same
  Is this sad world to me.
The flowery Spring, the linnet's song
  Cease not for all its badness,
And one pure maiden-soul may touch
  The whole round globe with gladness !

COMFORT FOR THE BEREAVED.

In Memory of John Webster Smith.

You mourn for me, and think me far away,
But I am near you as the air you breathe ;
As glides into your room the light of day
So glide I in to your sad souls—to stay.
My home is not above, nor yours beneath,
For we are all more lovingly united ;
I know 'tis true, but understand it not,
Our hopes bloom best when we esteem them blighted.
I dwell with you until I am forgot ;—
Forgot ! you answer with a flood of tears,—
To me they are most beautiful, I see
The promise there of peace for coming years,—
The richer Christ that is, and is to be,
All for my sake, because you mourn for me !

FROM THE GREEK.

PRIDE.

A proud little gnat,
   One summer morn,
For a moment sat
   On a bullock's horn.

"Oh friend!" quoth she,
   "Am I heavy, pray?
If I weary thee,
   I will go away."

"Pooh! you need not go,"
   Said he of the stall;
"For I did not know
   You were there at all!"

So little souls flare
   In their own vain eyes;
But are neither here nor there
   To the great and wise.

FROM THE GREEK.

ENVY.

In a field one day,
  While near to a bog,
An ox crossed the way
  Of a haughty frog.

Sore vex'd and surpris'd
  Was the frog to see
That a beast bigger-sized
  Than herself could be.

So in a great flum,
  She drew her breath in,
Till tight as a drum
  Was her wrinkled skin.

To her offspring near :
  " I'm as big as he,—
You cubs ! do you here,
  Am I not ?" said she.

" Lor', mother !" said they,
  " You're big as a hill ;
But blow, blow away,—
  He is bigger still."

In rage unsurpassed
  A great gasp she drew;
But this was her last,
  For she burst in two.

And her cubs, poor things!
  Thro' their tears learnt then
What grief envy brings
  On froggies and men.

CHORUS, FROM EURIPIDES. (Iph. in Aul.)

O'er the strait from where alone
Stands the town I call my own,
Chalcis, guardian of the spring,
The waters by the sea that sing
Of Arethusa, dear to Fame,
To the sandy shore I came
   Of Aulis by the sea,—
Euripean billows dashing thro'
The gather'd Grecian arms to view,
To the sandy shore I came
   Of Aulis by the sea,—
The galleys by the plashing oar
The hero-gods of Greece that bore,
And lash'd with leaping waves the shore
   Of Aulis by the sea.

  Borne in a thousand ships of pine
Against the treacherous Trojan line,
The heroes whom our mates declare
Young Men'laus with the golden hair,
And Agamemnon, kingly bred,
For Helen, loved and lost, have led;
Fair Helen whom the herdsman gay,
The Trojan Paris, bore away
From reed-o'erspread Eurotas' wave,
The gift the vaunting Venus gave
When by the fountain's dancing dew
She sought the prize, and won it too,—

CHORUS, FROM EURIPIDES.

With stern Minerva stoutly strove
And with the lynx-eyed Queen of Jove,
Fast thro' the Artemesian grove,
With crowded victims reeking red,
(That flushed with shame my youthful cheek)
Spurring my quickening course I sped,
For ardent hope urged on to seek
Where meeting warriors filled the field
With clangings of the battered shield;
Where whitely the war-teeming train
Of tented Greece bestrewed the plain,
And pranced the troops of snorting steeds,
Proud partners of their masters' deeds.

But armless and at ease reclined
The Locrian cheiftain there I find
The doughty draft-board bending o'er
With Ajax from the Cycrian shore,
The statelier Ajax, boasted son
    Of Salamis and Telamon.

    I mark'd Protesilaus, and there
Saw whom Poseidon's daughter bare,
Eubœan Palamedes too,
The same inglorious war pursue;
Saw Di'med, like a play-bent boy,
The pleasures of the disk enjoy
With Mars-begot Merione,
Fairest of mortal men is he;
And there Ulysses, deep in wiles,
    From the rough mountains of the isles;

And Nireus from the Noxian coast,
The fairest of the Grecian host.
And lo! along the pebbly shore,
The while his heavy arms he wore,
I saw the chief whom Thetis bore
And Chiron trainéd, in the race
Urging his storm-outstripping pace;
Swift as a glance he swept the shore
And with his feet the contest bore
Against a chariot's horses four,
Fleeter than whom ne'er scour'd the plain,
Nor comelier knew the conquering rein,
Nor braver shook the shuddering mane,—
White spotted o'er the central two,
Join'd in the yoke, the chariot drew,
Whilst by their sides each dappled bay—
Its course diverging, glad to find
By the loose traces less confin'd—
Held thro' the windings of the way;
The foam flew from their bits of gold,
And widely o'er the trembling wold
Thunder'd their iron hoofs;—nor less I hear
Pheres, the frantic charioteer,
As, urging still their wild career,
To his brave steeds he lustier cried,
And the fierce lash more fiercely plied.
On foot, and with war-sheathéd limb,
Close by the chariot's bended rim,
By the swift steeds that rivall'd him,
    The fleet Achilles ran.

AN AYRSHIRE TRAGEDY.

In Memoriam, J. W. D., August 11, 1892.

On Lendalfoot the summer sea
   Flowed with mellifluent sound ;
And many a lark's unfettered glee
   Fell rippling to the ground.

Such joy there was in waving field,
   On rock and yellow shore,
As Nature's kindest mood can yield ;—
   Nor heart could wish for more.

O Ailsa ! lonely witness thou
   Of many a tragic woe,
When crooked lightnings wreathed thy brow,
   And tempests raged below.

To you, ye Arran hills and vales,
   In sun and shade so fair,
How often have the wandering gales
   Brought moanings of despair

Goatfell ! how oft, in feudal days,
   From yonder Carrick sands,
To thee the dying bent their gaze,
   And vainly stretched their hands !

But never Fear more held her breath,
  Nor deeper pang was wrung,
Than when that day 'twixt life and death
  The trembling balance hung.

Dear youth, a father's, mother's pride,
  Their ever-fresh delight,
Who sank beneath the smiling tide
  In their bewildered sight;

And almost on the hapless boy
  Might they have laid their hand!
Ah then! what sweet-voiced waves of joy
  Had cheered that mournful strand!

For ever had it worn a crown
  Of richest green and gold,
The sod whereon they laid him down .
  All stony-still and cold.

No sadder blight on Hope's young flower
  Could Misery contrive;
'Twas more than death to see that hour,—
  To see it, and survive.

But sure in God lie deeper things
  Than that deceitful wave;
And there are strong aspiring wings
  For gentle souls and brave.

Eternal Life ! Thou hast thy shrine
   Where our poor wreckage lies ;
And fathomless the peace divine
   In tears of mourners' eyes.

IN MEMORIAM:

W. P. PATON.

Now that the Vision like a dream is fled,
   Not hard it is the Grecian god to trace
   In stalwart frame, and in his blythesome face,
In manly stride, free step, the high-swung head,
The eye unconscious of the love it shed,
   The agile arm, the lip suffused with grace,
   The noble breadth that found fit dwelling-place
In soul and shoulder. But, alas ! he's dead.
So lusty Spring not seldom have we seen
   By one bleak night droop to untimely grave—
The laughing hopes that glinted on the green
   Gone at a glance, as he beneath the wave !
Yet Spring ne'er was that vainly spent her breath,
Nor ever harvest-home so bountiful as Death !

AN OLD BALFRON WORTHY:

MICHAEL ROBERTSON, BANKER.

'Twas his at last the silent stream to cross,
    And leave the murmuring haunts of living men ;
The strath that knew him well now mourns his loss,
    And never more will see his like again.

Like a rare mansion of the olden time
    That some forgotten art hath richly graced,
Crumbling at length beneath our wintry clime,
    It may be lost and mourned, but not replaced.

New men will come, grow old, and quickly go,
    As they have done through countless ages past ;
Old Endrick to the Queen of Lakes will flow,
    And the Black Wing its ancient shadow cast ;

The kine in fields, the wildfowl on the wold,
    Where the glad fairies ring the heather bells ;
The splendour of the upland green and gold,
    Where stand the soft feet of the Fintry Fells ;

The tiny ones that cluster at the well,
    The rush of happy children from the school ;
The rumour when the storm begins to swell,
    And showers of brown leaves fall upon the pool ;

The slow-paced funeral on the village brae,
  The solemn eyes that watch from every door,—
The last look downward, and the falling clay,—
  The hope to meet again to part no more;

The rapture when the swain has found his mate,
  And social mirth leaps unrestrained and wild;
The calmer joy within the cottage-gate
  When the fond mother first beholds her child;

The plough, the furrow that it leaves behind,
  The braird that Heaven doth never fail to send;
The food God brings for beast and human kind,—
  The poor who find in Him a helpful Friend;

The quiet Sabbath morn, the sober face,
  The decent dress, the common House of Prayer,
The talk outside, the awe within the place
  When all in unity have gathered there;

The week-day when the toiler brings his gain,
  With sweat and summer-dust upon his cheek,—
Or takes his last mite homeward through the rain,
  With a proud grief that will not deign to speak; —

These scenes that met the old man in his way,
  Engaged his kindly heart and searching eyes,
Still haunt the same old village of to-day,
  And will while unborn generations rise;—

But never, in the days that are to be,
　The same old type of true man will be found,—
Till winding stream roll upward from the sea,
　And pine-clad mountain sink into the ground!

The light of chivalry and old romance
　Had not departed from his honoured brow;
An angel in his hospitable glance
　Well known in Abraham's time, forgotten now.

He was as courteous as the knights of old,
　And softly gave the stroke that needs must fall;
His wit was keen, but it was never cold,
　And a rich humour sparkled in it all.

Gracious and affable, dignified and wise,
　None could so well the churlish soul beguile;
He pierced the quick, and the hot blood would rise,
　Yet those who felt the pain were forced to smile.

Zealous for God, and for his country's weal,
　For conscience, truth, and sacred liberty;
For Church and State his heart's wish true and leal
　That both be guided from above, and free!

The children by the roadside in their play
　Will miss the accustomed hand upon their hair;
And from the church he loved has passed away
　The benediction of his presence there.

The worship of his pious fathers bore
   Its joyous fruit within his heart again ;
And what he craved himself at Mercy's door
   He gave with liberal hand to other men.

Nor did this " old disciple" ever cease
   To give of Mnason's piety the proof,
For many a weary messenger of peace
   Found refuge and repose beneath his roof.

No guest will e'er forget the genial feast
   Prepared of God for body, heart, and mind,—
How the talk brightened, and the joy increased,
   While rarest wit and richest grace combined !

Farewell ! kind friend, last of a goodly race !
   Strath-Endrick holds not thee, but holds thy grave ;
Thy memory long shall haunt thy native place ;
   Thy rest is with the blessèd and the brave !

DR. JOHN BROWN:

AUTHOR OF "RAB AND HIS FRIENDS."

No shining morn but hastens to its ending,
   Nor sparking dew but seeks too soon the sky;
Half unperceived upon our steps attending
   The wise men hurry on and pass us by;
   We know not what the good are till they die,
Nor know the prophet-soul whom God is sending,
Till, like the sailor's bride in tears upon the shore,
Waving her last adieu, we see him nevermore.

Brightest of all the goodly race before him,
   Of all his worthy sires most worthy he,
Whom Genius loved, and cast her mantle o'er him,
   Whom from a child Faith nurtured on her knee.
   Pure Wisdom, Wit, and (richest of the three)
Kind Humour, everywhere on earth deplore him—
Gentle, devout John Brown, droll wizard of the pen,
The son of mirth and tears, the friend of dogs and men!

For thee the thankful heart and voice of weeping,
   Thou Queen of cities! that he loved so well;
For never one, fair-curtain'd 'neath thy keeping,
   A sadder, sweeter, merrier tale could tell,
   Or wield more deft than he the wizard spell,
Who on thy bosom nourished, now is sleeping
Upon the rocky steeps that guard thy glorious throne,
Waiting the envious world to claim him for its own!

He walked life's way like shadow softly stealing,
    With the glad Muses ever hovering by,
The shyest of their secret things revealing,
    Whilst he, their loved interpreter, was nigh
    With mystic pen and seer's far-piercing eye,
Deep in his heart the subtle craft concealing
Of serving sacred Truth with Fancy's drollest wiles,
Melting the soul to tears, and turning these to smiles.

O rare old man! to whom so much beholden,
    Our hearts refuse to rank thee with the dead:
Still break the truth, the beautiful, the golden,
    And when thou speakest naught else need be said!
    Not one bright beam of thy dear face hath fled,
Nor will have fled when these our times are olden,—
Homely and sober face, benevolent and sage,
Comely and silver-crowned with three times honoured age.

Laid in the tomb—not dead, but death-defying;
    Fount of perennial pathos, tender, true,—
A mother's pathos when her babe is dying;—
    Brief as the light'ning, and as brilliant too;
    His work immortal tho' his words were few.
Go, Fame! and kiss the sod where he is lying—
Genial, devout John Brown, whom human hearts revere
Till Mirth no more can smile, nor Sorrow shed a tear!

GEORGE ELIOT.

" Master, we saw one casting out devils in thy name, and we forbade him, because he followeth not us. But Jesus said, Forbid him not."

Teacher she was of frail and erring men
    Whom but the wise could love and understand ;
And made the magic touch of woman's pen,
    The riches of her gentle heart and hand,
    Well-known from age to age, from land to land :
Her like the world ne'er saw, nor hopes to see again !

Helper so strong, so tender, and so true,
    She must have hearkened at the Master's feet,
And sat, perchance, more nearly than she knew
    In shadow of His truth-girt mercy-seat—
    And what she learned He taught her to repeat,
And whom the kindly Wisdom called she gently drew.

Prophet who spoke, by heaven and earth inspired,
    What both did feel but found it hard to say—
With love divine and human passion fired—
    And said it in the brightest, kindliest way :
    So man, henceforth, will go less far astray :
The sweetest of his sins will now be less desired.

Well done, kind spirit ! hail, all hail to thee !
    The ages welcome and revere thy name ;
Lo ! millions wait thy touch to set them free
    From the sore thraldom and the bitter shame :
    Go, teach them whom to praise, and what to blame ;
What Christ was like, and what the Judgment Day will be.

ALEXANDER MACLEOD, D.D.

["Not many days ago, talking of his death, he said he would not care to be placed in a shroud, and expressed his wish that his body should be wrapped in his plaid like an old Highland soldier."]

No martial chief, in old romantic days,
Whose soul the rugged hills and foaming streams,
Dark storms and tender flowers, ancestral faith
And valorous deeds had nurtur'd, till at length,
Not grudgingly, he gave to weary age
And death his wealth of undishonoured scars,
Was ever, when the last cold stillness came,
Wrapt in his plaid (companion of his toils
And of his welcome rest), more worthily
Than thou in thine, True Man! to whom high aims,
The royal strength that rules in gentleness,
And all things fair and bright, kindly and brave,
Were native-born as sunbeams are to summer!
Farewell, most dear of friends, more true than steel!
Soldiers of Jesus! whose unyielding sword
Death wreathes in victory and eternal peace,—
We mourn in tears whilst thou art shedding smiles
Amidst the children who in evil ways
By thee, Great Heart! into the Fold of God
Were safely shepherded.   Farewell!   Farewell!

WILLIAM HOWIE WYLIE.

Heroic Friend, strong, strenuous, and brave,
  Whom hard and honest labour best could please,
No rest is thine, for rest thou did'st not crave,
  Nor placid Heaven of soft indulgent ease.

The stern unsmiling task awaits thee still,
  Eager undaunted wrestlings of the soul,
The heart-throes, and the stress of thought and will,
  Which ardent love can raise but not control.

The joy be thine that brightened boyhood's dream,
  Green fields, and flowers, and hosts of murmuring bees;
The limpid laughter of the mountain stream;
  Unwithering groves of scented hawthorn trees!

For still, perchance, within thy spirit's home,
  Old scenes not lost are like thyself renewed;
And there are meads where herds contented roam;
  And there are vistas glinting thro' the wood;

And there are cheerful dawnings of the day;
  And there are musings meek at evenfall;
And there are skies not warm but cold and grey;
  And there are captive souls to disenthrall!

Oh Friend! be thine the hero's Godlike joy
  Proudly to strive without reward or rest,—
To bear the cross and find it sweet employ,
  For ever struggling, and for ever blest!

ISAAC OLIVER JONES.

DIED, SEPT. 17, 1896.

I.

Like a sweet psalm when it has reached its close;
  Like the last smile of the declining sun;
  A Sabbath when its placid course is run;
A couch where weary limbs have found repose;
A table spread "in presence of our foes";
    The blessing softly breathed which leaves out none;
    The last "Amen" which marks the service done;
Like mother's love that comes but never goes,—
So thou, dear friend!—we strike no note of woe,
  For we have known thee; and thyself so good,
Our loss in losing thee we hardly know,—
  We are like hunger when refreshed with food;
Our souls, like thine, in peace, and satisfied;
Thou lived'st so well, we feel thou hast not died!

II.

My heart is sore, and yet well satisfied;
  I feel the weighty stroke so lightly given;
Still do I drink the cup, tho' now denied;
    The friend I mourn is beckoning me to Heaven;
Pierced to the quick, yet only half-way sad;
    The pain would be past durance were it less;

I am all sorrow for the joy I've had,
  And seraph wings relieve my loneliness :
The shadow came, and yet it only seemed
  My best sunlight in the contrasted ray
Which from the prophet's soft-wheel'd chariot gleam'd
  While wafting him to life's more brilliant day ;—
Oh, would that mantle, as it did of old,
Fall on my filial spirit manifold !

III.

At the grave-side the Patriarch Psalm was sung ;
  The silver notes from the same lips ascending
  That called him Father,—in melodious blending
The tremulous joy and solemn sweetness hung,
As heavenly music may on mortal tongue,—
  While snow-flake seraphs to and fro were wending
  On steps of sunbeam, as they did, attending
Long since on Jacob, when his heart was young,
And night-dews fell on him,—on viewless wings,
  And in their censers, wrought of mystic gold,
Each happy sprite his errand homeward brings,
  Love's incense, more than thankful heart can hold ;
That two enraptured souls in Paradise
Might see and breathe their children's sacrifice !

I. J.

DIED, MARCH 21, 1895.

The silent chamber, witness of her pain
  And weariness thro' many long, sad years,
  Was thrill'd at last with psalms and smiling tears,
The sweetest fall of resurrection rain
That ever brought spring-flowers to earth again,—
  And Death, soon as the music touched his ears,
  Himself alone felt stricken by his fears,
Folded his dark wings meekly at the strain,
And stood transfigured; for he well could trace
  The harmony of love and praise and prayer
Left by a lifetime in the still calm face,
  Seen at a glance, and fixed for ever there,—
Like the child's gift of lilies in her hand,
Pledge of the New Life in the Better Land!

BISHOP MOULE.

"The bishop has been out in China some thirty years, and has evidently attained to the quiet mind. He disclaimed the idea that he was a Bishop Hannington. He had not a spark of enthusiasm in him, he said. There were bishops and bishops, missionaries and missionaries: all were wanted. The great thing was to go and work where Christ sent one."—*Report of Meeting at Oxford.*

"We cannot all be friars; and many are the ways by which God carries His own to Heaven."—*Don Quixote to Sancho.*

Not for thy long years' task alone,
   Good bishop, from my heart I love thee;
But for the weakness thou dost own
   In meddling not with things above thee.

Not thine the swift unsparing zeal,
   Enthusiastic, fierce and fiery;
Nor thine what noble spirits feel
   When duty's path is hard and briery.

Mayhap thy toil of thrice ten years,
   With but an honest heart upholden,
No strain of nerve, no bursts of tears,
   Needed to make it pure and golden.

In God's great benison of good
   There is a gift of dulness given;
And when it worketh all it could,
   It findeth welcome back to Heaven.

Souls quiet, unimpassioned, slow,
   God bringeth to His royal city,
Not by the path the martyrs go,
   Blood-stained, and drenched with tears of pity.

Some do not know the grass is green,
   They only know that wrongs need righting;
And some the stars have never seen,
   So rapt are they with striving, fighting.

Some never rest and never tire;
   Some are who cannot work for thinking;—
Can God who feeds the soul on fire,
   Forsake when it is merely sinking?

Kind Heaven reserves a quiet place
   For plain and unaspiring people,
Who run but never win the race,—
   God loves the church not for the steeple.

Bright honour be to those who shine,
   The all-enduring soldier, stoic;
Good bishop, let us not repine—
   We were not born to be heroic.

So will we calmly walk our way,
   And humbly do the task assigned us;
Kind Heaven be praised! return we may
   And leave no hero's name behind us

WILLIAM PEDDIE, D.D.

For sixty-five years Minister of Bristo Church, Edinburgh.

LIKE some quaint cup, by antique art designed,
Full to the brim—nor yet quite overflows—
With wine of Hebrew faith and well refined,
Which mildly in the evening sunlight glows,
Most gracefully and in old Grecian kind
His life was lived in beautiful repose;
The noble face, the silvery voice, the mind,
All bore it, and the life's calm lingering close.
I loved as no son better did his sire—
I loved the genial, chivalrous old man;
With more than lover's self-respecting fire
Did I revere the blameless course he ran
With step so soft, and soul so undefiled,
Till Sleep took to her breast again her weary child.

A FULL-GROWN MAN.

In Memoriam: Rev. Hugh Stowell Brown.

Struck like a great oak in a day of thunder,
  When the strong arms are laid untimely low,
Swift by the lightning sword-stroke reft asunder,
  And all the nestled songsters by the blow
Struck too with mute and sorrow-laden wonder,
  From their loved shelter scattered to and fro,—
Such was thy strength, such they whom it defended,
And such the stroke of God whereby it ended,—
  Strong man of God, broad-breasted man of men,
A Pauline-Samson to our day descended,
  As little shamed to love the joys of life
  As gird thee for the truth in manly strife,—
Such as we prized thee, now the angels can—
Nature's own child, and Christ's own full-grown man!

TOO LATE FOR MARTYRDOM:

OR TOO SOON.

Firm as a rock, and gentle as the dew;
Genial as sunshine is in April showers;
A child of Truth, a son of Laughter too,—
   Well-placed, not long, in this sad world of ours;
A brave man, tender, generous, and true;
   As rich in charities as Summer is in flowers:
Of others' untold ills too much he knew
To care aught for his own, alas! not small nor few.
   With all his heart engaged, and all his powers,
Divinely served the neediest, and threw
   A common workman's years of service into hours:
His martyr-blood unspilled,—he came too late;
Or his, perchance, the sterner, nobler fate
Had Love but willed it so that he should wait!

SILVER WEDDING.

(TO B. AND M. S. W.)

May God who gave the silver give the gold,—
   Who said long since that Love should wed with Peace,
And live thro' endless years but ne'er grow old,
   In happy union bless'd with large increase;—
The courts of Heaven were new that bridal day,
   And wing'd with sunshine were the ardent hours;
Joy laugh'd to see the cherubs at their play,
   Sowing the sky with stars, the earth with flowers;
The frame of all things felt a strange new thrill,
   For Music then first drew her charming breath,
And lo! that wedding march is marching still
   Thro' hearts of sorrow and thro' halls of death;—
In all true homes of God, beneath, above,
Love owns all peace, and nothing lives but love!

IN WEST KILBRIDE U.P. CHURCH.

Only a rustic maiden's face,
Mingling with other means of grace,
To-day, within the House of Prayer,
Brought revelation to me there.
With true apocalypse it shined,
As sideways from the pew behind
I saw it, and I understood,
As ne'er before, that God is good.

No sign was there of consequence,
But quiet, plain, unlettered sense;
Yet something seem'd enshrin'd within
The sober eye and sun-brown'd skin,
Played on the lip, enwreath'd the brow—
I know not what, I know not how—
Suggesting thoughts beyond the spheres,
And wide as the eternal years.

Nor did I love or covet her,—
I was a simple worshipper
Of Him, who made the daisy spring,
The brooklet dance, the laverock sing,
And bade this face, this homely creature
Of artless mien, and honest feature,
By some sweet mystery of choice
Speak to me with a prophet's voice.

She saw me not, nor could she know
The spell that swayed my spirit so,
Nor hear the soft-breath'd symphony
Her own self made and wafted me,
Like far-off music to the ear
When moonlit air hangs calm and clear—
A silent music to my gaze,
A perfect Gospel-paraphrase!

For tho' I lent no languid care
To the psalm sung and offered prayer,
Listen'd to saving truth proclaim'd,
Paid every due that could be named,
Still did she, by some sacred thrall,
Move me and bless me more than all,—
With many a vision fresh and kind
For weary heart and worried mind,—
Of Father's love, and angels' wings,
Afloat through all earth's common things;
Of tables for the hungry spread;
Of sweeten'd tears by mourners shed;
Of pardon, Mercy's meek-eyed child;
Of hearts, long alien, reconciled;
Of suffering souls content to wait
Beneath the fires of lust and hate;—
The whole wide world, from shore to shore,
Seem'd with compassions mantled o'er;
All evil things were Virtue's food,
Dark shadows of approaching good,
The fruit of God, ripe underneath,
Like full corn in the blade's green sheath.

Thus did my thoughts meander on,
Till service closed, the vision gone,
The maiden passed, I know not where—
A melted cloud in vacant air :
I nevermore, perchance, to trace
The benediction of her face.

What hers may be of daily task
I know not, and I need not ask ;—
Heaven bless her in her humble cares !
While she the farmer's brose prepares,
Or mucks the byre, or binds the sheaf,
Or gives the lowing kine relief,
Churn she the butter, press the cheese,
Or ply such other tasks as these ;—
And if, as I fain hope may be,
'Neath fragrant shade of hawthorn tree,
Some kindly lad and she—not loth—
Have given and ta'en a lover's troth,—
Bless her, as in the twilight haze
She wanders on the heathery braes,
Or in some glen on brookside stone
Sits meditative—not alone ;
Or should they lift the unslippered heel
In rapturous din of social reel !

All this ungrudged, for was not she
God's priest anointed, teaching me
What holy gladness one might find
In being born of human kind ;

What psalms of peace Creation sings
In simple unintending things,—
How bless'd with beauty, and how rife
With hopes, the God-like gift of life;
And one great truth, the last and best,
More rich by far than all the rest—
In her sweet looks I saw it shine—
The face of God is feminine!

A THOUGHT OF SYMPATHY.

O Balm! which none but wintry blasts can bring
   To breathe the health of Heaven on human woe,
Thou art too tender for the zephyr's wing,
   We find thee in the sternest winds that blow—
   Chill ice can make thy warm compassions flow,
Thou sweet, miraculous, death-defying thing!
Balm of dear youth when we are growing old,
   When Life can see, well-pleased, her lamp burn low,
When at the brightening hearth the heart grows cold,
   And with our loved ones lost we fain would go,—
O Balm of Christ! our wounded friend behold,
   Who censer-like did waft thee to and fro,
And made thee to a thousand hearts well-known,—
Breathe now thy benediction on his own!

BREEZE HILL, BOOTLE.

A Letter to a Friend in Edinburgh.

Wellnigh the summit of this gradual hill
I please my roving eye and wanton will
With varied scenes that lie in prospect round
On lazy slope of slow-descending ground;
While from my gladsome window, gazing down,
I view the distant sea and neighbouring town.
    First, for my window-sill is broad and bare,
I see the vulgar sparrow strutting there,
Brisk as a would-be lord, ignobly sprung,
Yet spruce with prideful airs and clamorous tongue.
And often, when the ledge was laid with snow,
Trim robin I have seen trip to and fro,
In decent poverty, with look genteel,
Winking a sober prayer for morning meal.
    There, too, has lain the lamentable dead,
Dropped from the starling's nest high overhead,—
A shapeless, naked, melancholy thing,
All innocent of downy breast and feathered wing;
In kindly soil we laid the limp remains—
A long reward of rest for life's brief pains!
    Beneath, a modest length of garden lies,
With sod of welcome green for town-used eyes,
With brown walks bordered, and with beds of flowers;
But neighbouring gardens vie too well with ours.

I look beyond, and see the patient fields
All waiting for the dower that Autumn yields;
In some, long ridges, like the rippling wave,
Hold the earth-apple in its hopeful grave;
And some that now seem desolate and cold,
Will soon be corn-lakes warm with waving gold.
   I watch the hues of the chameleon soil,
And all the yearly round of labourer's toil;
As varying task, or varying season needs
The pruning-knife, or plough with prancing steeds.
   But ah! these pleasant fields will show not long
Sweet Nature's work inwoven with her song;
Harbour the groping mole in silent dark,
Or send, like fervent prayer, the heavenward lark;
Hear moanings of the oxen long and deep,
Or feel the tender lips of nibbling sheep.
All this God gave, but man forbids to stay—
The builder comes, and Nature steals away.
   What time begins the drone of yellow bee,
And scented snowflakes lie on hawthorn-tree,
And softening gales beneath the blinking moon
Tell us that brighter days are coming soon;
When Love's warm law through every creature glows,
The same that moves the heart of budding rose;
Then with the evening's gentle hour and still,
The frequent lover walks this quiet hill,
Content with aimless wand'rings to and fro,
Long silences, and whisp'ring soft and low.
   Break not the golden dream, undimmed with care,
That forms new Eden for each ardent pair;

Bring not too soon the melancholy years
Weighted with leaden griefs, and wet with tears!
　See, over all the reddening plain below,
The new town rise in many a checkered row;
The several villa, and the close-made street,
Where noisy Business toils at Leisure's feet,—
There would the pensive come—but comes no more—
To walk the green lanes and the lonely shore;
On native hills the rabbit gaily ran,
And all the scene was peace till plagued with man!
　So Time, where I expecting to behold
The mystic Summer weave her green with gold,
Will pave the soil and bring the busy throng,—
But if it must come, may it linger long!
　Beyond the field, I view with well-pleased eyes
Religion's finger lifted to the skies,
The plain church spire, from ostentation free,
And nearer Heaven than aught the eye can see:
True type of ancient seer, it serves to show
Whence man has come, and where he hopes to go.
　And oft the chimes, like rain on thirsty ground,
Pour down refreshing showers of cheerful sound;
Or execrate, with crash of dreadful din,
The hated Guy for well-remembered sin.
　The child of neighbouring church, wide space between,
Stands the loud school beside the happier green,
Where, loosed from bitter yoke of book and pen,
The tiny women brawl with tiny men;—
Myself not far, but far enough away
To lose the din and yet enjoy the play.

BREEZE HILL, BOOTLE.

O'er slanting roofs and many-windowed walls,
The belfry to the busy playground calls,
And with the church points heavenward as it can,—
So tries the child to emulate the man;
Thus by matured example in the wise
The lisping learn to speak, the low to rise.

Close by, columnal chimneys, grim and tall,
One lusty giant rising o'er them all,
Plying with fire and steam the grateful task
To draw old Adam's wine from earthen cask.

And lo! great lids hang darkly on the right
O'er gloomy wells that hold our evening light,
Sun-substitute that cunning man has found,
Whose rays through iron pipes run underground.
Ah, man! what canst thou see,—what canst thou know?
God's light is from above,—thine from below!

There, too, I watch the barges come and go
On smooth canal, monotonous and slow;
Yet sweet the liquid highway to my eye
With mirrored hues of many-tinted sky.

Oft in my walks, with sickening heart, I note
The poor lank brute-beast pull the lumbering boat,
Yet scarce can drag his limbs, or draw his breath,
Sad intermediate shadow both of life and death,—
Once played his part, perchance, in noble strife,
For this reward—these thankless dregs of life!

Beyond, I scan the varied landscape o'er
From distant lighthouse on the Crosby shore,
To Litherland and sea-washed Waterloo,
And Seaforth with its saintly church in view.

And like the white-winged spirit of the plain,
I mark the fluttering breath of frequent train
Fly o'er the land, and float upon the wind,
With roaring street of railway-cars behind.
How the heart beats, and brain distracted reels,
In modern men who rush through life on wheels!
   In constant haze the leftward scene appears
Where Liverpool his thriving greatness rears,
And nearer still his brawny arm extends,
And plucks our flowers with toil-stained finger-ends.
   A quarry near, of depth and width immense,
Startles the view and strikes the whirling sense,
Foul smoke ascending from the vast abyss,
Plutonic groans, demoniac shriek and hiss,
While human cries commingle in the din
Like final woe of unrepented sin.
Ah me! what thoughts the passing stranger fill
Of other nameless regions, deeper still!
   High o'er the crowding roofs in vale outspread
A mighty obelisk rears its classic head,
But holds no lustrous deeds, or patriot's name,
Proud heritage of death-defying Fame,—
Offspring of Art and Industry combined,
It bears to heaven the smoke that plagues mankind!
   Through openings in the builder's broken screen
Tall masts of well-protected fleets are seen;
And over these, beyond where, deep and wide,
Majestic Mersey rolls her surging tide,
The slopes of Wallasey and Oxton rise
With charms like some well-peopled Paradise;

When rays of early morn the scene unfold
The land is velvet green, the mansions gold,
And on the lofty landmark where he stands
The happy windmill seems to clap his hands.

 Then height o'er height, aspiring higher still,
Dim shades appear of distant Cambrian hill,
Whereon queen Mystery with magic sway
Rules o'er my idling fancy day by day.

 Now from the finite land, infinite sea!
I turn with reverential eye to thee,
Last theme of my unworthy song and best,
Thou radiant zone of wide far-reaching west!
Man fears but cannot harm thee or confine,
Image of his inviolate God, and thine;
No stain of ancient curse in human toil
Will e'er unsanctify thy virgin soil,
But pure as heaven will evermore be seen
Thy fields of blue, thy fringe of evergreen!

 Full-freighted Mersey straight in front of me
Bears down her burden to the imperial sea,
Who smiles afar where she can shun the eye,
And lifts her lip to kiss the bending sky.

 With naked vision, or convenient glass,
I watch the splendid panorama pass,—
Fleets taking leave the fluid earth to roam,
Or laden with the spoils returning home;—
Strange pilgrims in the desert of the deep,
Fantastic, various as the course they keep,
Both tail of fish and wing of bird they wear,
And navigate at once both sea and air;—

Wild ocean's Bedouins, wand'ring far and near,
White sail for hood, and mast for pointed spear.

How altered now in courage as in form
To face dread billows and defiant storm,
Since when, of old, propelled by plashing oar,
Seaward they looked with fear and hugged the shore !
Strength in their prow, and beauty at their crest,
Borne out upon the full tide's ample breast,
The great ships pass, and dwindle to the eye
Between the silver lines of sea and sky,—
So come delightful dreams before the mind,
Linger, and pass, and leave no trace behind.

Oft when the western gale has raged too long,
And fret in weary dock the windbound throng,
With breeze from friendly east to set them free,
Lo ! what a lengthened forest trails the sea !
Each noble ship, strong, beautiful, and brave,
Led by steam-tug, like despicable slave,
Till threatening shoals and crowded waters passed,
Sweet liberty and roomy sea are gained at last.

Less beautiful but greater far in strength,
In bulk immense, like very streets in length,
Giants that own grim Vulcan for their sire,
With ribs of iron and with heart of fire,
The tribes of ocean-steamers keep their way,
Winds blow their worst, and waves roll as they may !

God speed you ! bravest of your noble race,
Who meet the rude Atlantic face to face,
In wild mid-ocean, dauntlessly alone
Cope with his mighty strength and hold your own ;

Or when the awful icebergs gleam before,
Or dark fogs gather on Canadian shore.
God speed you! 'mid the fair West Indian Isles,
Where Nature's havoc mingles with her smiles ;
Or when, with heavy toil and look forlorn,
Adrip with ice ye round the desolate Horn ;
Or lie near tropic shore in sickening glare
While pestilent vapours load the stagnant air.
Or if to ancient East your course may be,
Where cyclone wave turns land to dreadful sea ;
Or prowl Malayan hordes to kill or sell
The storm-struck mariner—God speed you well !

   I watch with joy that only lovers know,
These wanderers of the deep sea come and go ;
Muse on the many-sided life they bear,
Man's all of good or evil gathered there ;—
Man's whole mixed family—some weak some strong,—
Some in good health who will be sick ere long ;
Some with the sanguine cheek and cheerful eye,
And some scarce wishful that their grief should die.
A maiden goes to make one blessed now,
Who keeps unbroken still a schoolboy's vow ;
Old age consents at last to leave the shore,
And meet a far-off son—who breathes no more.
A bridal pair on deck walk to and fro,—
An uncaught criminal retires below ;
Some are on business, some on pleasure bent,
And some go home no wiser than they went ;
Friendships are falsely made and fortunes lost
By luckless fools who count the rueful cost.

What full-phased life these floating isles contain
In hope and fear, in folly, love and pain;
No feature lost that can be mourned or prized,—
The world is there, and man epitomized!
 Thus do I mark the scene and meditate,
While fretful Ocean moans beneath her freight,—
Bearing with equal strength, but changeful mood,
The wave-worn, many-masted multitude,
On heaving breast of slowly-swelling tides,
Or when the gradual flood once more subsides.
 Oft I behold the war-clad training-ships
Send thunder-cloud and lighting from their lips;
While loyal hearts are taught with skilful hand
To strike the foe, and guard their native land;—
Behold the fishermen on perilous waves
That yield their bread, and oftentimes their graves;—
Or wanton pleasure-boat, with sun-tipped sail,
Smile at the rolling waves and flustering gale.
 The wintry scene is infinitely grand
When foaming billows rave along the strand;
While rapid tide and raging tempest meet,
And clouds of spray contend with clouds of sleet.
Perchance I notice then, with throbbing breast,
Some drifting ship alone and sorely pressed,
Amid the dreadful breakers rise and fall,
Or vanish in the gloom of sudden squall.
 But should the tempest rage at lone midnight,
A creeping horror chills me at the sight
Where, like some lurid demon standing by,
New Brighton lighthouse rolls his bloodshot eye.

Awestruck I stand, my heart aquake with fear
Lest some ill-fated crew are struggling near,
Cling to the mast or ply the useless oar,
Or float on fragile raft and seek the shore.
Haply the gallant lifeboat hurries there,
Defies the storm and triumphs o'er despair.
Yet some, alas! may perish in the foam
Who saw, e'er dark, and wept at sight of home!

 All-radiantly the summer ocean shines
At eventide when sultry day declines,
And weary Sun bends low his burning face,
While lines of liquid glory mark the place;
Glorious the spot his glowing cheek has pressed,
His many-curtained couch of gorgeous rest,—
Magnificent array, that well might vie
Splendours ineffable of tropic sky:
Lo! in the royal purple's opening fold
Gleam forth deep inner shrines of dazzling gold;
Pavilions multiform of saffron hue
Dappled with stars of empyrean blue,—
Wrought by the spirit of perpetual change
To grander glories ever new and strange.

 Sometimes the clouds of awful crimson spread
Like canopy of dripping blood o'erhead,
While man and beast look on with fearful eye,
And solemn stillness reigns in earth and sky;
But suddenly the tragic scene will cease,
And charms of beauty blend with charms of peace,
While answering blackbirds in the waning light
Warble a quiet note of sweet good-night,—

Till darkness mounts her many-spangled throne,
And holds all Nature's empire for her own.
When I retire to sleep, the vision seems
To linger in my soul in glorious dreams,
Wherein to me, all undeserved, 'tis given
To see the House of God and Gate of Heaven!

RETROSPECT.

*(Lines suggested on visiting an antique avenue of rare
beauty at Dalwick, near Peebles, September, 1892.*

The path where gods and men, once on a day,
  Were fain to wander, ere their love grew cold,—
  Each smiled on each, and wondrous tales were told,
The while this brook went on its rambling way,
And those old trees shook down the sun's warm ray
  In flickering waves of glory manifold,—
  Or Autumn shed her wrinkled leaves of gold,
Whilst plaintive winds made mournful roundelay;—
  As oft befell, in ages not so far,
When youth and maiden walked this green arcade,
  Pale as the moonlight, trembling as a star,
And fearful of the bliss-born vows they made;—
  Quaint Fancy boasts of yonder old stone chair,
  King Lear and sweet Cordelia rested there!

A REMINISCENCE OF CONTINENTAL TRAVEL, May, 1891.

My Brothers! we have travelled far,
   Through summer scenes and wintry too;
But no cold variance came to mar
   The love that made our friendship true.

Of all God gave to charm the soul
   Our brotherhood we prize not least—
The mutual trust that kept it whole,
   And made it a continual feast.

We meet, it may be, not again
   Till we have crossed the silent stream;
But this glad time will haunt us then
   In beauty like an angel's dream.

A thousand memories intertwine
   Of glowing heart and raptured eye,
Like tendrils of the budding vine,—
   To bear rich clusters by and bye.

God was our Teacher all the way,
   And we were learning well or ill;
But through life's long eternal day
   We humbly must be learning still.

We worshipped at their noblest shrine
   Nature below and God above,
With veneration so divine
   It seemed too great to call it love.

Yet is not this, for you and me,
   The best our foreign travel yields—
To know how sweet home is, and see
   Once more the sward of English fields,—

The hedge-rows, and the rolling seas
   Of undulating hills and vales,
Where Beauty waits in quiet ease
   To float her bark and trim her sails?

Fair smiling France, the Switzer's hills,
   The Rhine-land with romantic glow,
Italian lakes, Italian trills—
   We scorn them not, nor rank them low:

Mountain on mountain towering high
   Where never foot of man had trod,
Great stairs descending from the sky,
   Stained with the pure white feet of God:

Dark forests, and the streamlet's dance,
   The dizzy cliff where eagles flew,
Calm lake's poetic countenance
   Wherein the heavens and earth were new:

Milk-white meandering and roar
    Of torrents in their rocky home;
Broad river on its broken floor
    Surging in hills of dazzling foam :

The crag, the awful depth below,
    The bridge so tremulous and slim ;
Sweet peasant homes in many a row,
    And pendulous on the mountain's rim :

And where the avalanche dragged its way
    From barren height to cultured sod,
Caught the poor children at their play
    And snatched them swiftly home to God :

The grey old temples, dear to Art,
    With golden altars deck'd with flowers ;
Stored with the treasures of the heart,—
    Albeit, an alien faith to ours :

One step, and we forgot the street
    In the cool shade where God is known,—
So still, so gloriously complete
    In gleaming glass and sculptured stone !

And if, within the wide expanse,
    One solitary knelt in prayer,—
It spoke the Father's kindly glance
    Who numbers every straggling hair !

Were these by Superstition raised?
  Conceived in brain of sin, forsooth?—
Then be the Prince of Evil praised,
  And perish all our hopes for Truth!

Milan! thy priestly rites to me
  Are motes of dust in purest air;
Thy Pile, whate'er thy mummeries be,
  Itself is worship—God is there!

Those marble hosts, in magic rows,
  Do all but heave the human breast,—
Still choir, whose anthem ever flows—
  Our God is worthy of the best!

Cologne! beneath thy stately fane
  The children met in myriad throng,
Wafting in sweet angelic strain
  The fragrance of their Even-song.

A sudden spell was round me cast,—
  My steps were wandering soft and slow
Thro' dim lone cloisters of the past,
  And mystic glades of long ago.

With tears my mother's memory came,
  And, saving this, all else was dumb—
"Our Father, hallowed be Thy name,
  Thy will be done, Thy kingdom come!"

My Brothers! we have travelled far;
  May these fair scenes that charmed our sight
Still keep their lustre like a star,
  When Time has darkened into night!

A BIRTHDAY ODE.

The years glide by, and over saddening Youth
  Comes the chill sense that she is growing old;
But Time can never change a heart of truth
  Save but to take the tarnish from the gold;—
Come he with fifty winters on his crest,
His gloomy wing brings but a harmless guest,—
No flutter need arise in Virtue's breast,
  For Truth is ever young, and Love is never cold.

MEMORABILIA ROMANA.

I.

THE COLOSSEUM.

Here Silence mocks for once her fair good name,
    And with an echoing wonder thrills the soul;
This Pile, restored, thro' all its giant frame
    Trembles, as once it did beneath the roll
Of ebbing, flowing, thunder-like acclaim,
    As man or beast the sanguine slippery goal
Had gained, and hard-fought wreath of fame,
    With shouts all Heaven could hear but not control;
Nor is the gasp unheard that comes no more,
    And sigh so faint that it can reach no ear,—
Of him, of her who at her rustic door
    Naught can but kiss her babe and wipe the tear;
The cruel throng their plaudits will not stay,
And she still keeps lone vigil night and day.

We envy thee, and oh! we need thee still,
    Brave monk, who from the orient sped
With silent heart, grim hope, unflinching will,
    In no imprudent haste thy blood to shed
If but thou could'st the Master's love fulfil,
    And pluck the friend-laid sorrow from His head;

Here crowds hung o'er thee like a threatening hill;
  In brutal rage they howled and wished thee dead;
But when thy harmless hood swept in between,
  The swords that sought each other fell on thee,
What sudden awe-struck stillness changed the scene!
  Then could the stone-blind Christians clearly see
In blood of thine—the last that stained this floor—
The honour'd Cross of Him whose name they bore.

II.

THE MAMERTINE PRISON,

BENEATH THE CAPITOL, ROME,

Whence St. Paul is supposed to have been led to Execution.

Be this thy pride for ever, oh fair Queen
  Of countless triumphs! this, of all the rest
  Glutting thy gates with spoils from East and West,
With slaves who sceptred princes once had been,
This captive, whom thy heedless throngs have seen,
  Of all rare treasures ever yet possessed
  By vaunting conqueror, the first and best,
Saving his dearest Lord, the Nazarene;
Oh! blush, and name it as thy single boast,
  Proud Mistress of the earth, Imperial Rome!
That long time since thou wert this poor man's host,
  Lent him his honoured chain and latest home,
Where bread of tears the Christ and he might eat
Ungrudged, in this foul den beneath thy feet!

III.

THE EUCALYPTUS.

*Church of the Three Fountains, Roman Campagna,
Scene of St. Paul's Execution.*

Three fountains rose where fell the martyr's head,
   Offspring of life from the death-breathing ground;
Then, like a nurse who at the sufferer's bed
   Kneeleth to suck the poison from the wound,
This angel Eucalyptus came, to spread
   Soft wings of healing-unction all around,
Drink the foul juice the soil was wont to shed,
   And bid these cloisters ring with joyful sound,
Where once the morbid face, the sunken eye,
   Sepulchral cheek, dry lip, and sharpened chin
Of weary monk appall'd the passer-by;—
   Oh! is it thus, amidst malarial sin,
The friend of Jesus bears, thro' pain and loss,
The healing tree of his unmurmuring cross!

IV.

THE CATACOMBS AND ST. PETER'S.

Not now Thou livest with the dead men's bones
   In temples dark and sinuous of the tomb;
Thine is the sun-lit, loftiest, largest room,
   The jewell'd altars, tribunes, golden thrones,

Showers of sweet chimes, triumphant organ tones,
  The glowing fresco for sepulchral gloom,
  And all the arts' bright summer-time of bloom
In pictured splendours and in sculptured stones,—
Faith of the Son of God, the Crucified!
  Not now more low than Lazarus at the gate,
Thine is the purple robe,—perchance the pride,
  The hollow-hearted feast and lordly state;—
Of all save dogs forsaken, oh! wert thou
More near to Abraham's bosom then than now?

v.

THE PANTHEON.

This, too, is Upper-Room and festal hall
  Where supper-table for the Christ is spread;—
  The pagan gods here own Him for their Head,—
They went before, obedient to His call,
Prepared the feast till the fit time should fall,
  When "Master, all things ready now" they said;—
  He came, He poured the wine, He brake the bread,
He bless'd, and held communion with them all:
The lord of power, the queen of female grace
  Are here, and he whose altar drips with blood,
The god of fluent speech and rapid pace,
  The god of fire, and he who rules the flood,
She of the serpent-swathing helm and shield,
  They of the peaceful hearth and fruitful field.

VI.

THE CARICATURE

(Of the Crucifixion sketched on the wall in slaves' apartments under Imperial Palace, Palatine Hill).

Whilst high o'erhead great Cæsar kept his feast,
   Here was no mirth for thee, thou honoured slave!
   Not thine who felt the wound, but his who gave;
And if long since both pain and spite have ceased,
Here lie in graphic plaster unreleased
   The rude insulting lines of scribbling knave,
   Deriding thee, and Him who came to save,
As tho' His Cross held mongrel man and beast;—
Alexamēnus! thine was woe indeed,
   No silver-tongued reproach, nor silken shame;—
Poor slave, we pity thee, we praise thy creed,
   We laud the Christ, we laud His Cross with fame
Loud as the world is wide,—yet still, alas!
The Christian bearing *his* we deem—an ass!

VII.

THE CRUCIFIXION

(Of Guido Reni, in church of St. Lorenzo, Rome).

Sorrow and Peace meet here at Heaven's door
   In this pale Form suffused with silvery light;
   I never knew a sadder, holier sight;
I never heard persuasive speech before
Of Love's low whisperings—Go, and sin no more:

The bleeding Love that makes my crimson white,
From depths of woe and sweetness infinite,
As moonlit waves come moaning to the shore ;—
It draws me as a trembling captive near ;
It veils with beauty all I would not see ;
Subdues the horror, brings the better fear ;
And greets me with the new song yet to be
When self-effulgent shines His Cross of pain,
And all hearts hail the Lamb that once was slain.

VIII.

THE COMMUNION.

AT ST. PETER'S, ROME.

There was an angel in the old priest's face,
　If angel bless'd might be with snow-white years,
　And eyes all dewy-wet with unshed tears ;
He, only he, did consecrate the place
With breathing balm, and founts of heavenly grace ;
　To look on him was death to low-bred fears,
　And life to hopes laid out upon their biers :
His every feature bore in every trace
Melchisedec : his smile a sacrament,
　The gorgeous edifice had been but poor
Awanting it, and Art's great wealth ill-spent ;
　Some old-time minister on Scottish moor
He might have been, when martyr blood was shed,
And 'neath the lapwing's cry the feast was spread !

IX.

THE PILGRIMS,

AT THE COMMUNION.

In crowds they came, and on their bended knees
   Crept near, and nearer still, row after row,
   Moving in solemn ranks, subdued and slow,—
Nor aught had they the carnal sense to please,
Mere dregs, and social "wines upon the lees"
   Not well-refined, but drugg'd with toil and woe;
   Each one the Father bless'd, and did it so
As tho' he felt 'twere done "to one of these";—
Their plaintive song the meanwhile rose and fell,
   Now fainting, now reviving, deep and shrill,
Such as the woman's heart at Jacob's Well
   Might yield, or the long wail from Calvary's hill
Which through the ages never yet could cease
Its tuneful tears and pantings after peace!

X.

AT SHELLEY'S GRAVE,

IN THE ENGLISH CEMETERY, ROME.

The gentle stars on thee shake down their dews,
   Pure and unfettered Soul of liquid song!
   Less free than none thou minglest in the throng
Whom Light no eye e'er saw doth interfuse
And robe for evermore with rainbow hues;

It were to Immortality a wrong
To say *Here*, *There*, of thee, *How brief*, *How long ;*
Nor shall one thrill the less o'ertake thy Muse
Till lustre find a grave in Beauty's eye,
  Till woman's bosom spurn her child's caress,
  Till Thought forsake the dreaming wilderness,
And Life repine when the sweet Spring draws nigh ;
  Till yon fair cloud forswear her shining dress,
And this bright lark his pathway to the sky !

XI.

AT KEATS'S GRAVE,

NOT FAR FROM SHELLEY'S.

Thy name is "writ in water"—writ in tears,
  As that Name is to whom all creatures bow ;
  In shades of Sorrow's temple dwellest thou
Where Fame no tablet to her children rears,
But there are choirs of the melodious years
  To weep for aye, as they are weeping now,
  For thee, and bear thy name upon their brow,
And waft thy music round and round the spheres ;—
Oh for a draught of that immortal wine
  Which he, for thy sole self, filled to the brim,
Whose "heart of hearts," now laid not far from thine,
  Once bled for thee, as thou had'st bled for him !
Oh choicest boon that friendliest Fate could bring—
To be as sweetly sung as thou thyself could'st sing !

PROVIDENCE.

An Incident of Earthquake in Italy.

High Carnival begins to cloy;—
With less of madness, more of joy,
Behold! our bright-eyed peasant boy
  Within his own home lingers;
The crowd may vent their pious rage,—
Far humbler things his soul engage—
Lures his pet sparrow from the cage
  And feeds it on his fingers.

Beneath that fair Italian sky,
While soft the evening shadows lie,
How bright the little flutterer's eye,
  And how the throat is swelling
To trill out thanks with all his might!
Love never saw a prettier sight,—
His ecstacy of warm delight
  Each to the other telling!

Thro' haze the morning sun arose,
Thro' sultry air grown thick with woes,
For in the earthquake's awful throes
  The Carnival has ended;
Ruin's black mantle covereth all,
The lowly cot, the princely hall,
The labouring brute-beasts in the stall,
  In one great horror blended!

Poor peasant boy! he breathes his last,
A brother's arms around him cast;—
Thus lovingly his life he passed,—
    Thus piously he perished;
All hid beneath the ghastly mound,
Only his hand above the ground,
And there, as on a perch, is found
    The little bird he cherished!

The God of earthquakes, driving o'er
Bewildered sea and groaning shore,
Unlatched the little captive's door
    With just a touch so slender,—
The great, the good God over all,
Who guards the sparrow from its fall,
And when His ways do most appal—
    Most mercifully tender!

Thou tiny prophet from the tomb,—
Thou bud of an immortal bloom,—
Hope's flower, upon the bed of doom
    In deathless glory springing,—
Thee, little bird! I carry hence,—
A sign,—a charm,—a Providence,—
A flood of heavenly affluence
    Upon my pathway flinging!

A MEMORABLE DAY.

*On Coaching Tour, G. & S.-W. R., Dalmellington
and New Galloway, May 27, 1896.*

To think of it is like a glorious dream ;
Nature beguiled us with her ample best ;
The White Thorn might have robed an angel's breast;
Grand organ-tones were in the tumbling stream ;
In deep Ness Glen came down the glinting beam
　　Like hope for some poor prisoner; on crest
Of the wild moor we might have been possess'd
With wings, so brisk the buoyant air did seem ;—
Cairnsmuir, The Kells, the quiet Lake of Doon,
　　The jewell'd fields all glittering gold and white,
The very graves, wherein alas ! too soon
　　Lie all, were fraught with visions of delight ;—
Serene, like us, the sun that day arose,—
He sank, not more content than we, in calm repose.

THE LANGUAGE OF FLOWERS.

A ROADSIDE ROMANCE.

A floweret by the brookside grew,
It was a dainty, blue-eyed thing;
    (Alas! the happy moments flew
      As swiftly as a bird on wing!)
A sweet lass led me to the spot.
I wished she would forget-me-not;
To speak I did not dare to do,
My wish in secret harbouring.
    (And still the moments flew, they flew
      As swiftly as a bird on wing!)
She stood, she turned her sharply round,
She stooped, she touched the dewy ground;
I saw the deepening colour speak
Faintly upon her nut-brown cheek;
She murmured, and the tune I knew
Such as alone true love could sing.
    (Alas! the happy moments flew
      As swiftly as a bird on wing!)
We rested by the green hillside;
Fain both to show it and to hide,
She held the floweret in her hand
Silent, but I could understand
She wished I would forget her not;
And ever will I love the spot
Where by the brook the floweret grew—
It was a dainty, blue-eyed thing.
    (Alas! the moments flew, they flew
      As swiftly as a bird on wing!)

MY FRIEND. MY RESTING-PLACE.

I.

The heart of God lies near to me in thee,
  Dear Friend, my hope, more bright with fleeting years;
Nor hath the love of mother ceased to be,
  Though she long since hath dwelt beyond the spheres;
Her love still lives in thine, celestial, free,
  Full of unfathomed gladness and of tears ;
Breathe thou but one kind word to greet my ears,
It speaks of all the friends I ever knew—
Thyself more rich to me than all the rest,
  More high than highest, better than the best ;—
Bear thou me up, Kind Heart, and bear me through ;
Thy loving deeds, though great, are all too few ;
  Were any flower of half thy charms possess'd,
  'Twere fit to grace—not mine—an angel's breast !

II.

Here, from the strain of toil too strong for me,
Thankful, I turn aside to rest awhile ;—
Within a space not large but well-embower'd
With trees, and rich in fragrant flowers,
My peaceful dwelling stands ;—it is a place
To me all redolent of sweeter balm
Than worship ever found in golden fanes ;—

This flower-bespangled sod my temple is,
Girt round by leafy walls of evergreen,
And arch'd by that blue Infinite above :
Great God, my God, permit my own poor praise
To mingle with the incense of the rose,
And worship of assiduous ants and bees,
For all my work is Thine, and Thine my rest.

AT WORDSWORTH'S GRAVE.

Of Immortality he sang, and here
   Sleeps he right well amid immortal things ;
No fane is this that mortal hands can rear,
   And crowd with monumental priests and kings ;—
Better that grassy mound than marble floor,
   Those hills for walls, for roof that ample sky,
For song the singing birds, the thunder's roar,
   Or the bright angel-brook that bubbles by ;—
With common folk he lies in common ground,
   That was and is their common dwelling-place,
God's whisper in the forest trees around,.
   And on the lake His calm benignant face,—
Sweet fragrant House of God that poets know,
And thine, Immortal Bard, to make it so !

A BIRTHDAY IDYL.

CONCERNING MATRIMONY AND SHEARS.

Take these scissors, my poor gift,
Use them well with hand of thrift ;
When thy daily task is found,
Shape it neatly, clip it round:
From thy habits, day by day,
Snip some naughty fringe away ;
When thy thoughts on high would wing,
Unclasp the cage, and cut the string :
Words may wound like thorn in hedge,
Deftly trim them round the edge ;
Walkest thou where scandal rails ?
Hold thy toes and prune thy nails :
Wherever truth is said or sung,
Prick thine ears and clip thy tongue ;
Thy scissors can, with unshamed face,
Fold meekly in this humble case,—
A little oil, a gentle squeeze,
And thou thyself might vie with these :
Cast no reproaches, else beware,
The point will turn, and will not spare ;
Forgive me what my fancy draws,
Scissors transformed to rasping saws ;
My Muse, poor duck ! of sluggish wing,
Can quack, but neither soar nor sing.

Long, long, by old Time's rusty knife,
Unsevered be thy thread of life!
We two, my darling, hold together
Like these two blades each to the other;
Unlock them, each would useless be,
So were it, love, 'twixt thee and me;
Each helping each, both serving both,
Discreetly thus we cut our cloth,
Till in Death's ocean drops the sun,
And Life's whole happy task is done.

A BIRTHDAY OFFERING.

If Love her best can yield when least is said,
   And be her kindliest when thought is still,
   Earning her highest boon by mere sweet will,
And thrive on trust as on her daily bread,
Then would I, like a rose whose leaves are shed,
   Some little space within the memory fill
   With balm, which never cankering care would kill,
A fragrance when the flower is long since dead;
For other gift from me, alas! is none,—
   With full heart only and with empty hands,
Walking between thee and the evening sun
   Adown the misty way of Hope's waste lands,
I greet thee, dearest soul of all that live,
With Love's poor self when Love naught else can give!

TEMPUS FUGIT.

This young and happy year will soon grow old,
    And sadden as the hurrying days go by;
Angel of snowy breast and wing of gold,
    'Twill wither all too soon, and droop and die;—
    We list to hear the message from the sky,
    When lo! the story is already told,
And on our lagging lips there rests a mournful spell,—
We mean to welcome, and we say a long farewell!

God of my life! not so, not so with me!
    I grow not old, but I grow young again;
My youth returns as I draw nearer Thee,
    Thrice-blessèd Hope of frail and guilty men!
    Old Time, my foe, I glide far past thy ken,
    And from thy wrinkled finger I am free;
Cloud not my heart's young dawn with thy bewildering fears,
I walk unhurt the wilderness of wasting years!

Me, born of God, the lovely angels bring
    Back to the child's true Home of long ago;
Now elfin-joys peep forth from each plain thing,
    The daisy-chain delights that children know,
    When sunbeams dance and piping breezes blow!
    Mine are the snowy breast and golden wing,
Not thine, to whom adieu ere yet thou hast been here,
Thou brief sad angel of the new and waning year

A NEW-YEAR MEDITATION.

No stranger thou, whom God doth send
   In mercy to my open door,—
New Year! I hail thee as a friend
   Whom I have known and loved before.

The memory of bygone years
   Is Hope's best promise for to-day;
And while I mount to yonder spheres
   It seems an old familiar way.

A new path; yet it must be old,—
   The same wherein I learnt to roam;
It leads the lost sheep to the fold,—
   The lost child backward to its home.

Hail to thee, gracious, glad New Year!
   The mask thou takest from my woe;
The rich ripe future bringest here
   With the lost friends of long ago.

Nay; my lost self thou dost restore,
   And all the false grows real and true;—
My Friend, I love thee as of yore,
   For are we not both old—and new?

New Year! thou art a mystic thing;—
   Like the brown leaves that make the mould,
Then in the green and balmy Spring
   Come forth so young,—and yet so old!

AULD YEAR AND NEW.

Not altogether ill, nor good,
The Auld Year helped us as he could ;
What sins were done, and what withstood,
                We cannot tell,—
He helped us to our daily food ;—
                So far, so well.

He shivered in the winter snows,
Frost-bit his fingers and his toes,—
And the cauld quivering drop had froze
                As hard as steel,
At thin end of his hookit nose,—
                The puir auld chiel!

But buried prophets rise again ;—
What shall the Auld Year tell us then?
God gave us talents five or ten,—
                What fools were we
To squander in the idler's den
                Heaven's noble fee !—

Who cometh? Mercy! who is this
With rosy face brimful of bliss,—
Lips pleading for a sonsy kiss,—
                And laughing eyes ?
Some cherub whom they needs must miss
                In Paradise !

Come hither, hail! Hope's dainty flower!
Child-king, who rul'st the festive hour!
Child-god, girt with a giant's power
    Of large increase!
Oh, to each cottage, kirk, and tower,
    Send swift-wing'd Peace!

Old age with joyous youth renew;
Restore false hearts, and keep them true;
Where upas-tree of Error grew,
    Cursing the plain,
Let Truth in fields of glistening dew
    Rear golden grain!

Brief life is thine; but ere it close,
Love reign where Strife's red ruin flows;
Nor hard Toil, from defeated throes,
    Lift hopeless cry;
Reft be the earth of half her woes
    Ere thou shalt die!

BEN HARDY'S BAIRN.

" A little child shall lead them."

In the deep shade of Silverwood
A cottar's humble dwelling stood,
And at the door one Summer's day
A little child was seen to play ;
And with a dark and roguish eye
A pedlar-loon was passing by,
And when he saw her sweet wee face
Stood like a statue in his place ;
Then quickly from his crookéd back
Tumbled the treasures from his pack,
And held them to her kindling eyes—
Trinkets of many shapes and dyes.

And thus he played his cunning part :
"What would you have, my little heart?"
She clapp'd her hands, " Gi'e little Nannie
That bonnie braw wee sodger mannie."
"Sweet little Nan, a gift so small
No better is than none at all,—
But this hot sun is killing me,
Come to the shade of yonder tree,
I'll give you there, my pretty pet,
A present that a queen might get."

So under the greenwood tree they sat,
But none ere saw them after that.
Oh! dark deed for so bright a day!
He stole the forest-flower away;—
No, peeping thro' life's morning hour
She had not grown to be a flower,
But just a bud and nothing more,
That promised at her father's door
With dewy lips and laughing eye
To be a sweet rose by-and-by.

Now homeward hied with heavy tread,
With sweaty brow and aching head,
Ben Hardy from his toil severe,
And home, sweet home, at length is near.
Tho' sorely rack'd in limbs without
Ben had a heart both brave and stout,
Unheld by weariness or care,
I trow there was no aching there;
For deep in his broad manly breast
A little bird had built her nest,
And there she sang the live-long day
The tune of "Drive dull care away;
Cheer up, cheer up, good honest Ben,
Here's home, and wife, and wean again."

So at a certain heap of stones
Ben used to leave his weary bones,
For there his sweet child every day
Met him and kissed him on the way;

And in his brawny arms he caught her
And home triumphantly he brought her;
And strange, as little Nan grew older,
She seemed no heavier on his shoulder.
Oh, such a ride! more joy it brings
Than splendid carriages of kings,
With panoply of wealth and power,
And clapping crowds to gape and glower;
Give me for all these vulgar charms
The carriage of Ben Hardy's arms!

Well, honest Ben came to the spot,
But there, alas! he found her not;
And tears rose in his anxious eyes,
And thus he cried with sad surprise;
"What ails thee,—why not at the cairn,
Sweet little Nan, my bonnie bairn?"

Oh, heavy was the woodman's tread,
And heavy hung his aching head;
A heavy weight his bosom bare
Because he had no burden there;
And when he neared his door at last
Maggie, his wife, came running fast,
And cried, "Oh, Ben! why, tell me, pray,
Where have you left wee Nan to-day?"
'Twas plain that some mischance had come,
And to her loud cries Ben was dumb.

Then each read in the other's face
The horrors of some dreadful case;

And then they hurried to and fro
Wherever Nan was used to go,—
In flowery nook and velvet green,
But not a footprint could be seen.

The startled hare leaps from the brake,
And sleepy songsters half-awake,
Aroused by Maggie's loud lament,
Chirp timidly their discontent;
And when she asks for " Nannie dear !"
Deceitful echoes answer " Here."
And Ben thus tries to check her moan
Though he could scarce hold in his own,—
" Be quiet, Mag,—what's this ado?
In some sweet nook not far from view
The child's asleep, you may be sure,
As cosy as it is secure ;—
But hark! No, Mag, she's not asleep,
I thought I heard her cry ' Bo-peep !'"
" Ah, Ben," quoth she, "'tis hard to tell,
She sleeps at bottom of the well."
Then straightway Ben he bolted in
Until the water touched his chin ;
But out he came all dripping wet,
And poor wee Nan was yet to get.

So through the wood and through the glade
Their frantic search was vainly made ;
By many a bank and downy dell
Dear to the daisy and blue-bell ;

And many a crag's outreaching crest
Where Nan's wee foot could not have press'd;
And deep down in the loch below
They grappled wildly to and fro;
And when the dark night drew her pall
Over the earth, wee Nan, and all,
Unwillingly they ceased to roam,
And in deep silence wandered home.

Alas! it was their home no more,
And scarcely had they crossed the floor
When up they rose, both Mag and Ben,
And forth they went and searched again—
And so they searched, and so they came,
And so they went and searched the same,
Hour after hour, and day by day,
Till many weeks had passed away;
But all in vain the search went on,
The rose-bud it was plucked and gone,
And all the greenwoods, blythe and fair,
Seemed joyless, desolate, and bare.

The warblers in the woods are dumb,
Chill Winter like a scourge has come,
And shorn with tempests keen and rude
The shaggy locks of Silverwood;
And everything on earth below
Is sanctified with saintly snow;
And giant oaks in ghostly charms
Lift up their white and naked arms;
And snow-flakes fall and gently rest,
Cold blessings, on the robin's crest.

Ben Hardy's cottage-walls and roof
Against the storm stood sturdy proof;
The fierce blast howled about the door,
But never dared to venture more;
And though a flake might chance to fall
Upon the hearthstone,—that was all;
'Twas tight and warm in every part
Like honest Ben's own trusty heart;
As quiet, cosy, neat, and clean
As Mag herself was always seen.
The languid Sun has ta'en his leave,
And all in white comes Christmas Eve;
In silence at the hearth they sat—
Maggie on this side, Ben on that;
The merry flame in mantling fog
Leaps up fantastic from the log,
And mimicking his rise and fall
Queer shadows dance upon the wall.

" Oh, Mag, how vacantly you stare,
Upon the fire-logs burning there!
Aye absent, absent, seeking still
The sweet wee flower that used to fill
That bosom half a year ago
With fragrance of a Heaven below!
Ay, ay, it is not hard to seek
The pale rose on your hollow cheek!"

Such thoughts as these ran through his head
Though not a word Ben Hardy said;

Nor did he stir from out his place,
But gazed in Maggie's absent face.
At last the crackling from the hearth
Recalled her from the sky to earth;
For when her bairn is found nowhere,
What mother would not seek it there?

Then when he saw her dream had passed
Good honest Ben outspoke at last:
"Now, tell me, Mag, where have you been?"
Quoth she, " I had a dream yestreen,
And fondly every hour since then
I've dreamt it o'er and o'er again.
Oh, Ben, I thought the angels came
And reft wee Nannie frae her hame,
And upward as they swiftly hied,
' Oh, mercy! leave me not!' I cried;
But a dark spirit drew a screen
Of terror and of wrath between;
The while my arms I madly toss'd,
With little Nannie all was lost.
But, lo! when I was nearly spent
The cloudy veil was quickly rent,
And there was Nan in royal state
Just entering the golden gate;
But when they looked and saw my woe
The angels seemed to let her go,
And down she came, the dear wee thing!
With ruby face and silver wing.
Oh, what a rapture! Oh, how brief!—
Oh, mockery of a mother's grief!"

With sore-bewildering hopes and fears
Maggie's voice melted into tears,
And like a thunder-shower they drap,
Alas! into her empty lap.
Ben's too, belike, in woeful race
Ran down his weather-waukit face;
In vain he offered to withstand,
Or hide it with his horny hand.

Now, Maggie had a secret spot,
Ben might suspect but knew it not,
More precious than the mint of kings,
Her treasury of sacred things;
And it was always there in chief
Her hungry sorrow sought relief.
She rose to bring them from their place
With sorrow smiling in her face.
" With tears," quoth she to honest Ben,—
" They need to be refreshed again."

And on the table ranged anew
They stood all wet in long review.
There was a pair of worn-out shoes
None but a little child could use;
A pinafore all stained and torn
Some little innocent had worn;
And dolls in trim from top to toe,
Or full-dress as the fashions go;
With many other trifles more,—
And Maggie kissed them o'er and o'er.

But all this while she little knew
That two dark eyes were peering through
The window, for she had forgot
Whether it had a blind or not.
In spite of cold and wind and showers
Those two dark eyes had watched for hours,
And not a shadow rose or fell
But they had seen and marked it well.

But hearken ! for the eyes have fled,—
A rapping at the door instead :
Ben opened, and a man came in—
Dark image of incarnate sin,
Whose tell-tale features, bold and bad,
Held all the honesty he had ;
His black hair hung in matted chains
Over a narrow brow like Cain's ;
His eye-glance, pitiless and fell
As any firebrand lit in Hell,
Gleamed in an instant every way,
Like wild beast roaming for its prey ;
His lips, it seemed he'd bit them small
Until he scarce had lips at all ;
And wrinkles criminal and base
Wriggled like serpents o'er his face ;
His dress, for fashion's sake, almost
Might have been worn in Pharoah's host,
And since 'twas rather worse for wear,
Perchance it did first flourish there ;
His mantle from the snowy wreath
Sheltered his tunic underneath ;

But hat and shoes, as one might know,
Were over head and heels in snow ;—
He was a man far past his prime,
But had been sturdy in his time.

What did he want ?   No good, no doubt ;
And Ben he would have thrust him out,
But Maggie held him by the sleeve :
" Be cautious, Ben, 'tis Christmas Eve,
And some, touch'd by the needy's prayers,
Have welcomed angels unawares."
" Angels," quoth Ben, " must want for bliss
Who come to us in shape like this."
" Pity,"—the stranger's words were these—
" My frozen blood and feeble knees."

And soon as Maggie knew his case
Her woman's heart leapt to her face ;
She hearkened to his mild desire,
She stirr'd for him the smouldering fire,
She set him in the coziest seat,
She stoop'd and wiped his frozen feet,
Hot-steaming from the chimney-nook
Her Ben's own supper forth she took,
And brought her uncut Christmas cake,—
All for the shivering stranger's sake.

And he did eat in sullen gloom
Like one next hour to meet his doom ;
Then on the table cast his eye
Where Nannie's rags and playthings lie,

And in a strange hoarse whisper, said,
" Has little birdie gone to bed ? "
The mother's breast began to swell ;
She told him how it all befell,
As to an angel's listening ear,
With many a mingled sob and tear.

Oh, what a groan the stranger gave,
As if some sword his bosom rave !
All ghastly pale his visage grew,
He gnashed his lips of livid hue ;
He had some woe he could not smother,
His knees they smote upon each other ;
Dog-like he sprang to reach the door,—
He stayed and staggered on the floor ;
And when he gaped as if to speak
His dry tongue clattered in his cheek ;
Once, twice, and yet again he tried
Till thus in fearful tones he cried :
"God ! it is dreadful here to sit,
It burns me like the brimstone pit ;
Your words, your tears, your hearth, your bread,
Heap coals of fire upon my head !
Oh, woman ! rise and strike and slay
The wretch who stole your child away ;
Beside our tents on Silverhill
The prayer you taught her rises still,—
No curse of mine could quench her cry ;
Go, bring her home, and let me die !"
He ceased, he reel'd, ere one could tell
Prone with a mighty thud he fell ;—

Mag held her breath, looked helpless on,—
And cried to Ben,—but Ben was gone;
Fast thro' the tangled wood he flew,
And dashed among the gipsy crew
Where, heedless of the snow and mire,
They crouched in revels round the fire;
Sped on, till midway through the camp,
In shelter from the cold and damp,
He saw a little bundle lie,
And stooping down, he knew not why,
Beneath the broad-wheeled caravan,
He took it up, and—there was Nan!
Oh, what a rapture filled his breast
As the wee birdie there he press'd;
And scarcely had he turned his face,
When lo! all breathless with the race,
His own dear Mag was close to view
And folded in his bosom too.

Now home at length, wee Nan, amazed,
Her sleepy eyelids slowly raised,
And cried, "My dad! my mammy dear!
Oh joy, joy, joy, to meet you here!"
Poor thing! she thought life's journey pass'd,
And all had met in Heaven at last.

The gipsy men, some three or four,
Had traced Ben's footprints to his door,—
They saw their mate, nor grieved were they,
Where on the ground stone-dead he lay;

They bore him to the self-same tree
Where first forgathered Nan and he;
They laid no wreaths upon his bier;
They buried him without a tear;
But many a time upon the spot
Small fingers laid "forget-me-not."

Far thro' that holy Christmas night
Ben Hardy's window flashed with light;
And the unwhispering trees around
Heard swellings of a joyful sound.
The silent angels, too, on high
Were listening to an infant's cry;
And joyfully recording there
A Father's penitential prayer.

For by his own babe's lisping tongue
Ben's heart with agony was wrung,—
Long had he ceased to pray himself;
So, raxing to a dusty shelf,
And from a dark sequester'd nook,
He brought his father's pride—The Book;
And ever after made to rise
Morning and evening sacrifice.

LITTLE NELLY NOBODY.

Little Nelly Nobody (she was six years old or so),
In the lonely street, with naked feet, was wading through the snow;
She was not going home that night, for home she never knew;
And if she had not many friends, her foes were also few.
While many a child crept cosily on many a velvet floor,
This ragged wean, this beggar bairn, did crawl from door to door;
And as they gave an orange here, and there a slice of cake,
Until, her little apron full, the string was like to break,
She wonder'd why they were this night so ready to relieve—
Poor silly thing! she did not know that it was Christmas eve.

At length upon a frozen step, with scarce a rag to hap,
She sat her down, and tried to count the bounties in her lap;
She had not been to school, you know, and so could scarcely say—
But three, or ten, or thereabout she thought the number lay;

Yet still how many oranges and crumbs of cake were there,
She did not want so much to find, as somebody to share;
The redbreast was asleep, no dog, nor sparrow could be seen,
No hungry creature came, or else how happy had she been!
Good Christian child! her little store was empty every day,
For when herself had just enough, she gave the rest away.

But soon by chance she lifted up her liquid languid eyes
And lo! a creature sure enough was there, of wondrous size;
By the street lamp's fitful glare she saw the features of a man,
And down his breast a hoary beard like silver streamlets ran;
His white locks leaped around his brow like wreaths of drifting snow,
And his mantle it was hemmed with stars in many a sparkling row.

And such a sight, so great a fright made Nelly quake and cry,
But there was laughter on his lip, and kindness in his eye;

And when she saw his face, and heard how tenderly he spoke,
She thought an angel was behind, and meant it for a joke.

"Weep not, my little lamb!" he cried, "and cast away your fear,
I'm come to take you home, my child, and give you better cheer;
On a bare stone, and all alone, so shelterless and bare,
'Twill never do for such as you to take your supper there.
Get up, my little dear, and haste, for if you only knew
What things are spread, how anxiously they wait at home for you."
"At home, Sir! why that is not me—they've told a wicked tale,
Unless you mean the workhouse home, or put me into jail;
I have not done no wrong, good Sir, pray let me from your door,
Forgive this once, and on the step I'll never sit no more."
"Oh, fie, my pet! you don't forget—don't you remember me?
Whom all good children ne'er forget, and like so much to see—
Old Father Christmas, don't you know, come back to town again,
To make them think of Christ, who died to save the sons of men?"

"Good Sir, I ne'er saw you before, and this I only know:
I begs for bread, and father's dead, and left me long ago."
"My heart! Oh no, it is not so, He lives not far away,
And now He sends for all His friends to sup with Him to-day;
Saying to all in His banquet-hall, and joyful was the sound,—
'Nelly was dead, and is alive—was lost, and now is found;
Go, Father Christmas, where she sits, outcast in rags and sin,
And bring her home, for till you come our feast shall not begin.'"

Then did Saint Christmas fold her up, poor lambie, in his breast,
No mother could more sweetly soothe her baby into rest;
And tho' his breast, by the frosty beard that from his chin did fall,
Seemed cold and bare, once you were there it was not cold at all.
I do not know the road he took, but Nelly scarce had laid
Her weary head upon the bed his snow-white bosom made,
When the dark night burst into light, breaking the gloomy bars,
As if it had been crowned with suns instead of twinkling stars;

And oh! what raptures rush'd at once on Nelly's
    ravish'd view,
For all old things had passed away, and everything
    was new.
No streets were there, nor palaces, nor such-like earth-
    ly things,
The crowds on living verdure walked, or flew on angel's
    wings;
And lifting her eyes (what a sweet surprise!) to her
    guardian old and grey,
Behold! his iciness, and oldness too, had melted quite
    away;
No seraphim could equal him, he seemed so young
    and fair;
Smooth was the skin of his dimpled chin, and locks of
    golden hair
Flow'd down his face, and took the place of those that
    time had stain'd,
But the loving-kindness of his eye, and that alone re-
    mained.

And thro' the sky these two did fly to where the feast
    was spread,
With guests all met, the table set, her Father at its
    head.
It was a place well furnished all with everything to
    please;
The roof was heaven, the walls were thighs and arms
    of noble trees.
First rose a hum, "Nelly is come!" and then the
    joyful sound

Of a thousand lyres from seraph choirs that floated all around;
And the glad Father rose in haste and left His lofty place,
And came and took her up, and gazed, and gazed into her face.
And Nelly knew His look at once, but how she could not tell;
She ne'er had seen her Father's face, and yet she knew Him well,—
The face of mother, sister, brother, long since dead and gone,
Lost not a trace upon the face that now she gazed upon.
There into one were blended all those old familiar faces,
For it was charmed with every charm, and graced with all the graces.
And the glad Father took her first with His own tender hands,
And robed her clean, till like a queen she shone among the bands;
And then He pressed each happy guest, and joyful was the sound,—
"Nelly was dead, and is alive—was lost, and now is found."

Now morning breaks on the snow-flakes that lie around the door
Where old Saint Christmas gathered up poor Nell the night before,
And the children all burst from the hall for snowballs on the stair.

One cries with a leap, "What a famous heap is in the
    corner there!
Ho, Dick! come quick, and let us roll this ball along
    the street."
They tried as much, but to their touch came two small
    frozen feet!—
O horror! what a fright it was! they stood and scarce
    could breathe,—
All stiff and cold, some six years old, a corpse lay
    underneath.
With what a noise the startled boys rushed back into
    the hall!
And all the rest cried, "What a pest these boys are to
    us all!"
But soon they came, and saw, and sighed, and then
    they did begin
To say, "Alas! what a pity 'twas we did not take her
    in."
It was not Nelly though, but just her broken cage of
    clay—
The bird had flown,—there on the stone the useless
    prison lay.
But the children cried, and nought they tried their tide
    of tears could stem;
How vain was this; but for her bliss, Nelly had wept
    for them!

The sexton dug a pauper's grave, and came to fetch
    the clay;
The robins they were there before, but them he chased
    away;

For in that lap and lifeless hand, that oft gave them
    their fill,
The oranges and little crumbs of cake were lying still.
And nobody laid the head in the grave, and nobody
    wept or prayed,
And nobody asks the sexton where that broken cage
    is laid;
For would you know who lies below, he says with a
    growl and a stare,
"Oh, nobody;—no matter who, 'tis neither here nor
    there."

TODDLIN' TAMMIE.

"Like as a father pitieth his children."

Twa-year-auld wee toddlin' Tammie,
   Fu' o' daffin, fu' o' din;
Winsomer wee sonsie lambie,
Brawer bairn to his ain mammie
   Never throve in halesome skin.

Dainty chiel! thy faither's crony!
   Pure thy breast, and sorrow-free;
His, alas! grown hard and stony!
Scant o' sense (if he has ony),
   Aye a sprinklin' o't in thee.

Angels in the Blue up yonder
   Nursed thee in their starry sheen;
Fond were they, but we, still fonder,
See it there the mair we ponder,—
   See it in thy bonnie e'en.

Many a blast o' windy blether
   Arts and Sciences can blaw;—
Thine to haud wi' mystic tether
In thy heart, like straps o' leather,
   Secrets darker than them a'.

Ugh! be hanged, ye splutt'rin' monkey!
 A' my ink clean whummelt ower!
Black my scrip as Satan's bunkie,—
Laugh! ye idiotic spunkie!
 Syne, I'll mak' ye gape an' glower!

Weel, weel; dinna ye be cryin'—
 After a', ye're but a wean;
Nae doubt, ye were only tryin'
To bring oot some thocht deep lyin'
 In your bannock o' a brain.

Wee bit sturdy, stacherin' chappie,
 Gleg wee man as e'er was seen,
Ken ye why the big saut drappie,
No ill spent, nor yet unhappy,
 Fa's doun frae your faither's e'en?

Thy wee roun' cheek, saft and callow
 Thy wee pow o' sunny hair;—
His is gettin' grey, puir fallow!
An' his face grows thin and sallow
 Wi' the bitter clytes o' care.

Shall he ever live to see thee
 Hale and strong on life's brae-tap,
Clad in a' the world can gie thee,—
Or in wae misfortune dree thee
 To the grave, thy mither's lap?

Speak nae mair the word o' sorrow!
  Bring nae mair the feckless tear!
Foolish wark it is to borrow
Frae the toom pouch o' to-morrow—
  God is guid—to-day is here!

My wee Tam, should ill befa' thee,
  Thole it weel till a' be dune;
Slander's tongue may oft misca' thee;
Pleasure's gilded toys withdraw thee
  Into slimy paths o' sin;—

But the Shepherd, kind and tender,
  Ance a wee bit lamb like thee,
Kens fu' weel what help to render—
A' the frail folks' ain Defender,
  Never Frien' sae staunch as He.

Soon shall cease thy childish prattle;
  Soon to sterner things give place
Spinning-top, and trump, and rattle,—
Gang thy gate, and fight thy battle,
  Gird thee weel, and win the race!

Here not long we bide thegither,
  But we a' shall gather there,
Unco blythe wi' ane anither—
Wee bairns wi' their faither, mither—
  In the lang, lang evermair.

GAVIN'S BIRTHDAY.

Little Gavin's first birthday—
Not his last we hope and pray.
Little roguish fairy bands
Rub their eyes and clap their hands,
And they say they hear him sigh:
"Oh, how quick my days do fly!
Life worth living? Nay, not so;
Born but one brief hour ago,
Wearily its length has run,
Empty, and already done;
Oh, how quick my days do fly!"

Little fairy rogues, you lie!
Never happier elf than he;
Sunbeam could not brighter be!
Hence, ye fools! ye silly things!
Tripping toes and sooty wings—
Would you, dare you, if you can,
Pessimise my little man?
Hence, I charge you! come not near;
Nevermore shall bless your ear
Doggie's bark and bairnie's coo,
Bow, wow, wow, and moo, moo, moo!

Sudden gust and merry peal
Thrilling me from head to heel,
What can this confusion be?

"Ha, ha, ha! and he, he, he!"
Laughter from the fairy bands,
Rubbing eyes and clapping hands:
"Fickle, frolicsome are we,
Little kettles filled with glee,
On the hot fire boiling o'er,
Up the chimney, on the floor;
Fickle, and of frolic full—
Sit you down, sir; with a pull
From below we snatch your chair,
Head on ground and heels in air!
Down with awful flop you go—
How you sprawl, and puff, and blow!
Ha, ha, ha! and he, he, he!
Of a crooked kind are we;
Take our supper, night and noon,
With the wrong end of the spoon;
Drink the goblet upside down;
Bless you with a wicked frown;
Pinch you with a sunny smile,
Mock your pain, and dance the while;
Crowd the hearth, and range the wood,
Doing aught but what we should;
Singing when we should be sad;
Melancholic most when glad;
Good-folks in our naughty ways,
Full of mischief, fond of praise;
Good nor bad as you might deem,
Naughtier, kinder than we seem.
Never more the harsh word say—
No; nor bid us hence away.

Merriest of romping elves,
Gavin, saucier than ourselves;
Gavin, bless his little pate!
Chosen for our own playmate.
Gifts we bring from far and near,
Beads of dewdrop, bright and clear;
Daisy-buds with silver frills,
Wholesome breezes from the hills;
Breath of roses, fresh and sweet,
Lady-slippers for his feet;
Elfin balls the fairies throw,
Frozen air and molten snow;
Jewels from the tropic seas,
Yellow gold from orange trees;
Fairy food brought from the moon,
Fairy saucer, cup and spoon;
Honey joys in crystal jars
From beyond the winking stars!"

Oh, but ye are brave, said I.
Would that ye could backward fly!
Idle rogues; run back and bring
Feather-dust from Gabriel's wing
On the flowers of Eden fell;
Bring a drop from Jacob's well;
Jacob's ladder, David's lyre,
Children's clothes that braved the fire;
Bring the horn from Shiloh's tent,
Where the High Priest, old and bent,
Poured the blessing undefiled,
Holy oil on Hannah's child;

Or beneath that later star,
Where a Babe lay, worthier far,
Angel-hosts mellifluent sang,
And the cold clear welkin rang.
Oh that ye, fond fays! might bring
Seraph song and cherub wing
Round my year-old baby's head,
With the Saviour's unction shed
On the happy lambs who played,
Under vine and olive shade,
On the slopes of Zion hill!

And the rogues replied—" *We will!*"

INNOCENCE.

Sweetly the summer morn may shine,
   But sweeter, brighter far to me
The love o' that wee lass o' mine,
   The blinkin' o' my bairnie's e'e;
Let me but pree her dainty mou',
   Let me but press her sonsy cheek,
Fresh roses drench'd wi' honey-dew
   I winna hae, I carena seek!

Lang syne a fragrant lily sprang
   In frailty at the Saviour's feet;
He saw it as He stept alang,
   And with a smile divinely sweet,
"Wee flower," quoth He, " I bid thee cheer—
   Tho' in the dust thy bed is laid,
King Solomon wi' a' his gear
   Was no' sae handsomely arrayed '

Kind Saviour! ne'er be far awa'
   Amid the stour o' earthly ways,
To keep my bairnie clean and braw
   In handsomest o' saintly claes;
That men in this wee flower may find,
   When love is low and troubles rife,
The beauty of a heavenly mind,
   The incense of eternal life!

A GOOD FIGHTER.

A special favourite of mine
Is that sharp-witted boy of nine,
Who in his crib in sickness lay,
And many a wicked prank would play.
The Doctor when he came to heal,
In megrim pain or sullen mood,
Was cured himself by laughter-peal,
Much more than his own physic would;
And oft he swallowed 'gainst his will
The tonic jest and frolic pill.

One morn the little chap was found
In winding-sheet all smoothly wound;
More stiff, more spik-and-span than he
No decent corpse could wish to be;
And on a paper at his head
In pencil roundly writ they read
How John had died on such a date;
How sadly mourned his cruel fate;
The place where first he saw the light,
The time, and then from mortal sight
Had passed away, in nine short years,
'Mid groans and moans and floods of tears;
And at the close in compact phrase,
    None could be brighter,
Accorded the due meed of praise
    To—"A Good Fighter!"

A MAN OF WEIGHT.

Upon the pedestal I stood
One day to make my true weight good :
Throw in my perfect stock of health,
My purse with all its weight of wealth,
My chimney towering black aloft,
My understandings limp and soft,
The burden of my cares and pains,
The bad blood coursing in my veins ;
Sermons in rude unshapen blocks
(Some more and some less orthodox),
The wine that made me somewhat heady,
My faithful crook to keep me steady,
My brain, my thick impervious hide,
And all my vanity and pride,
A heart too hard for axe of miner,
Sins that might sink a steam-ship liner ;—
Take them, and throw them one and all
Upon that groaning pedestal,
You'll not believe me tho' I swear it,
The iron ribs could hardly bear it !
Alas ! old Pharoah's lanky kine,
My whole gross weight was nine stone nine !

MOTHERHOOD.

Ah! my blue-eyed baby-boy!
Tiny fount of tears and joy,
   Whither art thou tending?
Whither go thy dainty feet?
Here thy heart began to beat—
   Where will it be ending?

Oft my foolish heart will quake
Lest the world should thee forsake,
   Or forget to love thee;—
Peace, O peace! for this I know,
Still hast thou, where'er thou go,
   God and Heaven above thee

Come, my ruby cup of wine!
Put thy pretty lips to mine,
   Feast me with thy kisses!
Ne'er were they so sweet before:
Now I know, yes, know far more
   What an angel's bliss is!

Sheltered from a thousand harms,
In the silk of thy soft arms
   Sweetly, safely folden,—
Better shielded then am I
Though ten legions from the sky
   Round me were beholden!

Merry stars are in thine eyes;
Music in thy sorrow's cries,
    Piercing me like lances,
Agony all full of joy!
O my brightest baby-boy,
    Kill me with thy glances!

Happy, happy little thing!
All a cherub save the wing,
    What hast thou with sorrow?
Trusting God will ever be
Kind each day to thee and me,
    Kinder each to-morrow!

BE STILL.

Poor child ! so hard, so hard bestead
Ere yet tired Life took up her flickering lamp
        And fled !
    Now, now, rest, rest thy head
On this the sweetest pillow ever laid, tho' damp
With many a drop from founts of bitter tears !
Is not life lived by feeling more than years ?
Poor child ! we measure not thy struggle by its length,
Greater it had not been with all a giant's strength.
      So still ! so still !
      It is the Father's will
For mighty nations, for the vex'd earth itself,
For the bright hosts night-marshall'd in the sky,
They have their life to live, their death to die,—
All have their agony, sooner or later past,
    Then there is peace at last !
    Poor babe, thou had'st thy cares
    Not less divine than theirs !
      Now, now,
      On that once ruffled brow,
      And in the eyes that sleep
Within those two pale curtains half revealed,
And on those tiny lips the God of Peace hath sealed,
    There is a new-made throne,
Another new, vast empire added to thy realm,
    Sweet Silence, lovely, sad, and lone,
    Thou saddest, holiest Empress ever known,
Daughter of God, and Heir of all God's own !
      Oh ! come,
      And teach us to be dumb !

VICTORY.

She is not here, and yet I dare not say
    That she has passed away;
Her presence like an angel in the gloom
    Haunts me from room to room.

Her very absence brings her doubly near
    Tho' mourned with many a tear;
And now I know, while she was heard and seen
    How distant we had been.

Distant! I grieve to call it distance, when
    We lived so closely then;
But that was like a dream to this,—now, she
    Is more like God to me.

From these complaining eyes she went apart,
    And crept into my heart;
The poor lost lamb that I can see nowhere
    Is seven times folded there.

To meet her was a daybreak of delight
    At morning, noon, or night;
I never meet her now,—no space can screen us,—
    No partings now between us!

There is a change in those old lonely hours,—
    They are not mine, but ours;
In sun or shade, in calm or stormy weather,
    We two are still together.

VICTORY.

Earth has a lovely face, and at the core
    Kindness unknown before;
All things are good and pure—my child, so be it!
    Thou hast the eye to see it.

Mine ears are not my own, with her clean eyes
    I scan both earth and skies;—
God sings in every warbler of the bowers,—
    God's face is in the flowers.

O Death! how good it is, how blest a thing
    To nestle 'neath thy wing!
Thy sunny face 'tis Heaven to behold,—
    Thy touch turns all to gold.

Had she been harsh and fretful in her ways,
    That now had been her praise;
Her very faults had been more dear than graces
    Worn in high Heavenly places.

But she was meek and patient as the dove,—
    Her only fault was love;—
I thought I knew,—yet first I found it so
    Deep in the vale of woe.

When earth is rack'd with storms that still increase,
    We know thee, gentle Peace!
Sweet Death! I thank thee for the parting groan,—
    My child is now mine own!

A REVERIE OF THE BEREAVED.

It was soon told, the child's own simple story—
   Twas hardly yet begun till it was ended
And from this gloomy vale to heights of glory
   The softly-falling footsteps had ascended;
   What wondrous power with weakness here was blended !
No sainted prophet, Heaven-inspired and hoary,
Laden with some deep secret from the Lord to tell,
E'er had so much to say, or said it half so well !

Panting, we press the little feet before us,
   Led by a way we never should have taken—
Light from the better country breaking o'er us,
   And the old world we seem to have forsaken;
   The meanwhile in our weary hearts awaken
   Strange echoes of the old angelic chorus,
When from the Father came a Child of peace to men,
As if it had revived when one returned again.

Yet for our child how can we cease repining?
   More than he brought he took when he was dying—
From the bright sun he took the golden shining,
   And beauty from the green earth underlying,
   And freshness where the open breeze was flying;
   Wherever light and love were intertwining
They sank, as daylight-sheen in Arctic ocean dips,
When the soul passed the stainless marble of his lips.

We could believe, in one so frail and tender
   A true Omnipotence was calmly sleeping,
The universal Maker and Defender
   Who holds all creatures in His all-wise keeping;
   He dwelt in one scarce old enough for weeping,
And when we tried our poor vain help to render,
The child-eye glowed with utterance: it seemed to be—
Ye do it unto " one of these," and unto Me!

Oft of the future we were fondly dreaming,—
   All trials—we, for his dear sake, could bear them;
And when he rose where Fame's high goal is gleaming,
   His honours too—we humbly hoped to share
      them;—
   The dreams are past and gone, and we can spare
      them;
There is a land where life needs no redeeming
From errors of the child, and from the parents' pain,
And where the hope of loving hearts doth never wane.

But oh! we could have kept him still beside us,
   A beam of love before our faces playing;
We recked not what the future might betide us
   While he his soft cheek close to ours was laying,
   With babbling lip some kindly thing was saying,
Or stretched his hand to fondle or to guide us!
O God! he made us know how loving Thou must be,
And now we find and follow him in seeking Thee!

HOME-GOING.

Our little one, our hope and care,
　　The angels took away,—
The little spirit could not bear
　　The burden of the clay.

We said, "Sweet one, O leave us not!"
　　And angels answer'd thus:
" Earth is a cold and dreary spot,—
　　Nay, sweet one, come with us;

" For earth, perchance, would cast away,—
　　Thy friends may be unwise,
And we can better keep than they,
　　Their treasure in the skies.

" Thou art, sweet one, like Mary's Son,
　　Who says, 'Come unto Me:'
And parents dear shall come up here
　　When they are like to thee."

And so amid our sobs and tears
　　They took our babe away;
And looking thro' the lapse of years
　　How could we answer nay?

Dear babe! in better hands than ours,
  We know thou'rt happy there;
Yet bitter tears we shed in showers,
  And how can we forbear?

We can forbear, by Jesus' grace;
  Now drawn by holier charms,
Sweet lamb! we seek thy hiding-place
  In the Redeemer's arms.

THE GRACES.

A Queen stands at her palace gates,
    Radiant and kind,
And many a poor one on her bounty waits—
    The maimed, the halt, the blind.

A blind old man and maiden fair,
    Faintly and slow,
Come crouching to her feet, and murmur there
    Their unpretending woe.

The Queen looks on with moistened eyes,
    A little while;
Then takes them by the hand, and bids them rise,
    With a most welcome smile.

Her sweet mouth speaks to them of rest,
    And daily food;
She takes them in, she clasps them to her breast;
    She is Divinely good!

She claims them as of kindred race,
    Calls them her own;
They find her palace an enchanted place,
    With an enchanted throne;

She robes the maiden all in white,
    Sparkling with gold;
She gives the blind such visions of delight
    As never yet were told.

And oh! how these two poor ones praise
    Their queenly Giver!
He growing lustier with his length of days,—
    She fair and young for ever.

O Faith! O fair young Hope! his child
    Born from above!
Ye had been dead long since had she not smiled
    Whose sovereign name is Love!

A CHILD'S PRAYER.

The little star by night,
  Shining in heaven,
Always doth shed the light
  Jesus hath given.
      Father, I pray
        That it may be
        Even so with me
      From day to day!

The little drop of dew,
  In lonely place,
Worketh for Jesus too,
  By Jesus' grace.
      Father, I pray
        That it may be
        Even so with me
      From day to day!

The lily, fair and bright,
  Grows by the flood,
Like saints, washed clean and white
  In Jesus' blood.
      Father, I pray
        That it may be
        Even so with me
      From day to day!

The sweet rose all around
  Sendeth its smell;
But sweeter scent is found
  Where Christ doth dwell.
    Father, I pray
      That it may be
      Even so with me
    From day to day.

The meek lamb, suffering sore,
  Doth ne'er complain,
Like Jesus when He bore
  Our sin and pain.
    Father, I pray
      That it may be
      Even so with me
    From day to day.

The lark doth gaily rise
  And sweetly sing,
Up where the spirit flies
  On prayerful wing.
    Father, I pray
      That it may be
      Even so with me
    From day to day.

The little birds all think,
  When sorely pressed
For shelter, meat or drink,
  That God knows best.

Father, I pray
  That it may be
  Even so with me
From day to day.

The little rills all flow
  To one great sea,
As all Thy children go,
  Lord, nearer Thee.
    Father, I pray
      That it may be
      Even so with me
    From day to day.

All things work out Thy will,
  And give Thee praise;
For love abideth still
  In all Thy ways.
    Father, I pray
      That it may be
      Even so with me
    From day to day.

Our fathers in the sky,
  Ere life was passed,
All hoped to reach on high
  Sweet Home at last.
    Father, I pray
      That it may be
      Even so with me
    From day to day.

A VISION OF FINAL JUDGMENT.

God gave a new King to the wintry world,
   Gentle of heart, and Bountiful his name;
Dark hosts of clouds their loyal flags unfurl'd,
   And hailstorms rattled forth their fierce acclaim;
Wild winds arose and their allegiance told,--
They meant warm welcome, tho' their breath was cold.

The courtly Sun looked down with watery eye,
   And the meek Moon, and gave their homage due;
Slow Mists, grey-mantled, kneel'd while passing by;
   Frosts came with silent step and saintly hue;
Great Floods on their deep organs played the while,
And not in vain the dull Hours tried to smile.

He was a priestly King—love filled his heart,
   And gifts both great and good were in his hand;
Right royally his purpose was to play his part,
   So spake he thus to all in every land:
"Honours I seek not, save in your behests,—
'Tis mine to serve, 'tis yours to be my guests."

Ah! then he was besieged by selfish cries;
   By pleading mouths already filled with greed;
By deadly hopes that glared in hungry eyes:
   By souls who knew their lust but not their need,—
Fond souls who craved the foulest for their good,
And weary hearts that swelled in prideful mood.

Some came in wine and clamour'd loud for more;
　Some were exceeding rich and cried for gold;
Some shriek'd for Pleasure from her gilded door;
　For Pity some, as wolves do in the fold:
"Freedom!" they cried who kept their brethren slaves;
And "Honour! honour!" who were branded knaves.

Lo! faintly seen outside the surging crowd,
　In silence stood a meek man, pale and thin,—
Him did the King espy, and thus aloud,
　With firm and friendly voice: "Come in, come in!
Back, back, ye brawlers!" Then with drooping eye,
With slow and faltering step the man drew nigh.

"What wouldest thou, my friend, most welcome guest?"
　Enquired the Royal Priest in accents mild.
"Thy will, not mine," he said, "Thou knowest best;
　Let me be loved and treated as a child,—
Only if good befall me, this I pray:
Good let it be that I can give away."

Then from his seat the Priest, descending, said:
　"I give thee this; I give thee but thine own.
He placed his crown upon the meek man's head,
　And led him, dumb with wonder, to the Throne,
'Mid angel songs and trumpet blasts of fame;
This done, he smiled, and vanished whence he came.

EPHPHATHA.

Oh ! Realm of Life remote, where Silence reigns
   Mute as the dead are in their lonesome halls;
Where lowing herds are heard not in the plains,
   And on the hills are voiceless waterfalls !

No song salutes the Morning at her gates
   From soaring lark or linnet in the vale;
On drowsy Noon no droning creature waits,—
   Eve has no thrush and Night no nightingale.

The sea is heard, the thunder-riven sky,
   The groaning forest when the tempest swells,
As in a dream one hears an angel sigh,
   Or hears the tinkling of the heather bells.

Ye favour'd ones ! well nursed on Fortune's knees,
   Who know Love's voice and grasp her jewell'd hand,
Your unbless'd brothers—oh ! remember these
   In the lone chambers of the Silent Land !

Sad land ! where never yet did shepherd hear
   The plaintive lamb, nor dog, nor cooing dove;
Nor ever yet did fall on mother's ear
   The music of her child's distress or love.

Nor fireside mirth is heard, nor sacred song
   Which pious hearts from family altar raise;
Nor psalm of strength ascending from the throng
   In courts of God's house on the best of days.

Lips never know the weary heart's complaint,—
　Life ebbs unheard by weeping friends around,—
Soft as the soul-step of departing saint
　His orphans' cries—all innocent of sound.

The city silent, with its rushing wheels
　And tread of myriads hurrying to and fro,
As when thro' haunted house a phantom steals,—
　All silent as the sound of falling snow.

Is Mercy silent? Doth she there alone
　Refuse fair Truth and bind her silver tongue—
Strike Pity deaf and speechless as a stone—
　Forbid the Saviour's triumph to be sung?

Nay; God be praised for what His grace denies!
　The boon miraculous His wisdom brings,
And Sight hath gifts of hearing in her eyes,
　And with her fingers, lo! she speaks and sings!

Oh! never were so beautiful the feet
　Of messenger on mountain sides of old
As when even here in tones divinely sweet
　The story of Redeeming Love is told!

Unrivalled harvests spring from iron sod
　Once the soft showers of heavenly blessing fall;
So let the deaf best know the voice of God,
　And souls with dumb lips praise Him most of all!

THE VICTORY OF LOVE:

A LAY OF ANCIENT ISRAEL.

Like far-off storm thro' forest faintly sweeping,
  Or distant moan of ever-murmuring sea,
I hear the wail of some sad mourner's weeping,
  Fast by the rocks of lonely Engedi.

I see the fresh day touch with rosy fingers
  The hills where gentle flocks all night have lain;
Perchance it is some thorn-caught lamb that lingers,
  And pours its rippling sorrow to the plain.

Their caves the bittern and the owl are keeping,
  No dove by eagle press'd there seems to be,—
I hear the wail of some sad mourner's weeping,
  Fast by the rocks of lonely Engedi.

From yonder cave shot forth with sudden screaming
  The bittern like an arrow cleaves the sky;
And many a startled owl in darkness dreaming
  Opes to the hated light his drowsy eye.

From rock to rock a thousand echoes leaping
  Dash on the breast of distant hills and die,—
I hear it swelling still, that voice of weeping,
  As tho' some fallen seraphim were passing by.

Lo! from the cave with faltering step advancing
  Among the tangled vines a tall form stands,
The joy of morn upon his helm is glancing,
  His face bent low and buried in his hands.

Is he the mourner? Wounded have I found him?
  A lonely man, mail-clad; but he is not alone,—
See, troops of grim-faced warriors rise around him,
  Awed by his unused tears and grief unknown.

With noble countenance, and close beside him,
  Forth from the cave a comely youth appears,
Jesse's fair son, with God to guard and guide him,
  In prowess unapproached tho' young in years.

A shepherd boy—the king gave him his daughter,
  And she gave love, for that no sire can give;
Now cursed by envy and pursued by slaughter,
  For Saul, the king, hath sworn "He shall not live."

From Salem yesterday, with trumpet sounding,
  The furious king three thousand soldiers led,—
But see! yon mourner, 'mong the host surrounding,
  Like Saul among the people lifts his head;

And stretching forth his tear-stained hands to David:
  "'Tis thou, my son, unjustly doomed to die,—
Thee had I slain, but thou my soul hast savéd—
  My son! my son! more righteous thou than I!"

Oh cruel spite, thou art thyself no longer!
    Changed is thy brow, thine eye that seldom sleeps,—
There is indeed in breast of kings a stronger
    Than jealousy and hate,—lo! it is Saul that weeps!

And David clasps the king, and cries, "My Father!"
    And Saul with royal tears, "My son, my son!
Round thee, most gallant youth, the tribes shall gather;
    Belov'd of Israel, the Lord's anointed one!"

Men of Gibeah! leave your ploughs and cattle,
    Ye Bethlehemites! your flocks, and come and see,
For Saul and David have drawn near to battle
    Fast by the rocks of lonely Engedi.

No bucklers clang, no hungry swords are clashing,
    No soul-exciting cry the trumpet gives,
Nor that high crest is seen thro' deep ranks dashing,
    For stalwart Saul is slain—and still he lives!

The king has perished, but the man is living,
    And with the king revenge and slaughter cease;
He perished in the glance that love was giving,
    And Saul and David now depart in peace.

Oh David! this of all thy deeds was greatest,
    When sword of mercy drew not blood but tears;
All ages shall record thee to the latest,
    Mightier by love than kings with swords and spears!

SONG OF THE HEBREW MAID.

1 Sam. vii.

A happy Hebrew maid,
Roaming the forest shade,
And soft green-mantled glade,
　　The berries and the flowers I bring, I bring;
And as I taste the vine,
And the pretty flowers entwine,
Of the dark-browed Philistine
　　　　　I sing, I sing.

One time, 'twas long ago,
Came up the deadly foe,
As swiftly as the roe,
　　Like locusts from the desert they came, they came;
Then every cheek was pale
When they saw the sunny vale
With shield, and spear, and mail
　　　　　Aflame, aflame.

We had many men of might,
But none with armour dight,—
No signal for the fight,
　　No banner waving over them had they, had they;
They had come with garments rent,
Their heads with dust besprent,
It was not war—they meant
　　　　　To pray, to pray.

SONG OF THE HEBREW MAID.

Then Samuel the Seer
With hasty step drew near,
With loud voice calm and clear,
 He bade their coward faithlessness to go, to go;
He lifted up the prayer:
"Wilt thou, Lord, leave us bare
To Gentile swords, and spare
      The foe, the foe!"

To save His chosen race
Came down the God of grace,
Clouding the sky's bright face,
 His thunder-chariot rolling on the flood, the flood;
The mountains shook with dread,
The valleys overspread
With lightning flashing red,
      Like blood, like blood.

On waters swelling high
Under the angry sky,
"Oh Dagon!" was the cry
 From the shattered ranks that rose that day, that day;—
As the torrents wide and deep
With restless dash and sweep
Dart headlong down the steep
      Away, away,—

So from the hills, behold!
The foemen's ranks were rolled,

When rushed our yeomen bold
  With psalm and shout of triumph from the gate,
    the gate;
The dead lay (overthrown
With weapons of their own),
Like berries, tempest-blown,
              Of the date, the date.

The groves all mourned the dead;
The lily hung her head;
The white rose turned to red;
  The dove had purple stains upon her breast, her
    breast;
And the spoiler's roving band
Came no more with sword or brand;—
Our homes and fatherland
              Had rest, had rest.

Ye groves! rejoice instead;
O lily! lift your head;
White rose! no more turn red;—
  Your snowy breast no more be stained, ye doves!
    ye doves!
Tho' great and high is He
Who hath made His people free,
Yet a little maid like me
              He loves, He loves.

THE SUNBEAM.

I.

It leapt down from the summer sky
   When zephyr winds were blowing;
It glittered in the eagle's eye,
   And danced where flowers were growing.

It gave the gleaming buttercup
   Its golden sheen so glossy;
It darted down and darted up
   On sweet banks green and mossy.

It flickered round by many a bower
   Where bloom'd the blushing roses,—
And where the little daisy-flower
   Its dewy lips discloses.

Adown the vale with prattling brook
   It glistened, oh so brightly!
And danced in many a shady nook,
   So modestly and lightly!

I saw it chase the icy spring
   With blasts of balmy weather,
And shake the gold dust from its wing
   Upon the purple heather.

There on the moor upon a stone
   I sat and saw it meeting
A beauty fairer than its own,
   Nor seemed one half so fleeting.

A bonnie lass came briskly by,
  With mirth her lip was laden;
The Sunbeam caught her laughing eye,—
  She was a sprightly maiden.

"Ho! ho!" he cried, "this very week
  This maid and I will marry;"
He kissed the dimple on her cheek,
  "And here," quoth he, "I'll tarry!"

Then rose fair music far and wide
  From birds of many a feather,
To greet the sunbeam and his bride,—
  And off they danced together!

II.

Why, Summer, are thy transports fled?
  Why drags life on so slowly?
The pretty woods with gloom are wed,
  And I with melancholy.

The silent snows of Winter come
  On yonder shepherd's dwelling;
And Death, while all things else are dumb,
  His time-worn tale is telling.

But o'er the maid and Sunbeam dead
  He tells no saddening story—
Hope with Immortal Bliss is wed,
  And Grace with Heavenly Glory!

MAJORITY.

" And Pharaoh said unto Jacob, How old art thou?"

The world's old coach that will not stay,
Just one-and-twenty years to-day
Took up a parcel by the way
    As on it roll'd ;
It was a book, and there it lay,
    With clasp of gold.

The trav'llers fain would read the book,
And many a curious glance they took ;
But still at every turn and look
    " Tush ! " was the cry ;
They found no letter—" hook or crook "—
    Save one—'twas " I ! "

They gave it an unfragrant name ;
Its empty pages filled with blame ;
Until at length the book became
    Of large dimension,
With many a tale of sin and shame
    I blush to mention.

But one with wings—like angel fair—
Wrote pardon, and the New Name there,—
Then it became a book of prayer :
    So let it be !
O Christ ! the " I " it used to wear
    Has turned to " Thee ! "

FAINTHEARTED.

" Work while it is day."

Weakness overwhelming,
   Sorrows multiply;
Bruisèd reed is broken;
   Frailty fain would die.
Life is heavy-laden,
   O that it would cease!
Death is long in coming
   With its welcome peace.

Can it be, the Master
   Blind to our behest?
To His servant lending
   Neither work nor rest?
Hush thee, fainting spirit!
   Hear the voice Divine:
"Work!" the Master's watchword;
   "Work and Wait!" be thine!

Soon enough for dying
   When our work is done;
When the war is ended,
   And the battle won;
When the wrong is suffered,
   And the wrong forgiven,
Time enough to languish,
   Soon enough for Heaven

Soon enough for dying
  When our strength is dead ;
When the sick have comfort,
  And the hungry bread ;
When the weary stranger,
  Reft of every stay,
Coming poor and needy,
  Goes in peace away.

Soon enough for resting
  When, the daylight past,
We have toil'd our utmost,
  And have prayed our last ;
Then the trooping angels
  Earthward floating down,—
Well-done !" from the Master,
  And the martyr's crown !

WISDOM FROM BELOW.

> God Almighty!
> There is some soul of goodness in things evil,
> Would men observingly distil it out:
> *   *   *   *   *   *
> Thus may we gather honey from the weed,
> And make a moral of the Devil himself.
> —*King Henry V.*

> And the evil spirit answered and said, Jesus I know, and Paul I know, but who are ye?
> —*Acts of the Apostles.*

Let thanks be given where thanks are due,—
For sun and shadow in the wood;
Both for the false and for the true,
Both for the evil and the good.

We trust God where we cannot trace,
We see Him frown, and love Him still;
To every other darken'd face
Is there a heart that knows no ill?

O might we but the evil trust
For what it holds in secret hiding,—
Good not begotten of the dust,
But nobly born, of God's providing!

None like the false can venerate
The honest truth for being true;
And still the wrong, tho' wrong be great,
Draws hope from what the right can do.

Courage, my heart ! tho' evil things
   Be round thee like an ocean swelling ;
To thee no ill the evil brings,
   Nor to thy happy truth-bound dwelling !

Still from the first the world hath seen
   One hypocrite thrust down another ;
And the poor child of lust or spleen
   Correct in truth his erring brother.

Ill hath no kingdom of its own,
   No church, and no communion-table ;
A bubble is its only throne,
   Its language and its home a Babel.

In secret ever doth it yield
   To God the sceptre and the crown ;
Its followers in the battlefield
   Can only beat each other down.

Be still ! God reigneth everywhere ;
   The patient Christ still bears the Cross ;
His foes with triumph fill the air,—
   'Tis they—not He—who bear the loss.

Are the vile heathen sunken low ?
   They know the Gospel when they hear it ;—
No heart in sin can deeper go
   Than the pure love of God can cheer it.

Man's nature like the brute may be,
　An infant Christ is at the core ;
Hell may be bad, but God can see
　His angel standing at the door.

Yea, Truth within that dismal realm
　In quiet lifts her shining face,
A glittering honour on her helm
　Which Heaven itself could not replace.

What need we fear tho' tumult rolls
　And wicked men are mischief making ?
Come, patient Hope ! preserve our souls,—
　We give thy hand a hearty shaking !

WAR!

War, thou art fearful, but we will not fear thee;
    Come, if thou must, we will not say thee nay;
Stern god! we need our strength when we are near thee,
    Nor need we quail e'en tho' our strength decay.

We are too proud to tremble,—weak we may be,
    Too weak to win, yet strong to yield our breath,—
Brave hearts are bright however dark the day be,
    And never are too weak to conquer death!

We neither bless nor curse thee, dark-brow'd duty!
    Thou com'st unwelcome in thy hideous guise;
Yet thy grim visage hath its gleams of beauty,
    And mercy tames the fierceness of thine eyes.

Is not the gentle Christ in all our trouble?
    And thro' our pains His mild compassions flow,
To cheer poor Frailty when her toils redouble,
    And bring forth music from the groans of woe.

So dost thou come unbid, thou scourge of nations!
    Nor like an unbless'd sorrow comest thou;
Fruitful and fair thy field of desolations,
    As are the thorns that crown the Saviour's brow.

O War! 'tis thine to make true sons of pity,
    Who know too well to love the shining brand;—
So let thy thunders roll o'er sea and city,
    Our only cry is—God and Fatherland!

THE FLOWERS;

AND WHAT THE FLOWERS BEAR WITNESS TO.

I.—THE CHANGEFULNESS OF PROVIDENCE.

Vision of God, oh lovely Flowers !
A dream of life where hope is dead ;
Light of the old Edenic bowers
   Still flickering on the path we tread !
Ye burst forth smilingly and gay
   As children do from cloister'd school ;
Only a flash, and then away
   Like swallows mirror'd in the pool ;
Only a smile ere going hence,
   Dear partners of our weal and woe !—
How seeming harsh is Providence !
   How merciful—for being so !

II.—THE FAITHFULNESS OF GOD.

Faithful, ye never fail to come ;
   The frowning heavens grow always fair ;
The singing birds are never dumb ;
   The autumn fields are never bare.
When trembling Noah left the Ark
   In fear lest God might fail to bless,
He saw upon the waters dark
   The rainbow of His faithfulness ;—
And still, in many a sparkling hue,
   Begotten of the sun and showers,
The same old Covenant shines in you,
   Ye earthly rainbows of the Flowers !

III.—The Spirituality of Man.

In open mead, or tangled wood,
   In garden trim, or mossy dell,
Priests, ye provide the spirit's food,
   And human souls ye nurture well ;—
Adorned, your dewy altars rise
   In temple grove, or lonesome hill,—
The incense of your sacrifice
   Is on the poor man's window-sill ;—
And we are sure, who, for your sake,
   Treads warily the spangled sod,
From Nature's bosom ne'er can break,
   Nor be a wanderer far from God.

IV.—The Father's Discipline.

Oh patient Flowers ! who bear the cross,
   Who feel the knife and murmur not,
Made beautiful beneath your loss,
   The trouble past, the pain forgot,
When ye approach the sufferer's bed
   With healing for the tainted air,
Pale sickness lifts her drooping head,
   And scents the future Eden there.
Father of all ! Thy deep design
   Who of Thy flowers can understand ?
To hurt us healingly is Thine,
   And bleeding Love controls Thy hand.

V.—THE CHARACTER OF JESUS.

Why did ye, Flowers, so idly lie
In shadowy glades, or desert moors,
Whilst He, your Prince, was passing by
In sweeter innocence than yours?
Ye came not crowding to His feet,
Nor cast your rainbow round His head;
The mocking thorns came, most unmeet,
And wondered whither ye had fled;—
Ah no! ye only shared His blame,—
Ye shared so well His likeness too;
Nowhere the beauty of His name
Shines meekly as it shines in you!

VI.—THE FRAILTY OF MAN.

Breathe love, kind Sisterhood of Flowers!
On brother Man in frailty cast,
The infant of a few short hours,
And then—a little dust at last!
His struggling spirit mounts on high,
Rose-visions throng his teeming brain,
But soon like last year's leaves they lie
In Ruin's heap and Sorrow's rain;—
Yet shall they nobly bloom at length,
And last while Heaven itself remains,
For God, who needs not creature strength,
Is honoured most where weakness reigns!

VII.—The Incarnation of God.

'Tis even so,—in frailest reed,
   Wild rose, or ruddy pimpernel,
In every unprotected weed
   The Highest condescends to dwell.
But of them all was never one
   So frail, forlorn, and bruised as He ;
God veiled in His Incarnate Son,
   The Flower of all Humanity !
Whose wing of holy balm is spread,
   His meek omnipotence laid bare,
Wherever Shame may hide her head,
   Or Weakness crouch in dumb despair !

VIII.—The Resurrection of the Dead.

Minstrels of every shape and hue,
   None ring the Resurrection bells
So worthily as ye can do,
   Who in the seed's unshapely cells
Once lay within death's lonely mound,
   In sure decay, in silent gloom,
But now in living splendour crowned,
   Miraculous offspring of the tomb !
Fit emblems for the dying bed,
   The fittest weeds to drape the bier,—
The bloom is on our Christian dead,
   They were but seeds while living here.

IX.—THE SAVIOUR'S LOVE FOR CHILDREN.

The plant grows old from stage to stage,
    But ye, blithe Flowers ! are always young,—
The children's friends, in every age
    Ye on their jewell'd necks have hung,
In Nature's pure sweet fellowship
    Where lambkin plays and brooklet runs ;—
So spake in love the Saviour's lip
    Of "lilies" and of "little ones."
May we that happy kingdom seek
    Where both are clustering at the door—
Where bloom is on the children's cheek,
    And lilies fade not, evermore !

X.—THE FREENESS OF THE GOSPEL.

Fair Flowers ! a Gospel rich with grace,
    And free for all hearts everywhere,
Like the broad heaven's impartial face,
    The sunlight, or untrammell'd air ;
To you, as to the saintly stars,
    There is no high or low estate,
Ye twine around the prisoner's bars
    As sweetly as the gilded gate ;—
In some old baron's ruined hall
    Forget-me-not is welcome guest,—
So love, the fairest flower of all,
    In desolate chambers of the breast !

XI.—The Finest of Christian Service.

Oh silent Flowers! in calm repose
    Ye ever do your noblest things;
Your savour, when the rough wind blows,
    Is wafted on unrustling wings;
And this, in many a sick-room, lends
    Fit pinions for the soul to rise
When lo! its prison-garb it rends,
    As do the ripening butterflies.
Like Mary at the Master's feet,
    The better service makes no sound;
The Christian's work when most complete
    Is but a fragrance circling round.

XII.—The Wideness of God's Fatherhood.

True Flowers! our friends whate'er befall;
    Pledge of a Universal Good,
Who in His love enfoldeth all
    With arms of wondrous Fatherhood!
Nor man alone ye fain would please,
    But wandering hosts of hill and plain,
Where oxen sniff the scented breeze,
    And gnat-life pours, like golden rain;—
All creatures, each to each, are bound
    In servitude's unselfish ties;
And the whole earth is girdled round
    With living chains of sacrifice!

HYMN OF DEDICATION.

I.

King of Zion ! God of Grace !
With Thy Glory fill this place :
Make this house we consecrate,
House of God and Heaven's gate ;
Here in all Thy beauty dwell,
God with us, Emmanuel !

What we give is all thine own—
Heart of love, and house of stone ;
Thou didst cause the work begin—
By Thy grace we enter in ;
Help, and we shall prosper well,
God with us, Emmanuel !

Grant communion when we meet ;
Solemn worship ; service sweet ;
Noble praise ; prevailing prayer ;
Gospel truth and joy to share
More than we can ask or tell,
God with us, Emmanuel !

Bind in one both great and small,
Rich and poor, and bless them all ;
Then let each, the blessing found,
Bear it hence, and spread it round,
Till Thy name all know full well,
God with us, Emmanuel !

Spare the lambs within our fold;
Strengthen youth, and cheer the old;
Every soul to new life raise;
Every mouth fill with Thy praise;
Let Thy love each bosom swell,
God with us, Emmanuel!

Helper and Belov'd of all!
When our charity is small,
Weak hands wish for idle ease,
Faints our zeal on feeble knees,
Let Thine own strong love compel,
God with us, Emmanuel!

Life of all that live or die!
Hear us when too weak to cry;
When doth fail our heavenward hymn;
When love cools, and light grows dim—
Show Thy face, and all is well,
God with us, Emmanuel!

II.

Thee we praise, by love's constraint,
Sinner's Friend, sweet Rest of saint;
Open Way, and Truth, and Life;
Joy of sorrow, End of strife;
Sure Defence from death and hell,
God with us, Emmanuel!

Wonderful, Thy works and ways;
Counsellor, beyond all praise;
Father's Love that ne'er shall cease;
Mighty God, and Prince of Peace;
Conqueror, whom none can quell,
God with us, Emmanuel!

Root of David; Morning Star;
Refuge near, and Hope afar;
Rose with all sweet Sharon's grace;
Lily in the lowliest place;
Lamb of God; Salvation's Well,
God with us, Emmanuel!

In the ages long ago
Thou did'st come, a Child of woe;
Sharing with us sorrow's bread;
Thorns upon Thy righteous head;
From the Cross Thy life's blood fell,
God with us, Emmanuel!

Ours the sin, and Thine the pain;
Thy great agony our gain;
Guilt of sin Thou tak'st away;
Love of sin no more will stay
When Thy Spirit breaks the spell,
God with us, Emmanuel!

Sick in body or in soul,
Thou our Health, shalt make us whole;
Nought can harm when Thou art near;

Future ill we need not fear;
Ne'er in loneliness we dwell,
God with us, Emmanuel!

Death, by Thee, is dawn of light,
Change of hope for welcome sight,
Faltering faith for perfect love,
Church below for Church above—
There at home with Thee to dwell
Evermore—Emmanuel!

LUX IN TENEBRIS.

"If I say, Surely the darkness shall cover me; even the night shall be light about me."—Psa. cxxxix. 11.

All silent lie this breast within
Undreaded depths of secret sin;
Dark realms of unsuspected woe,
Mine own, yet not for me to know;
Mine eyes are mercifully blind,—
Thank God! my guilt is hard to find!
    Unseen, All-seeing, Thou art there
    Alone to witness and to bear;
    To cleanse the breast, and clear the sight,
    My God, my Everlasting Light!

My secret sorrows unconfessed
Lift up to God their dumb behest;
Never to mortal ear revealed,
To my own spirit half-concealed;
I bear till I can bear no more,—
And there are sharper pangs in store
    Unseen, All-seeing, Thou art there
    Kindling Thy candle, my despair;
    Brighter than noonday shines the night,
    My God, my Everlasting Light!

Depressed, maligned, misunderstood,
I fail to do the task I would;
Though aimed with prayer I miss the mark,—

Struggling like Jacob in the dark;
Life void of fruit, and filled with gloom,
More dead than the unconscious tomb:
    Unseen, All-seeing, Thou art there,
    Thy Cross my burden and my care;
    I hear Thee groan,—then all is bright,
    My God, my Everlasting Light!

My cry for knowledge will not cease,
Yet darkness comes, and doubts increase;
Truth to my soul bleak Winter brings
With chill blasts of her blighting wings;
Night thickens o'er me, fold on fold,—
And blind Life staggers in the cold:
    Unseen, All-seeing, Thou art there,
    Only Thyself those clouds can wear,
    They are Thy mantle glistening white,
    My God, my Everlasting Light!

"I WILL NOT LET THEE GO."

Jesus, I cannot, will not let Thee go,
                I love Thee so ;
Far less Thy love will ever suffer Thee
                To part with me.

I know Thou lovest me, but cannot tell
                How long, how well ;
And all the love that fills this heart of mine
                Is drawn from Thine.

I feel no sorrow, and I fear no fear
                When Thou art near ;
And all my sinful feelings droop and die
                Beneath Thine eye.

O let my weary head sink down to rest
                Upon Thy breast ;
And let me drink in flowing words my fill
                Of Thy sweet will.

Thou hast, Thy dear self, of the pain I bear
                The largest share ;
My sorest agony is very bliss
                When I think this.

When my weak spirit cannot rise in song,
        O make me strong!
And when uneasy murmurings will not cease,
        O whisper peace!

Upon Thy bosom leaning, let me there
        Lose all my care;
And gazing on Thy glory, let me be
        Made like to Thee.

O love of Christ! that I can never know,
        Nor yet let go;
With Thee all sorrow from my life is driven,
        And death is Heaven.

PATIENCE.

Wae for the weary feet and sore !
Wae for the rough road travelled o'er !
But now the agony she bore
   Is overpast,
And she hath gained for evermore
   God's rest at last !

O Patience ! in the golden street
Where throngs of men and angels meet,
Hark ! how a thousand praises greet
   Thy meek pale face,
Once thou hast run, with bleeding feet,
   The saintly race.

Long waiting, suffering to the end,
Trusting the sorrow He could send
Who 'neath the bitter Cross did bend—
   Wherever known,
In footprints of the sinner's Friend
   Were placed thine own.

Thy voice in heavenly choirs He hears
Who treasured up thy secret tears
Thro' the long waste of sickening years,
   Thou patient one !
Thine only murmur in His ears—
   " Thy will be done !"

From Him great help thou had'st to crave,
And what His own heart richly gave
From thine to succour and to save
     Went forth as free—
'Rose Phoebe from her ancient grave
     And lived in thee!

They come, the dear ones thou hast known,
Whither thy gentle heart hath flown,
In some nook nestling near the Throne
     To meet again—
Brief hour of toil, a parting groan
     For us, till then.

THE WILDERNESS MADE GLAD.

"The Lord of Peace Himself give you peace always, by all means."

Foul, wretched, frail, deep-dyed and dreary
   With sins and woes that will not cease;
Laid in the dust, forlorn and weary,
   With gropings for the God of peace!

Hush thee, my soul! be still, expending
   Thy strength in fretful sighs like these!
Peace, at the Master's hand attending,
   Waits meekly till the Master please.

He bids, nor will the servant tarry—
   Swift as a sunbeam cometh He;
Nor ever sunbeam yet could carry
   The soft sweet light He brings to thee.

Warm, rich, most beautiful and tender
   The service of this gentle Friend!
None but His very Self can render;
   None else the servant He will send.

Even so, Lord Jesus! come, come quickly!
   Light of indwelling Peace, draw near;
And when my lamp burns low and sickly,
   Always let Thine be strong and clear.

Fresh rills of hope Thou bringest ever
   From lonely wastes of pain and tears;
They meet, they flow like God's own river,
   Calm and eternal as His years!

THE MYSTERY OF MYSTERIES.

" Verily Thou art a God that hidest Thyself."

" Yea, our God is merciful."

How darkly God hides from our sight
   In the sorrow that round us lies,
In the terrors of day and night,
   In the ruin of earth and skies,—
In the whirlwind's wild career,
   In the blast of the blinding sleet,
When His tread brings the earthquake near,
   And "clouds are the dust of His feet!"

Oh, where can His tenderness be
   When the thunderbolt fire He flings,
In the hungry roar of the sea,
   In the hurricane's fateful wings,
In the famine that stalks with death,
   In the flood o'er the weltering plain,
When the pestilence breathes his breath,
   And war finds his feast of the slain !

Dark, dark is the covering veil,
   But behind it the Bleeding Heart,
Whence the mercies that never fail,
   For His is the Sufferer's part ;—

There is kindness that cannot harm,
  There is sympathy pure and wide
In the stroke of the nail-pierced arm,
  In the feet of the Crucified !

His strength is the strength of His love,
  And His love is in all around,
In the orbs that glitter above,
  And sparrow that falls to the ground ;
Let Him bring the worst of His ill
  To His creatures the great or small,—
For the roughest of God's good-will
  Is the tenderest way for all !

MISERERE!

Dark was the night and cold,
   And in the silent street
The weary traveller, thin and old,
   Wandered with naked feet.

Panting at my closed door,
   Most pitiful to see,
"Mercy!" he muttered o'er and o'er,
   "Have mercy upon me!"

"O wretched man and worn,
   Whence comest thou?" said I.
"In Bethlehem city was I born
   Two thousand years gone by."

"Nay, sooth, that cannot be;
   But who art thou?" I cried.
"I am the lost soul," muttered he,
   "For whom the Saviour died."

The vision of despair
   Thus spoke and ceased,—to be
Only a quivering in the air,
   "Have mercy upon me!"

An agonising plaint
   As from a storm-vext tree,—
A moaning like a dying saint,
   "Have mercy on me!"

A shade more dark than night
  Wailing and hurrying on ;
One moment it appalled my sight,
  And in the next was gone.

Fierce grew the gathering storm
  As I made fast my door ;—
Oh, whose may be that voice, that form ?
  They haunt me evermore !

Saviour ! is this Thy moan ?
  And cravest Thou from me
The mercy that is all Thine own ?
  Oh ! have I none for Thee ?

NIGHTFALL.

It is my happiness in life
    God's purpose to fulfil;
My happiness in death to die
    According to His will.

If He should give me painless death,
    With thankful heart I take;
If agony, then I shall try
    To suffer for His sake.

I know it is my heart's desire
    To die in my own bed;
But God, where'er I fall asleep,
    Will hold my sinking head.

I fain would die with undimm'd sense,
    Clear mind, and active will;
But if not this, whate'er God give
    It must be better still.

If sudden death be in my lot,
    My God will order well
For all I have not strength to do
    Or have not time to tell.

I wish not to have aught in death
    But worthlessness to plead;
The Saviour died not for my worth,
    But only for my need.

On the sure merits of my Lord
I firmly take my stand,
And hope in my last hours to feel
That He is close at hand.

But this I crave, whate'er my God
For me may have in store,
That life may be a journey home,
And death the entrance door

DAYBREAK.

My God Thy glory breaking on my view
        Makes all things new ;
And lays a sweet distress of welcome kind
        On heart and mind.

I cannot tell, nor yet can I conceal
        The joy I feel,
Whilst unto Thee in worship, Lord, I call,
        And trust my all.

I had, while thoughts of self-praise clung to me,
        Hard thoughts of Thee ;
But now, in Thy pure light, and clad with shame,
        I mourn my blame.

Low in the depths I lay, and did not cry
        To call Thee nigh ;
Yet Thou did'st come, and all my trouble take,
        For pity's sake.

My sin I felt not, and I could not own
        My heart of stone ;
My soul, in deep sleep, at the gates of hell,
        Dreamt all was well.

O God of love ! and Thou didst come so low
        To save a foe ;
And when in mercy Thou had st set me free,
        Didst waken me.

Had I but known how dreadful was my case
        In that low place,—
Not knowing Thee, I must have known despair,
        And perished there.

Now Thou dost show to me the past alarms
        From Thy safe arms;
And show, in saving light which Thou hast lit,
        How deep my pit.

Great God! who succoured when I could not plead
        My unknown need,—
Help me, so strong to feel, so weak to raise
        My untold praise!

So poor am I to give Thee what is Thine,
        Saviour Divine!
Let me but beg in silence at the door,—
        I ask no more!

GRACE.

Fed from heavenly sources,
  Where God's river runs
Down thro' myriad courses
  Of the trembling suns,

In the soft green meadow
  Grows the Flower of Grace;
And the yew-tree shadow
  Falls upon the place.

Odour sweet it sendeth
  On the air around;
And the fair head bendeth
  Towards the dewy ground.

Say, oh lonely weeper,
  In the twlight hour,
While the dark grows deeper,
  Knowest thou this Flower,

With its breath of healing
  Breathed for human woe;
Fragrant peace, revealing
  More than angels know?

Yes!—this Flower hath crowned thee,—
  Joyfully it flings
Love's aroma round thee
  With its viewless wings!

AT THE CHURCH DOOR—ENTERING.

My God! into Thy House I go,
   And seek that I, in tranquil fear,
Thy Presence not far off may know—
     Nor yet too near.

Let me be shielded in Thy sight;
   Thy shadow only let me share;
The fulness of the Truth's fierce light
     I could not bear.

O come, kind Spirit! brooding Dove!
   The healing breath of mercy bring;
The soft sweet glow of sheltering love
     Beneath Thy wing.

I am all weakness, guilt, and sin;
   No word of worthiness have I;
In pity, Lord, O bring me in,
     And hear my cry!

Old Jacob saw Thee wrapt in gloom;
   Thy voice was heard on Sinai's hill—
Here speak, as in the Upper-room,
     Thy "Peace, be still!"

My God! into Thy House I go,
   And seek that I, in tranquil fear,
In love, and solemn joy, may know
     That Thou art here!

AT THE CHURCH DOOR—LEAVING.

I thank Thee for this hour of rest,
   Spent in the quiet courts of grace :
Lord, lead me as Thou knowest best,
And everywhere be Thou my guest
   Within the heart's most holy place.

The path untrod Thou knowest all,
   The task untried, the secret snare,
The sudden stroke that may befall,
The need that dare not on Thee call,
   The stony heart of dumb despair ;—

In things approved or things amiss ;
   In hopes beneath the sod that lie,
Or rise on glistering wings of bliss,—
Let my poor life shew only this—
   How saints can live and heroes die.

I may not tread these courts again ;
   But I would serve Thee—see Thee dwell
In sad and suffering souls of men,—
Come death, it is but blending then
   Heaven's welcome with the world's farewell !

AT THE THRESHOLD.

When heart and flesh are failing,
  O Lord, I look to Thee;
Let Thy grace, all-prevailing,
  Revive and comfort me.
This sad world all so dreary
  No resting can supply;
Thrice welcome to the weary
  It is in Christ to die.

O happy, happy landing,
  Safe on the other shore,
Where white-robed friends are standing
  Around my Father's door,
With ready and sweet greeting
  To grace my raptured eyes,
All on the threshold meeting
  Of long lost Paradise.

O tender ties that bind me
  To this drear earth of woe!
O friends I leave behind me
  To follow where I go!
Kind Jesus, all-forgiving,
  Calls me in tender love,
Not to the dead, but living,
  In His bright home above.

Even so, come, precious Jesus,
  Sweet Promiser of rest!
Thy goodwill may well please us
  That works all for the best.
It is brief time for sorrow
  To you, dear friends, who stay;
For ye go home to-morrow,
  And I go home to-day.

AT THE COMMUNION.

If any guest this banquet-hall within
Hath broken bread in unbelief and sin,
And to his lips the sacramental wine
Lifted, with alien heart, and love—not Thine ;—
Kind Lord, forgive ; nor let him leave this place
Unborn, unbless'd of Thy redeeming grace.

If any, worn with penitential fears,
Once more at this glad feast have sown in tears,
Mourning the path his wayward feet have trod,
Mourning an angry or an absent God ;—
Now may he find the balm for his distress
In Thee, our Peace, our blood-bought Righteousness.

If in some breast pent up the secret groan
Grieve over sins and sorrows not his own ;
Bewail some wanderer from Mercy's door,
Some loved one, loved in vain, yet loved the more ;—
Oh teach the faithful, in his agony,
How sweet it is to suffer, Lord, with Thee !

If now the weary heart can soar and sing,
As tho' with linnet's voice and eagle's wing ;
And Joy's fair children, fearless of control,
Roam thro' the sun-lit chambers of the soul ;—
See Thou, O Christ ! tho' cares of life increase,
The spirit droop not, nor the music cease !

And if to some, life's journey well-nigh past,
This feast in earthly tent shall be the last;
While strangers come to fill their vacant place,
And oh! how soon forgot the vanished face!—
Grant them, dear Lord, to meet, lost friend with friend,
Where true love-feasts begin, but never end!

PROPHECY.

He can the Future things foretell
 Who scans the Present well;
Nor is the mystery of Good
 Hard to be understood;
No good thing, let the heart be pure,
 Is lost or insecure;
Weak never is the simple mind,
 Nor can its eye be blind;
Be thou content but to obey
 In meekest humblest way,
The bliss, from heavenly fountains pour'd,
 Comes of its own accord;—
The Power, all other powers above,
 Is simple silent Love;
Its own it never lauds nor seeks,
 Nor of itself it speaks—
Yet, to the lowliest soul when sent,
 More than omnipotent;
The Unseen opens to its view,
 The Past and Future too.

TRANSFIGURED.

Weary and fever-worn a youth was lying
  On his vain couch, thence never more to rise;
Yet there not he but Death itself was dying,—
  The light of life was hastening to his eyes;
And eager angels stood with half-spread wings,
Their harps in hand, their fingers on the strings.

He was a gifted youth, and Hope was wreathing,
  With many smiles, rich honours for his brow;
But faint and fainter grew her loved one's breathing,
  And these from her fair hands were dropping now,
Like bloom which gentle Spring most fain would hold,
Reft by some sudden blast of Winter's cold.

Far distant was his home, where sat his mother
  Silent, and hardly knew that she was there;
His soul and hers changed places with each other,—
  In thought he laid his hand upon her hair,
And she in thought was kneeling where he lay,
Cooling his fevered temples night and day.

Yet was he there as lovingly attended
  As ever was the infant at the breast,—
Full hands and tender hearts were sweetly blended
  With skill, for he was no mere welcome guest,
But watch'd and fondly cherish'd like a son,
When Love has one to lose, and only one.

The foe, alas ! was pitiless, and stronger
   Than all that Love sought vainly to impart ;
And now the warfare youth could wage no longer
   Was fought more fiercely in the father's heart,
Who came in bleak bewilderment and fear
To stand beside the sufferer's bed—or bier :

As one doth stand whose ravish'd eyes are holden
   When falls in thousand fragments at his feet
Some legendary vase, enwreathed and olden,
   With spoils of unremembered art replete,
With forms of gods and men so deftly graced
As nevermore, once lost, might be replaced.

And as he gazed on life's young tide receding,
   The languid eyes met his with mystic spell,
With some deep soul of utterance in their pleading
   The still wan lips had tried but failed to tell ;
Did it concern his last long resting-place ?—
No change brought beaming answer from the face.

Or might it be some message for his mother ?—
   Oh ! ne'er did lightning break its gloomy bars
More swift than darkling Death sent forth this other
   From eyes made lustrous from beyond the stars,—
Ethereal eloquence no tongue could reach ;—
God said, Let there be light ! and light was speech.

Was it his wish that she might cease repining,
   And of his peaceful rest in Jesus know ?—

Then did Shekinah with its holy shining
  Burst from his face with beatific glow,—
One gleam, no more,—Elijah's chariot-flame
Wafting the spirit homeward whence it came.

O God! forgive us for our thankless grieving
  When Thou dost walk the vale in robes of light;
And we behold our loved ones there achieving
  The crown victorious faith bequeaths to sight,—
Children of earth no more but of the skies,
It is not they but Death itself that dies!

And in their speech will our sad words be spoken
  Where heavenly Love finds light her only tongue;
Where life's bright promise never can be broken,
  And God is God, and Youth is ever young,
And Hope can only die in meek despair
To find herself so blissful and so fair!

PRESENT NEEDS AND PATRIARCHAL MEMORIES.

"The God of Abraham, and of Isaac, and of Jacob, the God of our fathers, hath gloried His Son Jesus."—*Acts iii. 13.*

Life one long unrest,
By trouble overpress'd ;
Rugged path, and lurking danger,
To the lone unfriended stranger,—
    God of Abraham ! see
    My panting misery !

Love I can but trace
In her averted face,—
Self-rejected, faint and fretful,
Friends deceiving or forgetful,
    God of Isaac ! hear
    The weakling's cry of fear !

Sin, deceitful sin,
Foully I fall therein,
Deeper still in wallowing meanness,—
Oh ! this curse of my uncleanness,
    God of Jacob ! break,—
    For weeping Mercy's sake !

Saviour, still the same,
Who to our fathers came,—
Woeful men in deserts dwelling,
Yet by faith their bosoms swelling
    With Messiah's praise,
    In far-off future days !

Grace abounding send,
Who art the patriarchs' Friend !
Newly come in sweeter story,
Gleaming bright in Gospel glory,
    God Incarnate now,
    The lowly Jesus Thou !

Let me know Thee well,
Brother Emmanuel !
Loving-eyed, and gently breathing,
Meekly on my brows enwreathing,
    Tranquil hour by hour,
    Snow-white Redemption's flower.

Let me know Thy Cross
Nor mourn the pain and loss ;
Bruis'd like Thee, my Friend, my Fellow,
Mine Thy fruitage rich and mellow,
    In communion wine,
    Blood of the Living Vine !

My reward but this—
One drop of Thy pure bliss,
Blessing me to bless another,
Some far-strayed and fainting brother ;—
    Then, before Thy face,
    The humblest servant's place !

DIVINE SERVICE.

I.

THE FAMILY IN THE CHURCH.

Enclosed as in a little fold,
Within the pew meet young and old:
Father, with reverential grace,
The meek-eye'd mother's tranquil face;
And on the children nestling near,
With sober pride and joyous fear,
Fresh, week by week, as heavenly dew,
The blessing of the family pew!

They sing, they read, they pray, they wait,
They hearken and they meditate;
Unstained the sacrifice and whole,
One heart, one mouth, one mind and soul;
As from a harp's responsive string,
From each the Master's fingers bring
Pure worship in melodious tone
And blending music all His own!

The angel of Jehovah smiled
Long since on Hannah and her child;
And shed sweet beams of peace and joy
On Mary and her mystic Boy;

His hovering wings are guarding still
The little groups on Zion's Hill,
Who come in Wisdom's humble way
Prepared to listen and obey.

O sacred bond, with grace replete !
Home lifted to the Mercy-seat ;
With other homes united there,
Where all the common blessing share ;
These families of living stones,
Excelling far all earthly thrones,
Build up the Church of God in truth,
With mellowed age and ardent youth.

Long after will the memory save,
When parents lie in hallowed grave ;
Where'er, in quest of daily bread,
The children's wandering steps are led ;
When griefs becloud and hopes decline,
The memory in their souls will shine,—
Will come again, like healing dew,
The blessing of the family pew.

II

THE CHURCH IN THE FAMILY.

The Sabbath hour at close of day
When sweat of sin is washed away ;
And at the fireside-altar wait,
With weary frame and soul sedate,

The sire unharnessed from the strife,
Proud mother and the patient wife ;
The quiet children gathering round,
While heart-bells chime the solemn sound.

The father-priest lifts up his voice ;
In choral strains they all rejoice ;
He reads the sacred page, and now
Before the spotless Throne they bow ;
Step after step their souls ascend
Up to the ladder's Heavenward end,
Where visions of the angels be,
Ev'n for the infant on the knee !

Oft as'the family board is spread,
Thankful they eat communion bread ;
And when in playful mood combine,
It is their Lord's communion wine ;
Not unprepared for weal or woe,
Forth at the call of morn they go,
Well-mantled with Shekinah's rays,
To walk the world's polluted ways.

Thus, in his grey-hair'd wisdom's prime,
Stood Joshua in the olden time
And vow'd, howe'er all else might swerve,
In heart and home his God to serve ;—
The self-same vow each day would rise
With Job's all-trembling sacrifice
For some poor child, caught unawares
In the soft web of silken snares.

Oh ! speed the day such tie shall bind
The family of all mankind !
Assembling at the Father's feet ;
His Son the living Bread they eat ;
His own the joyous cup they drink,
Love sparkling ever at the brink ;
And striving who shall serve Him best,
Each one outrivalling the rest !

SALVATION FOR THE SAVIOUR.

I love Thee, my Deliverer!
    I reverence and adore;
Oh! give me grace to help Thee,
    That I may love Thee more.

The chalice of salvation
    With rapture Thou dost fill;
But in Thy service find I
    A cup more blessed still.

Thou bringest wine of comfort
    To these parched lips of mine;
Yet am I faint with longing
    To hold that cup to Thine.

I seek Thee not on mountains
    With glory round Thy head;
But I would find Thee panting
    On some poor sufferer's bed.

I wish not to be mantled
    In robes of dazzling white;
If Thou wilt give Thy pity,
    I will not ask for light.

And still would I be groping
    In life's dark lanes below,
To ease the Cross Thou bearest
    In all our want and woe.

So would I serve Thy weakness
    With aidance of Thine own;
And for Thy pain bring patience
    Which Thou Thyself hast shown.

To see Thee throned in glory
    May be a blissful sight;
To feed Thee being hungry
    Were more my soul's delight.

Oh that at last my dying
    Like Thy decease may be,
A drawing near and nearer
    To human misery!

Then would I go with gladness
    That I might come again,
Like Thee, Good Spirit, bringing
    The better boon to men.

Their sin, their pain, their sorrow
    Is all for Thee to feel;
And so Thou need'st the healing,
    For Thou alone canst heal.

Oh service to the Saviour
    For my frail self to do,—
In life done all too feebly,—
    In death begun anew!

THE SMOKING FLAX.

I'll seek the rich man's gate no more ;
Lo ! here I see a humble door
   Along this narrow road ;--
I'll turn aside,—perchance it may
Give access to a castaway
   Into a friend's abode.

  I have no home, no resting here,
  No hand to help, no friend to cheer,—
  I'm weary of this world of sin ;
  O let me in ! O let me in !

  Hungry, I have no bread to eat ;
  Naked to Winter's wind and sleet ;
  Sore head above, sad heart within,—
  O let me in ! O let me in !

  If thou hast pity left in thee
  For a poor wastrel soul like me,
  Good watchman, if it be no sin,
  O let me in ! O let me in !

Hush, stranger ! cease thy useless prate,
Dost thou not know King Christian's gate ?
Think'st thou to grace, foul wretched thing !
The marriage banquet of the King ?

O sir, I ask—and that is all—
The crumbs that from His table fall;
Good watchman, if it be no sin,
O let me in ! O let me in !

Ah ! tremble not; cast off thy fear,—
Meek soul, thou art thrice welcome here ;
Behold King Christian's open door
To welcome rest for evermore !

The feast awaits thee ; take thy place
'Neath the bright shining of His face ;
He knows the sorrows thou hast had,
And His long-waiting heart is glad !

LOVE'S ONLY CHOICE.

All good things to Love belong ;
She alone is wise and strong ;
She alone can play her part
With a free and joyous heart ;—
Yet is this her constant cry—
Let me suffer, or I die !

Happiest of living things ;
Hers the sweetest voice that sings ;
Hers the burdened soul's release ;
And her face is perfect peace ;—
Yet is this her constant cry—
Let me suffer, or I die !

Love's fair eyes are always wet
For the grief she fain would get ;
And of all the pain we bear
Coveting the largest share,
Still is this her constant cry—
Let me suffer, or I die !

Wearisome the road and rough,
Thou hast borne it long enough ;
Here are all fit things to please,
Verdant banks of balmy ease,—
Speaks the Tempter ;—Love's reply—
Let me suffer, or I die !

Thine the need, and thine the power,
Save thee from this fatal hour,—
Cast away the thorny crown,
From the bitter cross come down;—
Jesus did not,—nor can I—
Let me suffer, or I die!

As the self-denying seed
Springs thro' death to life indeed;
So beneath the sin and shame
Springeth Love's immortal fame;—
God is Love,—Love can but cry—
Let me suffer, or I die!

Help us, O Thou Love Divine!
Till the realm of wrath be Thine,
Till the latest tear be shed,
Suffering itself be dead,—
Still with Thee to raise the cry—
Let me suffer, or I die!

ALLELUIA.

If Thy bruiséd hand but lead me,
　Pleased am I to stand or fall;
Sorrow's bread, if Thou dost feed me,
　Is the sweetest bread of all.

Give the cross, and I will bear it,
　Only shamed to lose my hold;
Give the crown, and I will wear it,
　Prouder of the thorns than gold.

Better far than all Thou givest
　From Thy love's unbounded store—
Thou art mine, who ever livest,
　Mine, and mine for evermore!

Thy compassions then are kindest
　When my love is leaving Thee;
And my preciousness Thou findest
　When my worth has ceased to be.

Could I as the star rejoices
　Million-fold on heaven's bright floor,—
Could I with as many voices
　As the sand on every shore,—

Could I with the joy that wingeth
　On the morn's unresting beams,—
Or the music Nature bringeth
　From her lyres, the woods and streams,—

ALLELUIA.

Could I blend those notes of wonder
    Which the lark uplifts on high,
With the deep, broad-breasted thunder
    Of the ocean and the sky,—

With the songs of lonely mountains
    Awful in their mystic strains,—
With the clouds, those lyric fountains
    Of the dew-drops and the rains,—

Each and all had I to praise Thee,
    Vain would be the sacrifice;
For the silent Cross displays Thee,
    And in shame the anthem dies.

Praises all have there their ending,
    Stricken dumb and turned to stone,
Till Thy shining steps ascending
    Tread the pathway to the Throne.

Then, with happier notes and clearer,
    Risen from the dead as well,
Alleluia stronger, dearer,
    For the love it fails to tell!

A LYRIC OF CHRISTIAN LIBERTY.

"Take My Yoke."

Hark! weary souls, beneath the thrall
   Of sin and sorrow bending,
Around you rings the trumpet-call
   The Lord of Love is sending,
With jubilant freedom for you all,
   And never-ending.

The iron gateways bursting thro',
   In cadent sweetness calling,
The silver music summons you
   From fetters vile and galling,
As gently as the healing dew
   On mown grass falling.

Ye weary, come to Me, He cries,
   Ye hearts in anguish breaking!
When in the dust your courage lies,
   And hope's last gleam forsaking,—
And Friendship with averted eyes
   Farewell is taking.

Trust ye My kindly yoke, it will
   From mortal woes relieve you;

The hope of Heavenly peace fulfil ;
   Nor fret tho' it should grieve you
In love that can be faithful still,
      But not deceive you.

Fear not affliction's fiery cross,
   My humble spirit shewing ;
The flames redeem you from the dross,
   With My compassions glowing ;
A Heavenly gain from earthly loss
      For ever flowing.

THE SECRET OF STRENGTH.

Almighty Power! whose meekness most we fear;
Omnipotent to suffer and endure;
Whose sceptred strength is strong for being pure;
Stronger than we to shed the human tear,
To pour forth helpless plaints that none can hear,
To feel the wound of wounds than none can cure;
Thou weakest Weakling, Poorest of the poor;
Power of all power, whom Heaven of heavens revere,—
Thy lowly Name in Jesus breathing sweet
Like fragrance from the broken casket spread,
Or some frail weed when crushed by brutal feet,—
Oh, let Thy timely unction bless our head,
And cleanse us from the servile dread of Thee,
For we ourselves, Thou Blameless One! would blameless be!

A LADY'S ADDRESS.

She spoke, and the whole ample space
    With melody was filled ;
Light from her own touched every face,
    And every heart was thrilled ;—
She seemed the very Gospel, come
    In human form and fair;
All other sound was stricken dumb,
    And turned to silent prayer.

She pled the missionary's grief,
    When comes the mournful day
His children needs must seek relief
    In strange homes far away;
Would that the little ones were taught
    And nurtured by the best,
With influence, near as might be, brought
    Fresh from the mother's breast!

No flower could lift its dewy eye
    To greet the rising moon
More plaintively than God drew nigh
    On that dim afternoon ;
His love was radiant in her face,
    His music in her tone,
Her manner mellowed by His grace,
    Her utterance all His own.

O Womanhood! unseal thy lips—
   God's mysteries are revealed;
Sin's cancer touch with finger-tips—
   Its hidden roots must yield;
Angelic minstrelsies attend
   Thy steps, where duty calls;
Long-lasting sorrows reach their end
   Where'er thy shadow falls.

She spoke; and evermore she speaks
   With liquid voice and low;
Fond Memory, with flushing cheeks,
   Will never let it go;—
Amid the wildest of the storm
   That music will not cease;
And like a mantle round her form
   The melody of peace!

www.ingramcontent.com/pod-product-compliance
Lightning Source LLC
Chambersburg PA
CBHW022052230426
43672CB00008B/1152

LIST OF ILLUSTRATIONS.

The New House on the Castle Moat	FRONTISPIECE
Map	PAGE
A Japanese Junk	8
The Tokaido, or Public High Road	16
Dai-Butz; the Bronze Idol, 50 feet high	20
Lake and Village of Hakone	24
Japanese Hotel in the Hakone Mountains	28
Temple Gateway	36
School House at Shidz-u-o-ka	44
Buddhist Temple and Pagoda	50
The New House with the Castle Grounds	58
Man Pounding Rice	76
Mode of Sleeping	80
Fuji-Yama, the Matchless Mountain, 11,500 feet high	96
Gathering Tea-leaves; Fuji-Yama in the Background	120
Heating and Firing the Leaves—4 views	124
Sifting and Sorting the Leaves	126
The Kaisei Gakko, or Imperial College	140
Entrance of the Kaisei Gakko	144
Tower and Moat of the Tokio Castle	148
Tomb of the First Tycoon	150
The Home in Tokio	162
Suruga-Yashiki, and College Building	166
The Mikado in Modern Dress	172
The Empress in Court Costume	176
Representative Classes of Society	180
A Japanese Gondola	196
Riding in a Kango	210
Mode of Carrying the Baby	214
American Mission Home	220
The Lord's Prayer in Japanese	228
Japanese Summer House and Garden	244

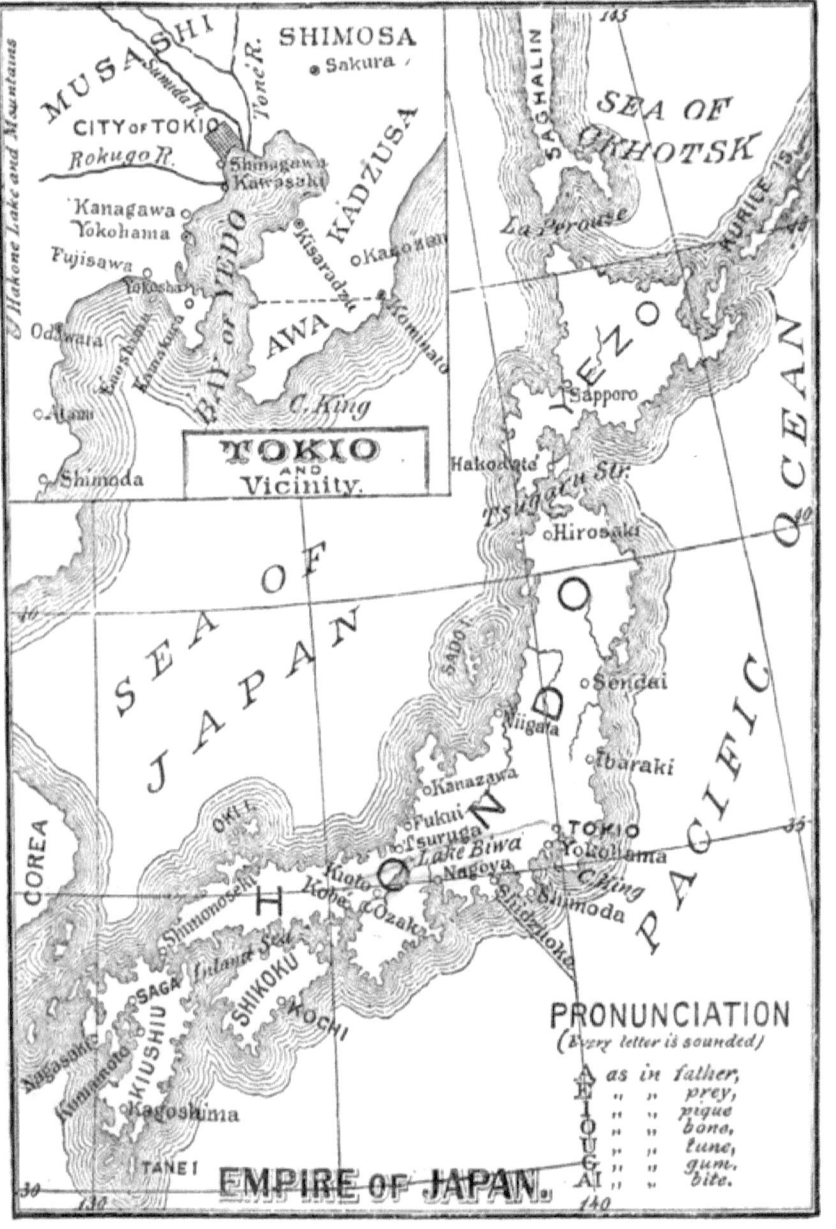

LIFE AND ADVENTURE IN JAPAN.

CHAPTER I.

FIRST SIGHT OF JAPAN.

At early dawn on Wednesday, October 25th, I looked out of my state-room window from the steamer Great Republic, and lo! the snow-white dome of Fuji-Yama, the "Matchless Mountain" of Japan, rising like a temple of beauty above the clouds and mist; and as I caught sight of it the sun rose higher and higher, causing the mountain to brighten up, and its face to smile a welcome to us in our approach to the old, old world.

Slowly we steamed up the great bay of Yedo, passing verdure-covered cliffs, rocky promontories, and small islets clothed in brightest green, while here and there the thatched-roof cottages of the fishermen were scattered along the shore.

A slight breeze rippled the surface of the water,

and Japanese junks came scudding by under full sail. The junks had low prows and very high sterns, with broad sails sometimes made of matting or bamboo, and having large characters inscribed on black bands of cloth, with which the main-sail was ornamented. The cargo of the junk was carried amidship, with a bamboo roof built over it ; and not a particle of paint appeared on the whole craft. The junks came quite near the steamer, dashing the spray from their low prows, and rocking violently in the rollers left in the wake of the Great Republic.

With the captain's permission I brought my new flag on deck, presented by friends far away, and up went my bright star-spangled banner in place of the ship's dilapidated ensign, and it flapped and fluttered proudly from the stern of the steamer.

As we passed vessel after vessel of various nationalities lying at anchor in the harbor, *that* flag was saluted with respect—German, Italian, English, French, Dutch, and other ships dipped their colors as we went by, and only ceased when the signal-gun from our steamer announced that we had made fast to our moorings in Yokohama Bay.

Swarms of little skiffs surrounded us, sculled by nearly naked Japanese, with brawny arms and brown skins. Dropping into one of these boats, I

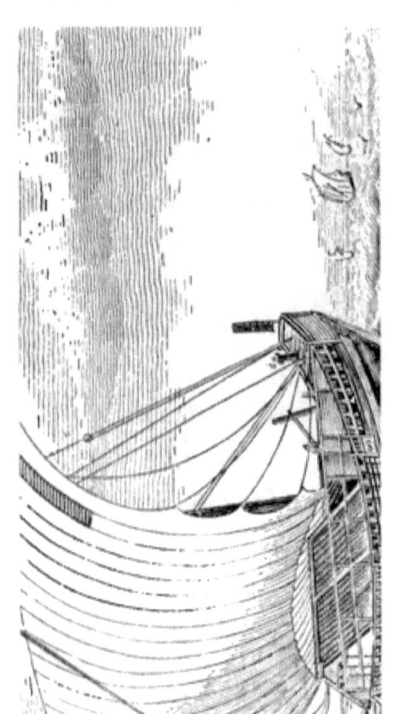

made for the shore. Alone I wandered off, and peculiar were my feelings as I wended my way among the strange sights and people.

It is said that the *sounds* of a place first attract the stranger's attention, and so it was here. I heard an unearthly shout or yell, repeated in quick and regular succession, and turning down the street I saw a line of rough wooden carts drawn by strong coolies, who tugged away like horses and gave these guttural yells in keeping step with each other.

Boxes of tea were piled on the carts, and as I passed by the stone houses on a side street I could smell the sweet aroma of the tea that was being "re-fired" within, and hear the merry prattle in a strange tongue of the tea-girls as they sang together and stirred the tea-leaves on the hot copper ovens.

Taking a straight street to the left, I passed through a portion of the foreign settlement, which was substantial and comfortable, and came to a bridge crossing the canal. On ascending a steep flight of steps I reached the top of "The Bluff," where many English and Americans live; from this point a beautiful view spread before me of the bay, shipping, city, and the native town of Yokohama.

I met many kind friends at the American

Mission Home, a beautiful building on "The Bluff," where Japanese girls are instructed in Christian truth, and where the first Sunday-school in Japan was established.

After a few days the Japanese officials arrived at Yokohama who were appointed to conduct me to their distant province in the interior of the country.

I had engaged to go to the city of Shidz-u-o-ka, one hundred miles south-west of To-kio, to take charge of a scientific school there, and teach the Japanese in chemistry, physics, and other branches of study. I was to be liberally paid by the Japanese Government, who were also to furnish my horses, guards, interpreters, philosophical apparatus, attendants, and give me a large temple in which to live. Thirteen long articles, written in Chinese, Japanese, and English, and forming three imposing-looking books, constituted the "contract" or agreement made between us for the space of three years.

But when I came to sign the agreement, I found that the "Dai-jo-kan"—as the Council of State is called—had slyly inserted a clause forbidding me to teach Christianity, and binding me to silence on all religious subjects for a space of three years. Many reasons prompted me to accept, and some of my friends urged me to sign the contract as it was. The interpreter said, "Sign the promise; but when you get way off in the country you can break it and teach what you please." Others said, "Sign it, or you will lose $300 a month, and all your good chances besides; some mere adventurer may get the position, who will do the people more harm than you can do them good."

It was a great dilemma, for I had spent all my money in coming to Japan and getting ready to go into the interior, and were the contract to fail I should find myself in a tight place.

Nevertheless I determined to stand firm on the principle at stake, and sent word to the government that unless the objectionable clause was withdrawn, the contract could not be accepted. "It is impossible," I added, "for a Christian to dwell three years in the midst of a pagan people, and yet keep entire silence on the subject nearest his heart."

To my surprise an answer was returned after three days, saying that the clause against Christianity should be stricken out; and the messenger who brought me the news exclaimed, "You have conquered, and have broken down a strong Japanese wall. Now you can also teach us the Bible and Christianity!"

I mention this to show that it pays to hold fast

to the right, at whatever apparent cost ; for, instead of thinking less of me, or being vexed at my obstinacy, the Japanese officials were more friendly than ever, and respected the "pluck" displayed.

They immediately advanced all the necessary funds to meet the heavy expenses incurred, and were so liberal and polite as to excite my gratitude and astonishment. Under their kindly assistance I was soon ready to start on the long journey.

But never before had I so many things to think of at once. Not only had I the care of perfecting my official arrangements, but I had all the minute details of "first going to housekeeping" beyond the range of civilization.

Imagine yourself preparing to keep house where a real house was never known ! Imagine yourself endeavoring to furnish said house where furniture was never heard of ; where bedsteads and beds and carpets and stoves were never seen ; where mirrors and windows and chimneys and coal had not even been dreamed of. Imagine yourself going to live a certain number of years in said house and place. The probability is you would want something to eat during your sojourn ; but there beef-steaks and mutton-chops are unknown, a loaf of bread is a myth, and milk, butter, and cheese are fairy tales.

Perhaps now and then you would like to know the time of day. But no town-clock ever strikes to inform you, no chronometer exists by which to set your watch when it stops, no almanac to tell the day of the week or month when you have forgotten them. In fact I frequently *did* forget the day of the week, and once kept the scientific school waiting several hours for me, supposing it was Sunday! After that I thought of cutting notches in a stick every day, after Robinson Crusoe's fashion; and when my watch stopped I would set it by a sun-dial, which I made with two sticks, a compass, and a string.

Na-ka-mu-ra was the name of one of the officers sent from the province where I was going; and although he was the most noted scholar of Chinese literature in Japan, he was as simple as a child, and quite amusing in his use of broken English. He called at the Mission Home to see me one day, while I was off making some purchases, and, as he awaited my return, the children of the Home volunteered to entertain him. "They take out several cards," he wrote, "singing the songs which are written on them" (Sunday-school hymns), "then passing the biblical pictures, very fine, to me, they said, 'While you look at them Mr. Clark will soon be returned.' The girls again merrily explained them to me, saying, 'This is John the Baptist,' 'This is dove,' 'This is Jesus,' 'This is Abraham sacrificing his son,' and the like. During one hour I feel myself to get some advantage from the surrounding children."

Not long after this Nakamura boldly presented a memorial to the imperial government suggesting that they build a Christian church in Tokio! in order that Japanese subjects might have an opportunity of being instructed in the truth. Of course the government did not quite see it in that light. Nakamura was appointed to go abroad with the Japanese embassy then starting for America, but he declined, saying that he had once lived in a Christian country—England —without learning Christianity, and now he wished to retire to his own province and study religious subjects with his new foreign teacher. He was subsequently my warmest friend and most intimate companion; he became a devout Christian under the instruction of my Bible-class, and frequently would sign himself, "Your most humble servant, and to be your future and forever friend in the spiritual world."

On my last Sabbath in Yokohama I attended the little chapel where foreigners are accustomed to assemble, and listened to an interesting sermon from Rev. Mr. H——, a missionary of North China. It was communion service, my first in Japan, and the last that I should have for a long, long time, as I was going where there were no Christians. On returning from church I wrote home, saying :

"The more I enjoyed the service, the more vividly it brought upon me the realization of the keen deprivation I am to suffer in being cut off from all holy associations, and how I shall long for the strength gained from Christian sympathy and the sound of the Gospel.

"You can scarcely imagine the impressions of one fresh from a Christian land at the first view of the heathenism of which he had heard but never seen. There is no more Sabbath here than if the Ten Commandments were never written. The sounds of labor are heard in every direction, and sin and corruption abound in their worst forms. Instead of church bells, I hear ever and anon the deep, prolonged sound of the great bell of the heathen temple, as it strikes to announce that another soul has entered to bow down to the idol. Instead of sacred music, I hear fire-crackers in an adjacent Chinese burying-ground, where worship is going on to the spirits of the dead. As I visited the temples of Yedo the other day, and saw the hundreds of human beings prostrated before their images and calling upon their gods, it did seem to me the most pitiable sight I ever witnessed ; and as I moved among the millions in the great capital of Japan who never heard the name of Christ, it seemed too solemn to be true. Possibly I may become so accustomed to heathenism and its accompaniments as not to feel their painful reality, but I trust I may never lose the earnest desire to turn these poor deluded souls from their errors."

On the following Monday the horses and guards appeared at the door, and as my furniture and freight had been sent by sea on a Japanese junk, I bade farewell to all my new-made friends at Yokohama, and started off with the guards to encounter the strange experiences and adventures of life in the heart of Japan.

THE "TOKAIDO," OR PUBLIC HIGH ROAD.

CHAPTER II.

A JOURNEY ON THE "TOKAIDO."

The great public thoroughfare of Japan is called the "To-kai-do." It is several hundred miles in length, and passes along the sea-shore and over the mountains, connecting the ancient capital, Kio-to, near Lake Biwa, with the modern capital, To-kio, at the head of Yedo Bay.

The road is flanked on either side with venerable pines, which have shaded generations of travellers and pilgrims who have passed to and fro through this beautiful country. Near the sea-shore it is protected by earthen embankments, and over the steep declivities of the mountains it is paved with stones. It runs through innumerable villages and towns, and its way-side is the best possible place to study the country life and character of the people.

Here you may meet the two-sworded "Sa-mou-rai," as the military gentlemen are called who wear long sharp swords thrust in their belts, and who sometimes look very fiercely at foreigners, whom they do not love overmuch for invading the sacred seclusion of their country. Here you meet the farmers also, carrying their produce to market, and the coolies, trudging along with their burdens suspended from the ends of a pole carried on the shoulder.

Here you meet bands of pilgrims clothed in white, wearing broad bamboo hats, and carrying a small bell in one hand and a long staff in the other. On the staff were strips of paper prayers, and the little bells tinkled continually to call the attention of the gods to the prayers while the pilgrims were on their journey to the various heathen shrines.

The country people were very polite, and as we passed them on the road each one would bow and exclaim, "O-hi-o!" (Good-morning). The children would also nod their little heads politely, and touch their foreheads as a mark of respect.

In passing through one of the towns on the "Tokaido"—shown in the accompanying picture—we saw a long ladder standing upright at the side of the street, upon which a man climbed whenever the fire-alarm sounded. The houses were simply wooden shanties, with paper sliding-doors, and when they caught fire, as they frequently did, the man on the ladder would shout to his neighbors, and they would run together and pull down the house, instead of attempting to extinguish the flames.

On the road-side a stream of water is seen, which the natives use in cooking and washing. The open space in front of each house is used for drying fish, sifting grain, and also for sunning the babies and children who swarm by the road-side, and who use this space frequently for a playground.

The mountain Fuji-Yama is seen in the distance.

We turned aside a few miles to visit "Dai-Butz," the great bronze idol of Japan, which is about fifty feet in height. It stands near the former site of an ancient city of great historic interest, but which passed away some centuries ago, leaving scarcely a vestige behind, except this idol and a large temple.

The colossal image represents Buddha sitting in a large lotus-lily, in the state called "nir-vana," which is a kind of divine sleep or unconsciousness. This is the heavenly state which the devout Buddhist hopes to attain. Not a heaven of holy activity and of joyous worship, but a *sleep* of eternal unconsciousness, an absorption into Buddha! Yet there is certainly something very peaceful and even beautiful in the expression of repose on that bronze face, and I do not wonder that multitudes of the ignorant pilgrims worship it with awe.

In front of the image are two vases containing large bronze lotus-lilies with expanding leaves, and between the vases is a bronze brazier where incense may be burnt. Dai-Butz is very imposing without, but he is entirely empty within; for you may go inside of him, by passing through a small door, and find his hollow form lined with shelves, on which small gilt images are ranged. His ears are very large, as all ears are on idols, and his massive head is covered with concentric rows of snail-shells, which gathered there to protect his sacred person from the sun when (in mythological times) he rose from the sea.

After studying the image as a work of art, I climbed up into his capacious lap, and sat upon one of his thumbs, which were placed together in a devout attitude. Here I began to sing the long-metre doxology, to the astonishment of the priest standing below, who could not understand the words, and wondered what the matter was! A year after this I sang the same hymn in Dai-Butz's lap, with half-a-dozen other people; and we told the priest we were praising the TRUE GOD, that the time was at hand when idolatry in Japan was going down, never to rise again, and

DAI-BUTZ, THE BRONZE IDOL, 50 FEET HIGH.

that even Dai-Butz would no longer be worshipped.

Not far from this great image is the beautiful island of In-o-shi-ma, close by the shore, where shrines and temples are found embowered among the trees high up on the rocky cliffs, and where you may descend to submarine caverns, to reach which I had to swim around the rocks and allow myself to be swept into a dark and dreary cavern by the waves. Here a naked priest stood by a stone altar. On the ledges of the rock, where the surf rolled and dashed high in the air, little Japanese urchins were diving for pennies in the deep green water, protected by the grottos formed at the foot of the cliff; they would catch a penny when thrown into the water long before it reached the bottom.

We spent the first night at a large city on the Tokaido, and the next morning found us galloping along the level road leading towards O-da-wa-ra, a city at the foot of the Hā-ko-né mountain pass. The whole journey to Shidz-u-o-ka required five days, for you must remember there were no steam-cars, coaches, or modern conveniences of travel. Besides, I very soon found that it was to be a journey of Japanese etiquette the whole way. As we approached the province where I was to live, whole villages appeared specially prepared for my reception. The native officials would come out to meet us, dressed in flowing robes, and salute me in the way they used to receive the dai-mios, or distinguished princes, in olden times. Although they were two-sworded men of rank, they would kneel in front of our horses and bow their heads to the earth, heaving a deep sigh of respect that sounded like a miniature typhoon!

These Yaconims, or officials, would escort us on foot through the whole length of the district under their jurisdiction, picking up any stray straw or stone that happened in the way, and motioning all carts and traffic to the side of the road with a wave of authority that made all plebeians drop on their knees at once, and keep there until our august presence was passed.

It tickled my Yankee glee not a little to touch up the horses now and then, causing these sedate officials to perform feats of pedestrianism such as they had scarcely before attempted. They took it in good part, and I usually favored them with an extra " smile" for their pains. If I started on a brisk trot, however, and shouted, " Sai-o-na-ra!" (Good-by), they would fall at once on their faces, keeping their heads bowed between their hands until we had disappeared from view.

At the next village we would have to go through the very same formalities, until, after a dozen or more were passed, it became rather monotonous. Whole neighborhoods were thrown into agitation by the arrival in their midst of such a strange-looking creature as the "foreigner," and I was evidently as great a curiosity to the people as they were to me. Long lines of awe-struck faces presented themselves at every window and door and crevice, and crowds of women and children thronged the narrow lanes as we galloped through the principal street, making the old town echo with the clatter of our horses' feet.

On crossing the Hakoné range of mountains it became necessary to change our horses for peculiar vehicles called "kan-gos," carried on men's shoulders. The "kan-go" is like a broad cane chair without legs, slung securely on a thick pole, and in which you must squat, with the happy alternative of breaking your neck above or twisting your legs out of joint below. How to get into it was a mystery, so I just gave a pitch and tumble, leaving it to chance whether I came in right side up or not.

When I was fairly stowed away in the kan-go, two naked coolies raised it from the ground and placed the ends of the pole on their brawny shoulders. Off they trudged, as though I were simply a bag of rice or a box of cheese, and, jolting me up and down like a bowlful of jelly, they slowly climbed the steep and stone-paved path of the mountains. Now and then they rested the ends of the pole upon their stout bamboo sticks, and after shifting the heavy burden to the other shoulder away they would go again. Though their naked bodies would fairly shine with the sweat that trickled down their backs, yet they went great distances without apparent fatigue, always shouting to each other in keeping step. There are half-way stations on the mountain, where they stop to rest and eat rice ; it is very amusing to see a dozen of their nude bodies dancing around the fire, each carrying a steaming bowl of rice in one hand and chop-sticks in the other. Their appetites are well earned, and after eating plenty they finish off with a cup of tea.

In coming down hill the coolies trot very fast, and jolt one almost to pieces ; but on level ground the kango goes easily, and when you get accustomed to keeping your legs tied up in knots for two or three hours at a time, and are reconciled to wearing an artificial stiff neck for the same period, it becomes quite comfortable, and you can soon imagine yourself being rocked to sleep.

On the pass we encountered naked runners, or

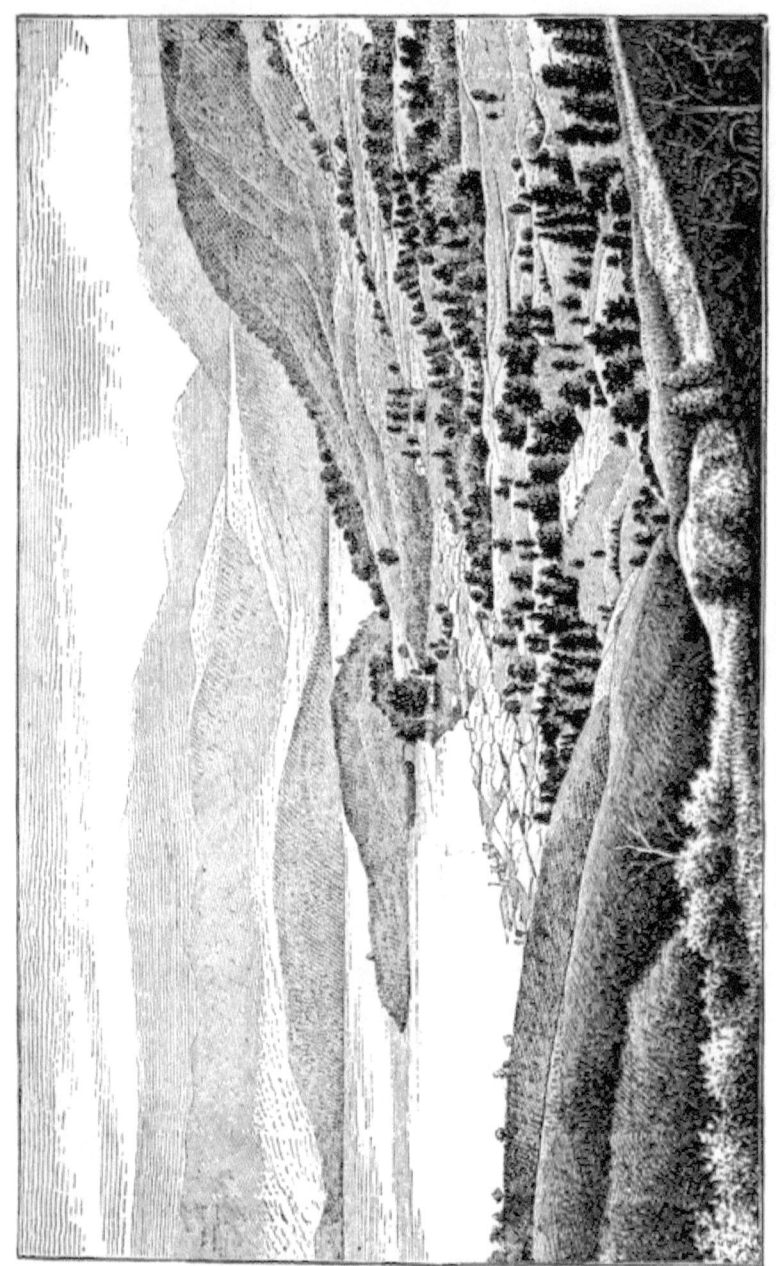

LAKE AND VILLAGE OF HAKONE.

post-carriers, with their broad-brimmed hats and their little post-boxes slung on a stick over their shoulders. These are the swift-footed fellows who afterwards brought me my home mails from Yokohama.

After ascending several thousand feet, through thickly wooded ravines, we reached the picturesque village of Hakoné, nestled among the mountains, at the head of a lovely lake of the same name. The whole vicinity of Lake Hakoné is perfectly charming, and I used to frequently stop here afterwards, as it was the "half-way" point between Shidz-u-o-ka and Yokohama.

The lake is six miles long, and the water is blue, clear, and cool; at one end of the lake is a small peninsula (seen in the picture), and near it are the thatched roofs of the houses of Hakoné village, close by the shore. They look like white patches in the distance. A clump of trees behind the peninsula marks the spot where the road comes down the hill-slope, through a grand avenue of pines and poplars, and enters the village near an ancient guard-house that used to be the military "key" of northern and eastern Japan. Only the foundations of this guard-house now remain. The whole village of Hakoné, like many of the towns scattered along the "Tokaido," is located entirely on one street. The houses are plain wooden huts with paper sliding-doors, matted floors on which people eat and sleep, and roofs covered with thatched straw, without chimneys, and having holes at the top to let out the smoke. Babies were sprawling around on the floors, or strapped upon their mothers' backs like an Indian's pappoose. Sometimes the baby's head was shaved, with tufts of hair left upon the sides and back of the head ; at other times the child wore a little red cap, which I used to think quite pretty until I found it signified small-pox !

The " hotel " at Hakoné was like most of the others we stopped at on the Tokaido ; the landlord was very polite, and the women of the house favored us with loud demonstrations of welcome by uttering a chorus of strange sounds we could not understand.

Our coolies turned us out of the kangos on the porch of the hotel as though we had been in wheel-barrows ; and taking off our shoes, as all Japanese do on entering the house, we walked across the clean straw mats to the inner apartments prepared for us.

Japanese houses are only one or two stories high, but cover a great deal of space, and have many rooms, separated from each other by framework and sliding-doors covered simply with rice paper. All these sliding-doors can be thrown open at once, making one large hall, so that from the street you can look straight through the house to the garden behind. The kitchen is at the very entrance, so that in coming in you pass through an array of pots and kettles, and see the women boiling rice and frying fish over a fire kindled on the floor, or in a stone fireplace where there is no chimney. Unsavory odors greet you of unmentionable Japanese dishes, and you are glad to escape the noise and smell by retiring to your room, which faces upon a small garden ; here you sit upon the floor and rest as well as you can, in the absence of beds, chairs, sofas, or common comforts. My cook prepared supper from the preserved provisions brought with us in tin cans, and every thing was served on tiny little tables, scarcely a foot high, in dishes no larger than saucers.

After tea soft quilts were spread upon the floor of the guest-chamber, which is one foot higher than the other rooms, and a wooden pillow-block, with a little round roll on top of it was placed at the head of the pile of quilts for a pillow ! When I placed my neck on the pillow-block I felt as if I were about to be decapitated ; but they covered me with a great stuffed quilt, shaped like a coat, with arms two feet wide that flapped over me. Then they hoisted a great mosquito-net, and tucked the edges under me to keep away the rats! I wondered at this, until I rolled from under the net, and found the rats at midnight playing tag over my face! Nor could I drive the creatures away until I struck a match, when they fled at the light.

At one of the villages we afterwards passed, the yaconims mourned greatly that in the whole place they could not find silk comforters for me to sleep in, so that for one night I had to condescend to cotton ones. Everywhere we met with the most marked attention and respect; couriers went ahead to "prepare the way," and officials vied with each other in courtesy to the stranger.

We left Hakoné Lake early the next morning, descending a portion of the way on foot. It is customary to start off while yet dark, so as to get well on the journey before the heat of the day. We had the path illuminated by huge torches made of bundles of dried reeds, which burned with a brilliant light, and were carried in advance by the coolies. It was a very weird sight: we wended our way through the dark forest and deep ravines, lighting up the rocks and trees, and causing shadows to flit along our path as the torches flared up or smouldered away in the hands of our guides. Ere long the morning light came creeping quietly over the neighbor-

JAPANESE HOTEL, IN THE HAKONE MOUNTAINS.

ing hills, chasing away the gray mist and shooting long bright streaks across the sky, until at last the golden fringe of the eastern sun, which skirted the mountain-top, gave place to one broad dazzling flash of light, and the king of day was ushered in with a perfect sea of glory. There was real romance in this early morning ramble, so far away from the rest of the world, with such strange and beautiful surroundings. We were now passing close along the foot of Fujiyama, and could see all the way up his sloping and regular sides, even to the spotless night-cap which he still kept on his crater-like head. The first thing that would strike a Yankee boy on being brought close up to Fujiyama would be the jolly sliding-place it would make from top to bottom for his winter sled ; in fact it looks as if it were shaved off for some such purpose, as well as to fit nicely on lacquer boxes and tea-chests. The appearance of the Tokaido throughout this section of the country is splendid ; it is lined all the way by a double row of massive and magnificent pines, whose overhanging branches have shaded the generations that have journeyed over this road for centuries. These old trees are among the most pleasing and interesting features of the whole country, and I like to hear the wind sighing through them, as though it were mourning over some strange and unknown scenes of the past. Passing through the villages so early, it was a peculiar sight to see all the houses shut up in front, their weather-beaten sliding-doors fitting into each other so closely as to make the whole town look like a succession of windowless barns. Now and then we met some old woman taking her morning walk, who was petrified with astonishment at the sudden apparition that greeted her.

Smoke issued from numberless crevices in the roofs, showing that the morning fires were being lighted within.

We stopped at a large tea-house, where breakfast was served in better style than usual, and then we reclined on the broad veranda overlooking a garden where dwarfed trees, miniature mountains, and rippling cascades were all placed in an incredibly small compass. We fed the finny tribe in the gold-fish pond close to the veranda, and then sent out for "Jin-reka-shas," or man-power carriages, and resumed our journey southward. The "Jin-reka-sha" is a two-wheeled vehicle, more than twice the size of a substantial baby-carriage, and is usually drawn by two men. One man gets into the thills, the other runs ahead with a rope. Both are finely tattooed with pictures pricked into the skin with ink of various colors. These pictures are similar to those seen on Japanese fans, but are more elegantly executed. The naked bodies of these human horses are browned by the sun, and you study the muscular proportions of their powerfully-developed limbs as they dash along the level road at a rate that fairly takes your breath away. By changing your men frequently you may have new pictures on their backs continually dancing before your eyes; and the varieties in art may thereby keep pace with the ever-changing beauties of nature through which you are passing! These fellows are very strong, and I have often had a single pair of them carry me forty miles on a stretch! They would stop every three hours to eat rice and refresh themselves; in this way they would run a whole day without showing signs of weariness.

The little carriage has a cushioned seat and short springs, but in going down hill where the road is worn rough from the rains you are liable to be bounced out if not very careful. Should a storm come up, you are protected from the wet by an oiled silk top drawn up over your head, completely covering you; through a little flap you can look out at the storm and see your coolies with dripping straw coats splashing through the mud.

We were now approaching the sea-shore skirting the head of the deep Gulf of Su-run-ga, which bears the same name as the province where I was destined to live. On our right towered the great snowy peak of Fujiyama, nearly 12,000 feet in height. All about us were waving fields of grain white for the harvest; bright landscapes met the eye in every direction; fleecy clouds decked the mountain-side; and sunlight and beauty filled the soul with joy, until some sad evidences of heathenism were passed, showing that though in the midst of God's bounties we were still in a pagan country.

The long journey drew to a close as we approached the suburbs of Shidz-u-o-ka. Several turbulent rivers had been crossed in flat-boats, propelled by bamboo poles, and now the last relay of Jinrekashas had been given up, and we found ourselves entering the city, mounted upon jet black Japanese ponies sent out to us by the local officials. The directors of the Scientific School met us some distance down the road, and bade us welcome.

The streets of the city were crowded with people anxious to catch the first glimpse of the strange-looking foreigner. All traffic was cleared to the side-streets, and the crowds were hushed into silence, as we rode slowly and in state toward the "ken-cho," or government house, where the official reception was to be given. Multitudes of faces peered at us from behind the sliding-doors, and from rows of people squat on their heels by the way-side, as we marched by. Crossing the drawbridge of the castle moat, we passed under an immense gate, and then turned toward an inclosure filled with spacious buildings.

We dismounted at the second gate, and walked across a paved court-yard to a broad porch where twenty or thirty officials stood waiting to receive us. I could immediately see by the demeanor of my guards and attendants, and by their profound bows, that I was in some very august presence; for they had received quite complacently all the salutations on the journey, but now they bobbed and scraped as though they could not get their heads low enough!

The "Gon-dai-san-je," governors of the province of Su-run-ga, welcomed me with all the dignity due their station, and after taking off my hat and boots I walked up to them and bowed respectfully. They returned the salutation, and then, without a word being spoken, conducted me into an inner chamber, where a bran new table with two plain wooden chairs had been provided. The chief official sat down with me, while all the rest stood by, and our first "interview" proceeded through interpreters ; the French language being used, which was then translated into Japanese.

The governors welcomed me, they said, to the province and city over which they ruled, and congratulated me upon the auspicious termination of the long and tiresome journey from my distant home. They expressed themselves particularly pleased that I had arrived in Japan so much sooner than they expected.

I replied that in America we were accustomed to do things very promptly, and that no sooner was their invitation received than I acted upon it. They seemed grateful and satisfied.

After further conversation they said I must be weary after my long ride, so they ordered my attendants to escort me to the great temple, which was hereafter to be my " home !"

CHAPTER III.

LIFE IN A BUDDHIST TEMPLE.

THE Buddhist temples usually occupy the most picturesque sites, enshrined among thickly shaded groves, and secluded from the noise and bustle of the large cities. Approaching them through an avenue of trees, or ascending the hill-slope, you may see their massive roofs, carved pagodas, and huge bell-towers rising abruptly through the green foliage. The very atmosphere of sacred solitude surrounds them.

In one of these temples I was destined to live during my first year in Japan. With all its heathen rites and pagan darkness, I yet learned to call it my home. Under almost the same roof with me were the priests of Buddha and the idols, before whom incense was continually burning, filling the house with fragrance. The grounds of the temple covered several acres, and contained nearly a dozen buildings. Some of these were temples, others were small shrines, and the central building was a temple and dwelling combined. Here most of the worship was performed by day and night, and here I lived.

Several massive gates led into the grounds. Under the largest stood two grim warriors, carved in wood and painted plaster, measuring fifteen feet in height, and holding giant spears, bows, and arrows, with which to guard the sacred portals of the temple. Colossal pines shaded the walks, and bamboo groves skirted the hill-side. To the left stood a Buddhist cemetery on the terraced slope of the hill. A great bronze bell in the tower tolled solemnly and slow, with a deep booming sound, every evening when the sun went down.

At first I thought it quite romantic; I liked the retirement and the peaceful stillness, broken only by the prayers of the priests and the measured beat of the drums accompanying the repetition of the musical words, " Buddha armida" and " Na-mi-o-ho-ren-gi-ko." The priests were very polite, and sent me fresh tea raised in their own garden, and boxes of eggs and sponge-cake. I thanked them, sent them some preserved peaches, and invited them to attend my Bible-class !

In fact I *had* a Bible-class, even in this stronghold of heathenism, with nothing to interrupt except the noise of the gongs and the pagan wor-

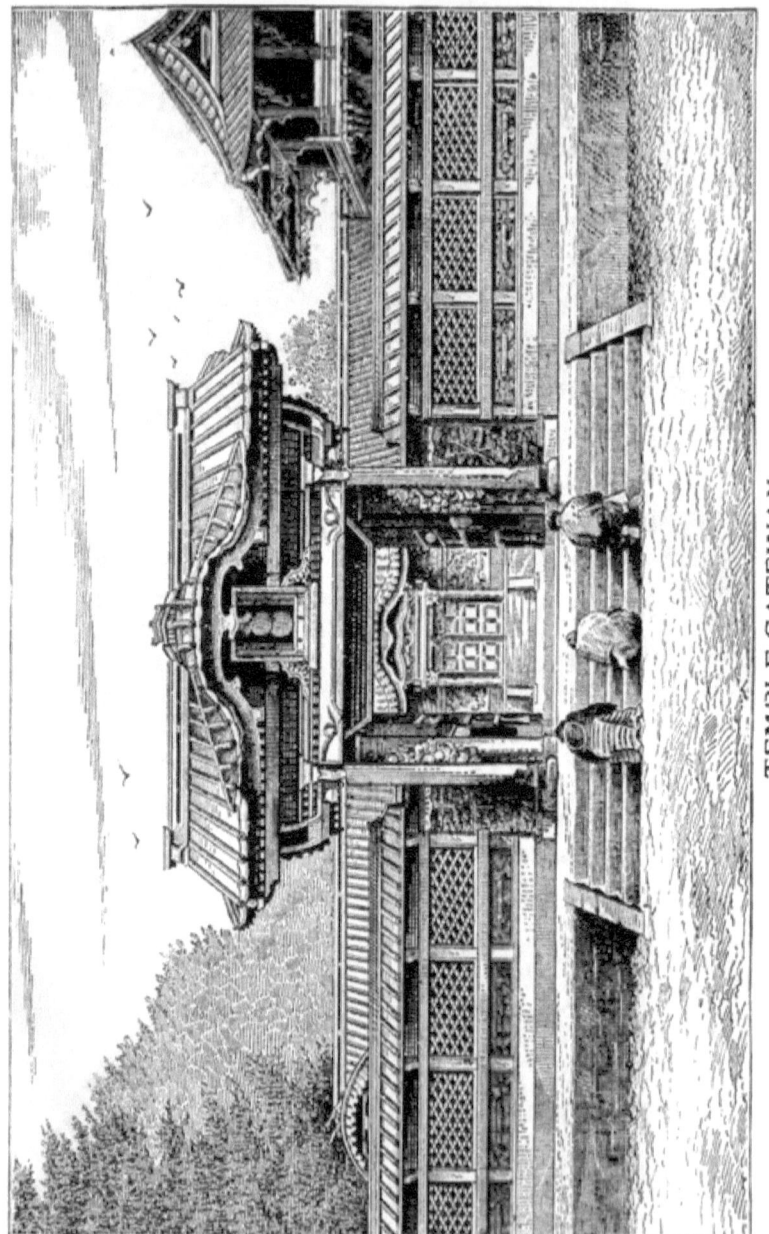
TEMPLE GATEWAY.

ship of the adjoining temple. On the very first Sabbath, at the request of many of my brightest pupils, I explained the teachings of Christianity to as earnest and intelligent a body of young men as it was ever my privilege to address. They listened for more than two hours to a careful presentation of Christian truth, warmly thanking me at the close, and gladly accepted a copy of the Scriptures, which I gave each one of them, promising to study the chapter assigned for the next Sabbath.

The happiest memories I have connected with my long exile in the interior of Japan are those of the hours regularly spent with my Sabbath-morning Bible-class. The eagerness with which the truth was received, the affectionate gratitude manifested by all who attended, the solemn assurance which the Divine Spirit gave of his presence, and the consciousness that I was presenting Christ to those who had never known him, but would soon rejoice in his salvation, filled me with awe and yet with enthusiasm, and gave an unction to my words far above the secular teachings of the week-day lecture-room or laboratory.

Of the difficulties experienced in presenting spiritual truth to minds entirely unaccustomed to it, and through a strange language, I need not speak ; but all obstacles were gradually overcome, and the students would write me grateful notes during the week, asking questions on the subject discussed, and usually closing with short exclamations like the following :

"These are golden truths you are giving us, and they satisfy the soul," said one student. " I have got very great important points yesterday, of which you have spoken to us from the faith," wrote another. A third wrote, " Alas ! my grandmother has died without knowing the greatness and glory of our God, and the comfort of the blessed Gospel of our Saviour Jesus Christ."

So engrossing were my duties during the week that it was impossible for me to meet the students more than once for systematic Bible study. But they became so interested in the subject that they voluntarily started a Japanese Bible-class, conducted by themselves ; the class was held on every Sunday afternoon, at the house of one of their number, and the Chinese and Japanese translations of the Scriptures were used.

Shi-mo-jo, my favorite interpreter, lived with me at the temple ; he was the brightest and most interesting young Japanese I ever met, and I learned to love him as a brother. He was invaluable to me in a thousand ways, and I bestowed great care on his education. In scientific studies he made rapid progress, and at my daily lectures in the class-room he rendered the work of instruction delightful by the clearness and enthusiasm with which he would expound to others the most abstruse scientific subjects.

But his health was delicate, and to my great sorrow he died in his twenty-fourth year, just as he was entering a life full of usefulness and promise. Over his grave, in a Japanese cemetery in Tokio, was raised a large stone, with a touching inscription written in Chinese by his friend Nakamura ; and having at the close a complete statement of the Christian faith, in the hope and comfort of which Shimojo died.

Two little boys also lived with me ; one was the son of Governor Okubo, and the other the son of the captain of a Japanese ship-of-war, which went down in the last naval battle fought in 1868 by the forces of the Tycoon. When the father of this little boy saw that his ship was going to sink, he sent his men away in the boats, and then set the ship on fire, and drew his sword and committed "ha-ra-ki-ru," which the Japanese consider a very brave and honorable way of terminating life.

I must not forget to mention another humble member of my household, who had quite a remarkable history even before I became acquainted with him. His name was "Sam Patch"! and he was my cook. He was nearly twice as old as any of the rest of us, and used to amuse us with his droll style and strange stories.

"Sam" was formerly a poor Jap sailor-boy, who drifted to sea in a terrible periodical storm—the "typhoon," which drove his frail junk far away from the shore. After many anxious days on the ocean he was picked up by an American sailing vessel and carried to San Francisco. Here he was friendless and alone, so he embarked on another ship and went to China, and afterwards to the Philippine Islands. When Commodore Perry went to Japan to make the first treaty, he took Sam on his flag-ship, the Mississippi; but as Sammy was afraid of losing his head if he landed, he fell on his face before Commodore Perry, and begged him to bring him back to America. In those days the Japanese were so barbarous in their feelings toward foreigners that they would even kill any of their own people who had been among foreigners and then come back again. Sammy was therefore permitted to take the long voyage around Cape Horn to New York, and it was on this journey that the sailors nicknamed him "Sam Patch," as they could not pronounce his real Japanese name, San-ta-ro.

Sammy was befriended by a missionary, who took him to his home in the central part of New York State. On their way Sam passed through

Albany and Syracuse, which he afterwards described to me as very queer places. Sam had great opportunities in the world, but he didn't have any brains to start on ; so after a while he was sent back to Japan, where he aspired to the position of " cook," in various missionary families. He liked to have his own way, however, and after many vicissitudes he became the chief of my kitchen department. He baked the bread, roasted the ducks, made pies and puddings, and his rice-cakes were everywhere famous. Finally, at the end of three years, I buried him in a Buddhist cemetery ; but of that I will speak by and by.

Perhaps you may wonder how I occupied myself during these long months away from society and civilization, without seeing an American or European face for half a year at a time.

You may even imagine that I had an easy and dreamy existence, in the midst of shady trees, fragrant incense, and oriental repose. On the contrary, I never before worked half so hard as I did during the months of exile in the interior of Japan. With an institution of nearly one thousand students, under the supervision of a single foreigner ; with fifty Japanese assistants to direct and instruct ; with classes in various scientific departments, both theoretical and practical ; with interpreters to be drilled, regulations to be made and enforced, experiments prepared, and lectures given through the threefold medium of English, French, and Japanese, you may believe I had my hands full.

My regular duties at the school began on Christmas-day, as much time had been spent in getting settled. During Christmas week the heathen festival occurred of offering first-fruits of the earth to the pagan deities, so that three holidays were given. We began again on New-year's-day, and I made out a programme of studies, which was accepted and printed in Japanese. I said nothing respecting the Sabbath, but left the space blank ; the officials inferred my wishes, however, and inserted the word "rest." It was quietly done, and an order was issued changing the previous arrangements, and closing the school on the Sabbath.

I usually rose at six o'clock in the morning, and after breakfast the horses and guards would appear at the gate. Passing across the little garden, with its dwarfed trees and gold-fish pond, I would mount my jet black Japanese pony and gallop down the road, preceded by my "bet-to," or groom, and followed by the guard. The "bet-to" was a well-formed young fellow, naked to the waist, and splendidly tattooed with colored figures and dragons ; he ran like a deer, and always kept ahead of the horse, clearing the road by a peculiar cry, which made everybody get out of the way. The distance from my temple to the school building was more than a mile, and as I frequently went over the ground four times a day, it was sometimes necessary to go very fast.

When I got tired of riding horseback—for the Jap ponies are very spirited and hard to hold—I borrowed a four-wheeled foreign carriage, which I found the ex-Tycoon had brought to the city. This carriage was the only one in the whole province, and was a great curiosity to the Japanese. It had been presented by the Dutch to the Tycoon, and now that it was no longer needed, he lent it to me, with the horse that had been trained to the harness. But Shidz-u-o-ka roads were never made for carriages, so the governors caused the way to be widened by building new bridges and small embankments.

If you could have seen the bewildered amazement of the natives as my chariot wheels dashed by their doors, you would suppose something frightful was coming. Mothers were running for their babies in the middle of the road, peasants flying into the ditches, ducks cackling, dogs barking, and stones rattling—all mingling in the wild *mêlée*. Yet nobody was hurt.

The two-sworded men on the road would prostrate themselves before the carriage, thinking that the ex-Tycoon was coming; but when they heard the laughter of my guards as we passed, they looked very fierce and straightened up immediately. They were as wrathful in the end as they were reverential in the beginning. These were the men who disliked foreigners.

To reach the school building we had to pass a drawbridge crossing a deep moat which skirted the outer embankment of the old castle grounds. Then riding a quarter of a mile through the inclosure, we passed under a wooden gate, and dismounted at the school. Here the directors and petty officials would meet us.

At the side entrance of the school are shelves upon which are ranged hundreds of wooden clog-shoes, which the scholars have taken off on entering; instead of a hat-rack (of which there would be no need), you see a sword-rack, with pegs in it, upon which rows of small swords are resting, some of which are sharp and elegantly ornamented. These belong to the Samourai scholars within, who, though small, are proud of their rank, and are entitled to wear swords in their little belts, with the ancient family crest on their clothing.

On entering the part of the building where Japanese instruction is going on in the old-fashioned style, you hear a great buzzing sound, such as might come from a colossal beehive, and as the

SCHOOLHOUSE AT SHIDZ-U-O-KA.

A BUDDHIST TEMPLE. 45

noise gets louder and louder you can distinguish the shrill voices of several hundred youngsters, who seem to vie with one another in studying aloud their Chinese and Japanese lessons.

Following the dignified steps of the director, you pass through various rooms with low ceilings and matted floors, finding in each room rows of tables a foot high, before which squat the little folks upon straw mats. The noise subsides somewhat as you enter the room, and all the scholars bow down in an instant before you, touching either the table or the floor with their foreheads. Each teacher greets you with " O-hi-o !" (Good-morning) and kneels beside you while inspecting the class, catching every glance of commendation you deign to give, and as you retire he draws a deep sigh, not of relief but of respect, and the next class goes through the same formality.

In the school and the family the children are trained to politeness and respect to their superiors as the first and most essential requirement ; and the dignified and gentle manner in which the young folks conduct themselves is really surprising. The Japanese are the most polite people in the world, and though they have bare feet and wear less clothing than we do in America, they certainly are more courteous and kind than many people who call themselves " civilized." The children especially are never quarrelsome or troublesome; they are obedient and dutiful to parents and teachers, and are all the happier for it. In the school you would not see any thing that even approached disorder, and there was an air of refinement about the commonest-clad child. The scholars wore loose dresses with long sleeves, which served as pockets, and in which they carried tops, strings, oranges, and rolls of brown paper, or any thing they needed. They tied up their books in pieces of cotton or silk, and carried them home to study at night in the same noisy way. All this loud study of former days simply filled their heads with long passages from classical Chinese and Japanese books, which they memorized by rote, without understanding half they studied. They had to learn a great many "moral precepts" also, such as obedience to parents and the elder brother, respect for the aged, worship at the graves of their ancestors, offerings at the shrines of pagan gods, and stories of romance and robbers, which were calculated to teach bravery and give them contempt of death.

The scholars in the Japanese and Chinese department came to school at six o'clock in the morning and were dismissed at nine. They also came again at five in the afternoon. My own classes of the more advanced students commenced at nine o'clock and continued until noon ; then I arranged the apparatus and experiments in the new laboratory built for me, preparatory to the afternoon lectures, which began at two o'clock and continued until five.

I wrote chemical formulas, and drew diagrams on the large black-board, which were copied by the students while I went home to dinner. On returning I would find fifty or sixty young men seated in the large lecture-room, ready for the experiments and the lecture in chemistry or physics. These young men were nearly all about my own age, enthusiastic in their pursuit of science, and diligent in their studies to a degree that astonished me. They mastered with facility text-books that had taxed all the energies of American college students, and were so thorough and devoted to their work that it was a pleasure to teach them.

The government had been very liberal in providing suitable scientific and philosophical apparatus, so that all the principles and problems in chemistry and physics could be proved and illustrated before their eyes. The experiments were at times a little dangerous, but the Japanese delight in excitement, and would face without fear the most hazardous "demonstrations."

One may easily imagine with what astonishment

and delight these people (who had hitherto known nothing of science and the marvellous inventions of our age) viewed for the first time the wonders of electricity, the steam-engine, the air-pump, the startling results of chemical combinations, and all the powers and appliances of modern physics. No wonder that rumors floated about among the common people outside the school that either I had " the gods" or " the devil " in my laboratory, they didn't know which ! While I was performing my experiments, Shimojo, my interpreter, would explain the principles to those students who only understood Japanese ; other students were taught in French or English. Between the three languages we usually got along very well : they always asked a great many questions.

When the duties of the day were over, the horses and bettos would appear at the door, and I would ride home to tea. I always found " Sam Patch" awaiting me at the temple with hot rice-cakes and honey, and plenty of nice things. The guards put up at the little house at the gate, and as night came on the servants closed the long line of sliding-doors, which ran in grooves on three sides of the building, so that the whole temple was shut up like a box ! No one could enter the grounds after dark.

At night I could hear the rats racing through

the great empty lofts of the temple ; hundreds of them would come scampering over the thin wooden ceiling at midnight, directly over my head, and I would wake up with a start, thinking that a small army was coming !

Earthquakes are very frequent in Japan, and often occur at night. Sometimes I would be aroused from my sleep by a strange motion of the bed, as though its four legs were about to walk off with me ! On listening, I would hear the heavy timbers in the roof creaking, and the whole building groaning and shivering like a ship at sea. Still, as there was no storm raging outside, I could not sometimes imagine what the commotion meant, until, on lying perfectly quiet, I could feel the earthquake waves passing under the temple at intervals of two or three minutes each. Usually there are three waves, and the second is the most severe ; so, if the first shock was heavy enough to shake things up badly, I would scamper out of bed, and try and get from under the massive roof of the temple before the second wave would have a chance to bring it down on my head. These roofs, being made of stone tiles, are exceedingly heavy, and are supported simply by uprights standing on the ground, without any foundation ; in fact the whole building stands on wooden legs. As the earthquake wave passes under, these timbers slip and creak and make a great fuss, but do not fall. When they *do* fall, however, woe to the unfortunate people who happen to be underneath ! In the destructive earthquake in Tokio, some years ago, more than sixty thousand persons perished by the falling of these tiled roofs and the opening of deep crevices in the earth.

One Saturday, after I had returned from the school, the gate-keeper, knowing that some money had been left in the building, undertook to become robber instead of guard. He slipped quietly into the room where the money was, and finding one of the guards sleeping with his head resting on a pillow-block, he attempted to decapitate him. The poor fellow seized the sword blade in trying to save himself ; but these Japanese weapons are as sharp as razors, and he only cut his fingers off. In another instant the robber had killed him and fled with the money, leaving a Buddhist book behind, which fell from his clothing. By this book he was afterwards detected in the next province, and brought back to Shidz-u-o-ka and beheaded. If it were not too terrible, I could describe the way they sometimes " try" such criminals by torture.

Earthquakes, robbers, and the romantic experiences of a strange country kept life in the old

BUDDHIST TEMPLE AND PAGODA.

Buddhist temple free from monotony for some time; but at last it became very lonely, as the romance and novelty faded out, and the clatter of drums and gongs in the temple, instead of being musical, became intolerable. I used to wander up through the woods, passing the Buddhist burying-ground, and sit down on top of the hill (on every Sabbath afternoon), and look off across the Pacific towards home.

The sullen roar of the ocean could be heard as the waves broke heavily upon the beach five miles away; that same sea washed the shores of my own country, nearly five thousand miles further east. The sun set over the western hills of Japan, and reappeared rising from the ocean, fresh from its journey across the continent of America. It came to me bright and cheery every morning from "home," though all my distant friends were in bed and asleep in America at the time it reached me in Japan.

Still the days and months rolled by, and though I worked hard and kept busy there were hours when the sense of loneliness seemed too oppressive to be borne. On the Sabbath especially I would pace to and fro on my temple porch, or climb alone to the hill-top, and think of the long months yet to come before I could hope to see a familiar face or hear a familiar American voice.

If I could only see a single foreigner like myself for "just a few minutes," I would often say, then I thought I would be happy and willing to stand another siege of seclusion from society. But when this did happen eventually, and two friends came all the way from Yokohama to visit me a few days, I felt all the more lonely after they left; for the solitude seemed more complete, in contrast to the merry social times which they said everybody was having in Yokohama and Tokio. Nevertheless I believe in solitude, and I like it, provided it comes in doses that can be endured. I believe that true development comes through some forms of solitude faster than through most forms of society. One can be happy alone, if he has the proper resources within himself; and I look back upon that old Buddhist temple as the brightest and happiest spot that I have yet seen in the world.

CHAPTER IV.

LIFE IN A FEUDAL CASTLE.

NEARLY three hundred years ago the founder of the Tycoon dynasty dwelt in a great castle. This castle was at Shidzuoka, and was surrounded with high walls and broad moats with water flowing through them. There was a double line of moats, stretching in a continuous circuit of half a mile or more, and faced with sold stone masonry. Within the inner inclosure there rose a massive tower and other lesser battlements. Upon the long line of embankments pine trees were planted, from which the archers might shoot their arrows at the foe. The trees were young then, but now are grand and stately in their old age. From these castle grounds a most impressive view was presented on either hand. To the north stood the "Matchless Mountain," ever fresh and glorious in its snowy robes, and capped with more silvery clouds than ever shadowed an Alpine peak. On the west stood a long range of bleak heights, which opened up into a valley rich in fertility and every tint of green.

All around the castle was spread out a broad expanse of rice fields and waving grain, while a few miles to the east lay the ocean, whose distant roar could easily be heard, and whose waves had so long broken upon the shores of a land locked in mystery. The thatched-roof houses and huts of Shidzuoka (then called *Futsiu*, or Chief Capital,) were scattered in great numbers about the castle ; and all the inhabitants rendered complete submission and homage to their feudal lord, the First Tycoon. This castle is now in ruins, and fire and earthquake have left little there save the walls and moats and crumbled towers shaded by patriarchal pines. The mail-clad warriors are gone who once walked these now deserted parapets ; the archers no longer shoot their arrows from the fir branches of the trees ; the spearmen and swordsmen who guarded the gates have gone to their graves long ago, leaving the copper-covered gates unbarred, the drawbridges tottering and decayed, and the wild foxes to roam among the ruins and vine-covered rocks of the once mighty fortress. For a century or more these castle grounds remained unoccupied, and the birds and wild animals had learned to make it their home ; while the city still thrived without

A FEUDAL CASTLE.   55

the walls, and grew in crescent form around the broad outer moat of the castle.

After I had lived a year at the Buddhist temple described in the last chapter, the government decided to build me a house in foreign style, and I was requested to select the most suitable site for its location. My two friends Katz and Okubo, who had been councillors in the court of the last Tycoon (and who were more recently instrumental in calling me to Japan), were the persons who built me the house, as a gift from San-mie-san, a little prince of the province, whom they had in charge. This little prince was greatly respected in the region, as he was descended from those who had ruled the country for three hundred years, and would have been the present Tycoon had not that power been overthrown.

Katz and Okubo thought my temple home too far away from the school and too unprotected, besides being inconvenient in many ways. They wisely proposed the new house, and I chose the deserted castle grounds as the best place upon which to build.

The Japanese carpenters had never seen a foreign house, nor were they familiar with modern methods of construction; neither did I consider myself an architect, or capable of very explicit directions. But I wanted a house well built, comfortable, and secure. So we determined to overcome all obstacles. I drew up the plans with care, and for nearly six months hundreds of stone-cutters and carpenters were engaged in executing them. A portion of the embankment on the corner of the castle moat was cut away and faced with solid masonry, constructed from stones drawn from the ruins of the old castle tower. The stones for the walls of the house were brought from a neighboring province.

I experienced much pleasure in watching the progress of my crude architectural ideas, as they slowly assumed solid reality. But the work was no child's play ; for not only did the ground plan and apartments have to be mapped out, but every thing inside and outside the house had to be explained, for the Japs had no more idea of their meaning than the man in the moon. Doors, windows, stairs, closets, chimneys, and other minor details had to be drawn and presented to the head-carpenter by pictures and measurements. Sometimes the most amusing mistakes would occur, owing to his never having seen the objects in question. The carpenters were skilful in imitation beyond any thing you could believe. They brought back the most perfect little models of the things described, and it was seldom necessary to correct them.

After the work of building was fairly commenced, the *roof* was completed in a month, and the heaviest part of the foundation in two months more; for you must know that it would be decidedly contrary to Japanese character to do any thing except in a manner directly opposite to all our preconceived notions on the subject. In a Japanese house the roof is always built first, and the other parts afterwards! With a kind of celestial instinct, they always commence at the highest point and work downwards. In all the lesser occupations of daily labor, such as digging, sawing, planing, cutting lumber, boring holes, or turning screws, the Japanese do just exactly the reverse of what people do on the other hemisphere; and it is consistent with the idea which children have at home respecting our antipodes, the queer folks that walk with their heads down and their feet sticking up, like flies on a ceiling.

After watching the manner in which they built the house, I felt as if they would be inclined to stand the whole thing on its chimneys, with kitchen and cellar skyward; but this was hardly convenient to do.

The chimneys, by the way, were the most mysterious part of the house to the carpenters. For a long time they could not be prevailed upon to build them; but at last they broke holes through the floors and roof, and, with the aid of the stone-cutters, put them in.

They regarded the building of the house as a wonderful achievement, and hundreds of people from all over the country came to see it, supposing that all houses in America were built in the same style.

The picture given of the house is taken from inside the castle grounds. On the right of the picture is a small Japanese house occupied by "Sam Patch," who is seen standing in front. The well is also seen, with the stone furnace where Sam heated the water for baths. In the foreground is a Japanese well, with a long bamboo stick, having a stone tied at the end, like the old Egyptian method of drawing water.

Four large pine trees stand near the house, between which I used to suspend a beautiful American flag, which the Japanese called the "flower flag," and which could be seen from the surrounding country. With it waved a small Japanese flag, having the "rising sun" upon it; the American "stars" and the Japanese "sun" floated very peacefully together, and in raising the flags I usually caused salutes to be fired.

The situation of the house was very picturesque. It stood upon the outer embankment of the castle moat, facing northward upon the

THE NEW HOUSE IN THE CASTLE GROUNDS.

"Matchless Mountain" of Japan; to the left, towards the sun-setting, were fertile valleys and verdant hills; and to the south—the side on which the picture is taken—its open outlook was towards the ruins and interior moats of the castle. On the south side of the house a court-yard is seen, where I gave a "stereopticon exhibition" on Christmas eve to several hundred delighted Japanese, the parents and friends of my students. The evening was beautiful, and the people came early with printed tickets that invited them to "a trip in imagination through foreign countries and the starry heavens"!

Not the least interesting part of the entertainment to them was the opportunity given of viewing the interior of my house. Ushers were appointed to guide them around, and for an hour the people poured in and out of the house, uttering all manner of exclamations of wonder at what they saw. And well they might, for the poor creatures had never been accustomed in their own homes to any thing we would call comfort. Living and sleeping, as they do, on straw mats, in simple wooden houses with paper windows and shutters, and without any thing that we could call furniture, except little lacquer tables a foot high, of course a foreign house, furnished in American style, appeared to them luxurious beyond description.

They examined every object with the minutest care; carpets, rocking-chairs, table-covers, writing-desk, mirrors, lace curtains, chandelier, beds, and bureaus—all were of great novelty to them. The brilliant-colored oil-cloth in the hall created astonishment as they walked upon it, for they could not imagine what it was or how it could be made. The walls and ceilings were covered with bright-tinted paper of various patterns—for we do not use plaster ceilings in this land of earthquakes—and the Japanese understood the wall paper very well, for it is from Japan that Europeans first got the idea of covering their walls with paper.

But when the Japs, especially the ladies, came to explore the kitchen, their admiration for the cooking-range and chimney was unbounded. They had never seen ovens, or appliances for baking, roasting, etc., and every thing in the culinary department was a revelation to them exceeding the novelties of the parlor, bedrooms, or well-stocked pantry.

When it was dark I seated the people on straw mats in the court-yard, and delighted them with the stereopticon entertainment. They had never seen such a sight before, and the beautiful pictures of scenes in America and Europe were like glimpses into another world. The revolving astronomical diagrams excited great astonishment. I tried to prove by the shadow of the earth on the moon, and by the ship sailing around the globe, that our world was round. But the old folks shook their heads, and were sceptical on that point ; for they had been in the world longer than I had, and *knew* it was flat !

After most of the people had gone home I gave a Christmas dinner—or supper rather—to forty of my friends and the officers of the province. The long tables, bountifully spread, proved a climax upon their astonishment and their appetites, and they pronounced the bill of fare as good as it was novel. There were roast ducks and chickens, corn, peas, beans, tomatoes, succotash, and potatoes, besides plenty of pies, cakes, jellies, and sweetmeats. All of these foreign provisions were imported from London and San Francisco. The Japanese market is limited to rice, fish, and a few unpalatable vegetables. Piles of oranges, apples, and other fruit loomed up among the casters and dishes, and the long white tables, lit up by lamps and countless candles, presented a cheery appearance, rendered doubly gay by the reflection of the large mirror hanging on the wall.

After half an hour the provisions began to grow beautifully less, and the clatter of unskilful knives and forks became less apparent. At this stage of the proceedings a large turkey appeared upon the scene, and was of course the rarest sight of all. Said turkey had been presented to me some time previous by one of the Daisanje, and had been purchased by him at a fabulous price from some enterprising Japanese, who had brought it from Yokohama, but had found it "a white elephant" upon his hands. I had kept and fattened my feathered friend especially for this Christmas occasion; and when he came in well stuffed and plump, with oyster-sauce accompaniment, I indulged the hope that I might strategically remove a nice slice or a "drumstick" to my own plate for private purposes. I had, moreover, ordained that two or three "courses" should intervene before the bringing on of the turkey, trusting thereby to stay the tide of demolition, so that when it came to turkey it would have to say, "Thus far, and no farther." But alas! vain was the hope for me and my drumsticks! The sight of the turkey only renewed their courage, and they set to work again with greater vigor. I was kept so busy carving that I had no time to realize that friend turkey was fast disappearing from my view, until when I at last came to my senses not a vestige remained save a few stuffing crumbs and that unmentionable appendage which goes over the fence last.

The only amusement I had as the long months passed away was in entertaining the Japanese and seeing them enjoy themselves. On various holidays I would give them dinners, scientific experiments, fireworks, or exhibitions with the microscope and the stereopticon. In return they would deluge me with presents and with expressions of gratitude, and take me to see any Japanese display that they supposed worth showing.

One of the students came to me one day and said there was a great Japanese "tournament" going on on the other side of the castle, and that it was like the "War of the Roses" which he had read of in English history, and like one which Japanese feudal history also tells about. So I went off with him, thinking it was a good chance to see the style of warfare which once prevailed about the very castle in which I was then living. We found a spacious inclosure, fitted up like a great circus ring, with a frail bamboo balcony running around it, upon which the spectators were seated. The first part of the fray consisted of single combats, in which the knights were arrayed in old-fashioned armor, the same as that worn in past feudal days. Instead of steel swords, however, they used a clumsy bamboo weapon shaped like a sword ; for they did not intend killing each other, though they struck very heavy blows. Before each pair of combatants engaged each other, a personage in flowing robes, and with a large black fan, would step forward and announce their names in a most ridiculous tone of voice, and then holding his open fan out towards them he bade them approach each other. Whereupon they advanced to the centre of the ring and saluted, and then, wetting the handles of their swords with water, went to work.

First they began fencing, until one attempted either a thrust or a blow, and then there came such a clatter and quick succession of foils and strokes that you could scarcely see who was getting the worst of it. Usually a fair and square blow on the head would settle the question, and one of the " braves" would jump backward with a triumphant yell. The person who got fairly struck twice out of three times was declared defeated, and a "judge" always stood by to decide any point in dispute.

The main feature of the show came about the middle of the afternoon, and it was this which my interpreter had called a little " War of the Roses." After a general clearing up of every thing for the coming strife, forty " knights" appeared upon the field, each with his armor, sword, and a hideous-looking mask. They were heralded by a trumpeter, who came with stately step into the middle of the ring, dressed in a rich white robe of silk, and carrying his horn in a silken net. This horn was a superb instrument, made from a natural sea-shell, and the notes it yielded were mournfully beautiful. My interpreter said this was the horn used in olden times to call the people to battle. So, as the notes of the horn died away, the forty knights began to file into the field for action.

First came the "Whites," all clad in armor, each having a white sash or ribbon tied over his head, and streaming down behind. In the centre stood their color-bearer, not with a flag, as you would suppose, but with three great plume-shaped things dancing over his helmet. Next came the "Reds," their chief walking in front with stately tread, and their red ribbons shaking in anticipation of the bloody fray. They too had a color-bearer of the same tripod style, and when he shook his head the scarlet banner waved like a tree in the wind. But the two parties did not stand long on ceremony; the line of battle was formed, and though it was of limited extent it made the conflict all the closer. Each party kept a reserve in the rear, and each color-bearer was also kept behind. Each knight had upon the top of his helmet a small piece of soft wood, tied loosely with a string.

Inasmuch as it was inexpedient for them to

break each other's *heads* in the fight, the next best thing they could do was to break this little piece of *wood* on top of the head. Whoever had his little piece of wood broken was considered as getting the equivalent of having his head smashed, and was therefore placed *hors du combat*, and must leave the ring!

The Japs are very polite, even in fighting, so the first thing the two lines of warriors did was to salute each other, and then, at a signal from their chiefs, they sprang upon each other like tigers. Such a *mêlée* as ensued I never before saw. There were shouts and yells, and rushing to and fro, and crashing of swords and sticks, and torn ribbons fluttering in the wind, till it became one bewildered scene of tumult and confusion.

For some time we could not tell which party would come out ahead, though one individual after another was seen leaving the ring with his helmet off and his piece of wood broken. But at last the "Reds" rushed into the reserve of the "Whites," and it looked as though things were getting rather hot for the latter. Nevertheless the "Whites" rallied and drove the "Reds" into their own camp, and then the scene was most exciting.

The crash of arms had reached its height, and scarcely a thing was to be seen save the dozens of uplifted swords which rose and fell repeatedly, making one think the Japs must have pretty thick skulls to withstand such a continuous thumping. But at last the color-bearer of the "Reds" got his tripod standard broken, and nearly half his comrades had already been driven from the field. So the fray ceased, and the "Whites" gave a shout of victory!

The open area of the castle was very much exposed to storms, and the elevated position of my new house gave me the full benefit of thunder and lightning, and sometimes of a typhoon. One Friday night we had a most terrific thunderstorm. It awoke the whole city from sleep, and at midnight raged with such fury as to threaten the frail Japanese houses with destruction. The rain poured in torrents, and was driven in every direction by the wind. The flashes of lightning followed each other with such rapidity and dazzling brightness that the whole neighborhood was one blaze of light, and the thunder shook the earth with its repeated reverberations. Such a succession of flashes I never saw—first here, then there, then everywhere, lighting up the sky with a ghastly and insupportable glow. The clouds were black and heavy, hanging very near the earth, while thunder and lightning came so close that sound and flash blended into each other with a rattle and roar that shook the house and bed on which I lay, causing me to quake in sympathy with them. The lightning struck a tall "fireproof" storehouse near by, setting it in a blaze notwithstanding the pouring rain. This building belonged to a covetous and rich old man, who kept all his goods locked up here, secure from fire or robbers from without; but the Japanese afterwards said that the fire of heaven "fell into" the storehouse for his withholding from the poor the food they so much needed.

I often thought of placing a lightning-rod on one of the tall trees near my house, as the position was very much exposed; but the Jap carpenter had never heard of such a contrivance for "catching fire from heaven," and I could not prevail upon him to put one up.

The storm finally passed off to the north-east, marking its course with the same vivid forks of light; while behind it left the blazing building, whose flames leaped higher and higher as the rain ceased, lighting up the scene with a different kind of glare.

The deep-toned gongs of the various temples chimed in one after the other, giving their musical but mournful signals of the fire-alarm. At one time it looked as though the conflagration would become general, like another fire we had a short time before, which laid waste quite a section of the city. But the "fire-proof" walls were thick and massive, and served to keep the flames inclosed, though they towered to a great height. As I looked about the outskirts of the castle walls everybody was turning out to the fire, and for a time there was a perfect procession of men and lanterns passing the house. But, true to their Jap instinct, there was no haste or hurry. They were as slow about this as about every thing else, and they all walked as though it would have been a sin for them to run even to a fire.

Soon the fire flickered away, darkness came again, and was only broken when the sun rose and gave us the morning as bright and clear as the night had been dark and terrible.

I close this chapter with a letter written by my good missionary friend, Rev. James Ballagh, of Yokohama, who came to see me in the summer of 1873, and who sent home an interesting description of the surroundings and historical associations of my house within the old Tycoon's castle.

"SHIDZUOKA, JAPAN, September 2, 1873.

"Yes, here I am, after a week's journey through baffling storms and floods.

"We were storm-stayed two days at Fujiyama, spent a day and a night in a hut on the mountains, and were detained a day and a half by flooded rivers, yet we had a very enjoyable time.

What with the company we fell in with, and the abundance and variety of good cheer provided in the shape of preserved meats and fruits, we have not lacked what was requisite to stay up the outer or inner man.

"I set out with brother Clark, partly to make experience of his trials in living in the interior, partly for a change, and partly to visit the homes and families of some of my Christian pupils, whose fathers reside at this place; and my highest anticipations have been more than realized.

"I feel grateful to my Heavenly Father for what his hand has here wrought. Let materialists try to legislate God out of his own universe, they cannot put him out of his wonder-working providence, nor out of the joyous confidence of the humblest believer. I feel this conviction very strongly here in this Christian home and its surroundings. It is located in the province of Surunga, which boasts not only of its 'peerless' Fujiyama, but of being the birth-place and home of *Ieasu*, the founder of the last dynasty of Tycoons. He was not only a great general, the friend and ally of the Great Taiko Sama—the George Washington of Japan—but was his successor in the government. This was his ancient capital. Here was his castle. Later he built Yedo, and made that the great northern capital of Japan. To it he brought together all the princes of the empire; there he compelled them to build palaces, and reside half of their time, alternating between the provinces and the capital. There he instituted a system of court etiquette, of counter-checks in government, etc., that truly entitled him to the appellation of the Jefferson of Japan. After his death he was buried at Kuno, near Shidzuoka, and here, at the splendid temples erected in his memory, he was worshipped as Great Go Ngen Sama.

"What makes his memory most important to us is that he formed the laws against Christianity that have existed without change for nearly three centuries. His predecessor, Taiko, persecuted the converts, and by the third Tycoon they were exterminated.

"His last successor, the seventeenth from Ieasu, now lives here in exile.

"Now the evidence that this is of God is shown by the remarkable change of government that took place when the last Tycoon was in the height of his power, and the results that have followed strike the most incredulous as the wonderful work of God.

"Here is my friend's home—the house a perfect gem of beauty and durability in itself, occupied by a young, joyous, decided Christian, with every room in it emblazoned with mottoes—located within Ieasu's old castle grounds, as a tower of Christianity and civilization, on the very corner of the moat! And there, if you lack further proof of what God has wrought, raise your eye to that well-filled bookcase standing in the room in which I write, with one shelf entirely filled with Bibles, and the others with works of 'science and religion;' while above the bookcase stands one of the board tablets on which is written the old edict against Christianity, and which by the late order of government has been removed from the public crossways, and now hangs up, as a memento of God's wonderful doings, in this Christian parlor. Yes, 'God reigns!' 'Let the earth rejoice!' 'None that ever put their trust in him shall be ashamed.' 'In the Lord Jehovah is everlasting strength.' Am I not right in feeling as in the presence of the wonder-working God in view of these things?

"Then I wish to note the decided Christian character of the house. Here are illuminated texts beautifying the walls, and speaking of 'Faith, Hope, and Charity,' of 'God is my salvation,' and giving 'Glory to God in the highest,' and on earth proclaiming 'Peace and good-will to men.' Here in every room hang hymns, texts, and daily promises; Christian works of practical piety lie side by side with those of science. This is as it ought to be, but alas! is seldom found elsewhere.

"September 3.

"I should close my letter before leaving this delightful home, but as it is now late, and I must start at dawn, it will be impossible to say all I could wish. Yesterday and to-day we spent in visiting scenes of interest in the locality, including the famous temples and the tomb of Ieasu, situated seven miles from here, on the sea-shore facing the Pacific, and located high up on a mountain—a flight of stone steps twelve feet wide winding up across the face of the lofty bluff, with hand railings of massive masonry. The temple where he is worshipped and the tomb itself are of wonderful workmanship.

" A lofty five-story tower has just been sold by order of government, and removed, although it was the crowning glory of this sublime mausoleum. This is owing to the tower being an emblem of Buddhism, and the government is trying to do away with it in favor of Shintoism. Ieasu had been a great patron of Buddhism. Its priests had given him aid in war, and he rewarded them in peace by making Buddhism the state religion.

" The removal of his dynasty, together with the system he established, is again the wonderful work of God. Mr. Clark tried hard to purchase material enough of the tower to make the pulpit of the first native Christian church in Japan. They were eager to sell, but finding we wanted it much they went up proportionately on the price.

" This afternoon I spent a couple of hours in the laboratory connected with the school. Here, too, were the walls illuminated with Scriptural and other appropriate texts. Over the clock and over the door was ' God bless our school,' supported by ' Prove all things, hold fast that which is good,' ' Let not your heart be troubled,' ' Peace I leave with you,' ' Speak the truth,' etc. Maps of the United States, presented by Commodore Perry twenty years ago, grace the walls. Rare works fill the library. Two immense Holland atlases of over one hundred years old show all parts of the then known world with a remarkable fidelity. All the maps had names written in Chinese characters on gilt paper, and pasted over the countries, showing that they had been carefully preserved for the Tycoon's use.

A FEUDAL CASTLE.

"The opening hours of school exercises were spent in singing 'Just as I am,' 'I was a wandering sheep,' 'Joyfully, joyfully,' 'From all that dwell,' and numerous other Sunday-school hymns. The boys first repeated the verses from memory with great ease and propriety. They sang well, brother Clark playing the organ and leading them. The long-metre doxology was on the black-board. It was their last exercise in closing. I gave them a Japanese translation of it, which I had made for our own use in Yokohama, and they sang it at once, and seemed pleased with it, the first time I presume they have ever heard God's praise attempted in the Japanese language."

CHAPTER V.

EXCURSIONS AND COMICAL EXPERIENCES.

The sights and scenery of a country can best be studied by roaming around on foot, and going to out-of-the-way places where primitive customs prevail, and where nature has had full play. Occasionally I would take a holiday and tramp off among the mountains, or go on hunting expeditions through districts never before visited by a foreigner. At other times I would be sent for to make some scientific researches in a neighboring province, where black stones suggested the proximity of coal, or shining fragments of iron or copper pyrites were kindled, by the Japanese imagination, into hidden mines of gold. "All is not gold that glitters," would be my usual response to the yellow missiles sent to me for analysis. Sometimes I was sent for to vaccinate a baby. Small-pox is very prevalent in Japan, and I was supposed to be equal to every emergency, whether to vaccinate a baby, find a coal mine, teach a school, build a house, or measure a mountain.

One day in July I started off on an excursion with a party of my students to visit a famous water-fall thirty miles distant, located in the region south-west of Fujiyama. I knew the young men needed exercise, for they studied too hard and walked too little ; so I planned that we should make the tour on foot after leaving the high-road, and I knew that no kind of conveyances could be obtained there for such as were inclined to be lazy.

We got along very well until the latter part of the afternoon, when, after traversing a great tea district, and resting at the ruins of an ancient Buddhist temple, one of the most beautiful I ever saw, we entered the rolling and hilly region leading towards the magnificent slope of the " Matchless Mountain."

Here we were overtaken by a storm, and the wind and rain nearly drenched the romance out of us. We entered the woods and made our way as fast as the steep and slippery nature of the ground would admit, hoping to arrive at some habitation where we might rest and spend a comfortable night. The water-fall was only three miles away, but as the rain was too much for us we decided to put off visiting it until next morning. The whole region abounded in rapid streams and miniature cataracts, and as we trudged along we could hear the thumping of a Japanese water-wheel turning on its rude axle and driving a heavy wooden hammer by means of projecting spokes, which pounded the rice into powder. Usually the rice is pounded into flour in the way shown in the accompanying illustration, where a man stands all day in the sun and pounds the rice in a wooden mortar with a large wooden hammer. It is very hard work, but he gets used to it, and simply stops now and then to wipe the perspiration from his naked body. The man in the picture has as much clothing upon him as most of the country people wear in the summer.

We passed Japanese farmers "ploughing" in the field. One man guided the plough, while another led the horse. But the men, the horse, and the plough were all in two feet of water and mud, and presented a ridiculous appearance as they rushed back and forth in the miry field, with the rain pouring upon them, and with only straw hats and straw coverings over their bodies. When the rice field is stirred up into a perfect mush of mud they consider it fit for planting.

At last we arrived at a thatched-roof farmhouse, which our guide said was the best place in that neighborhood for us to spend the night. But the two old women of the house did not welcome us very warmly, and said they had nothing for us

MAN POUNDING RICE.

to eat, and no good place for us to sleep. We were not going to be driven out again into the rain and cold, however, so we said we would manage to get along, and told the old folks to get a hot bath ready and then give us some supper. I was wet to the skin when I arrived at these uncomfortable quarters, and as there was not a thing for me to put on, I knew I must catch a severe cold unless I could manage to get my clothes dry. So I told them to build a good fire, and then said I would get into the hot bath and wait patiently till one of the students dried my clothes. Their bathing arrangements were of a decidedly primitive order; nevertheless I had to make the best of the circumstances. The bath-tub was a round wooden concern, with a little copper oven placed in its side, and in this oven a little fire was built, so that the person bathing and the fire itself are literally in the bath together! This big tub stood —not in some private corner, as you would imagine, but directly in the centre of the house, and in the most conspicuous place, close to the entrance door. Grouped about it were the women and children, all waiting for the fun of seeing the Tojin get into his bath! But modesty is at a discount in this part of the world, and I could not stand shivering in the cold while my wet clothes were drying; so after one or two futile attempts to drive the spectators away, I made a bold dash and succeeded in submerging myself in the scalding contents of the tub!

Here I thought I would be at ease for awhile; but I found as I reached the bottom of the tub that the mud of the region was by no means confined to their rice-fields, for such a slimy tub I never had the misfortune to be in before, and I wanted to get out immediately. Besides, the water smelled as though they had been boiling old fish in it, and if I turned about now and then to get a fresh sniff of air, I was sure to strike my legs against that hot copper oven with the fire in it! Then I would give a jump, but as I appeared above the rim of the tub a dozen eyes would be fixed upon me to see what was the matter. Now and then a farmer or neighbor would come in at the door, and be transfixed with astonishment at the strange apparition which greeted him in the tub. Not that the sight of cuticle was by any means new to him, but such a chalky creature as the one before him had never appeared in his zoological experience; and many of the farmers rubbed their eyes, as they came in and out, to see whether it were a ghost or not.

At last the clothes were dry, and I arose from the tub a little wiser, if not cleaner, from the operation. But hardly had I stepped out of the

COMICAL EXPERIENCES.   79

water before another person stepped in, and when he was through still another followed, till I counted during the evening at least a dozen different individuals who bathed in that same tub, and in the same water, one right after another!

The next thing on the programme was supper; but supper they had none to give us, and this was not the most agreeable information, inasmuch as we were cold and hungry, and had walked fifteen miles without any thing to eat. We also knew that we must walk the same distance next day, and it was necessary for us to get something substantial with which to build up our energies. One of the students proposed therefore to the old farmer, when he came in, that he should kill a chicken and make soup for us. But the old fellow shook his head in horror at the very idea of it, and whispered that it was well known to all the people of the region thereabouts that whosoever killed a fowl would have his house destroyed by the gods, and he besought us not to ever speak of such a thing lest destruction should be brought upon him. Neither could he be prevailed upon at first even to cook some eggs for us; but we tried to prove to him that eggs were not chickens, so at last he yielded, but said we must not *eat* them!

After a scanty supper of eggs and rice, and the poorest tea that ever was put over a fire, we prepared ourselves for bed. But going to bed in Japan is rather an indefinite expression for any one accustomed to sleep between sheets and comforters and upon snowy pillows. In fact you do not "go" to the bed at all, but the bed, such as it is, simply *comes* to you ; and the style of preparing for the night is about the same wherever you are. First, a cotton-stuffed mat is laid anywhere upon the floor, and a block or roll is placed at one end to rest (?) your head upon. Then you lie down, and a cotton-stuffed quilt is thrown over you.

This quilt is like a Jap dress on a big scale, with large and heavily stuffed sleeves which flap over you like wings. But the difficulty is that these capacious sleeves, with all the rest of the bedding, contain unnumbered legions of voracious fleas hid away in recesses known only to themselves, but which only wait till you get fairly nestled in sleep when they begin their onslaught on their defenceless and helpless victims. Awakened by the merciless havoc they are making upon you, it is in vain that you roll and toss and shake your clothes till you are wearied out ; that only increases the vigor with which they renew the battle, and though you may spend hours in the faint glare of the primitive oil-lantern, which is set in one corner of the room, and strive to rid yourself

JAPANESE MODE OF SLEEPING.

of the tiny tigers that are devouring you, it is all to no purpose, and you sink down at last asleep. But you are soon awakened again, only to undergo the same tribulation, and the long hours of night pass away as you pace up and down the narrow limits of the room listening to the snoring of the dozen or more tough-hided sleepers who surround you, and peep through the sliding shutters of the house to see if day is breaking or not. You cannot lie down again, for the floor is crawling with the creatures you dread, and you cannot *sit* down, for there is nothing to sit upon, and such a thing as a chair was never heard of in that region; neither can you take even a sniff of fresh air on the balcony, for the house is boxed up entirely with the windowless and doorless sliding-shutters, which you strive in vain to force open. Besides, the rain pours in torrents outside, and you would only be drenched in any attempt to change the situation. Such was the miserable and tiresome night I passed after the day's fatigue which preceded it. The morning found me sleepless, tired, and hungry, and with scarcely a square inch of my body which was not covered with bites innumerable. The rain was still pouring outside, and our prospects for the day were not very cheerful. Nevertheless we laughed at our misfortunes, and began tramping off again over the hills, though it was with difficulty we could keep our feet, for the paths were steep and slippery, and the wind blew the rain in our faces till we were half blind. We were bound to get to the water-fall which we had set out to see, though we had hardly reckoned upon such an abundant "water-fall" as that through which we were now passing.

As we drew near, the roar of many waters greeted us, and the sound grew louder and deeper as we passed under the dripping foliage and descended the precipitous and rocky path which led us to the bottom of a wild, romantic-looking cañon, completely shut in by steep rocky walls nearly a hundred feet high.

The main water-fall was situated at the innermost end of the circular-shaped gorge in which we stood, and though its height was not more than sixty or seventy feet it was very beautiful. The amount of water was considerable, and it fell in one solid column, which struck with great force in the oval basin below. The noise was almost deafening, because the sounds reverberated from the walls of the gorge which encircled us with a circumference of not more than five hundred feet. The Japs call this fall the great "White Rope," and the little fall close to it they call "Silver Threads," because there are so many of them spinning down over the rocks. The main fall reminded me somewhat of the *Staubbach* in Switzerland, for there are surely a thousand miniature fountains which leap from the rocky precipice to the right of the main fall, and these add greatly to the beauty and romance of the scene. Just to the left, also, there is a " Bridal Veil " fall—thin, smooth, and transparent in its airy descent. There is a rich border of foliage inclosing the whole gorge, and setting off the falls, the foam, and the cataracts to great advantage. It is, on the whole, the prettiest spot I have seen in Japan.

The ex-Tycoon lived not far from my house, near a temple founded by his illustrious ancestors. He was very fond of hunting and hawking, and as I wanted to make his acquaintance and see his trained hawks, I sent him a pretty chromo of a hunting scene and invited him to take tea with me.

He replied very politely in an elegant perfumed note, written with his own hand, saying that he wanted to come and see me in my new house, but that political difficulties were in the way, for he was an exile. He thanked me for the invitation, and for kindness in teaching his people ; and as a slight token of his regard sent me an immense aquarium bowl made of the finest Chinaware, and carried by four men. The bowl was beautifully ornamented with blue waves, fishes, and turtles, and was so large that I sat in it and had my photograph taken! "Sam Patch" attempted to extemporize a bath-tub out of this bowl one day by putting several gallons of hot water in it, when it exploded with a terrific noise, frightening the wits out of poor Sam, and leaving me only fragments of my present from the Tycoon!

Not succeeding in securing a hawk hunt with the Tycoon, I started off on a grand boar hunt in a wild mountainous section of the country, where no foreigner had ever penetrated before. I left the students behind this time, as they could not stand the fatigue, and took my most reliable guard with me. The governors of the province gave me guides, and ordered nearly two hundred armed men of that section to go with me and beat up the game.

When I reached the neighborhood of the hunting ground, I found myself at the head of a small army of wild-looking Japanese farmers, who carried old-fashioned guns which they fired with a slow match. They had never seen a foreigner, and gazed at me with as much curiosity as I did at them and their queer guns.

On arriving at the hunting ground we discovered several deer standing under a tree on top of the hill. The men divided into three parties and soon surrounded the three ravines in which the hunt was to take place, and through which they were to beat along in the underbrush, driving the game before them. I stood on a low cliff, at the base of which the ravines converged, and shot at the game started from the bush when I could do so without endangering the men below. The hunters were all hidden in the underbrush and tall grass, but the noise they made was frightful; they yelled like demons, and fired their guns incessantly, while the dogs kept barking furiously as the unseen but noisy circle closed slowly upon the game within the three ravines.

Now and then a wild boar would dash out and attempt to break through the line of fire by rushing headlong up the hill. Fifty balls would follow him before he reached ten paces, and, if he were not killed outright, the dogs would dash after him; but the dogs sometimes had the worst of it if they happened near his sharp tusks while he was yet alive. The frightened deer were driven down the glade and died without a struggle.

At noon all of the men came together on the side of the hill and ate balls of boiled rice which they carried in small boxes. This they considered a satisfactory dinner; each ball weighed half a pound and had a plum or raisin inside of it. They looked at my cake, crackers, and bread and butter with great wonder. After dinner I made them fire a salute of two hundred guns, to hear the marvellous echo of the valley and to end the day's sport.

They brought up three wild boars and two fine deer, which they laid at my feet, and I said this was sufficient to supply me with fresh meat for some time. The largest boar weighed nearly two hundred pounds, and was a fierce-looking fellow; it required eight men to carry him to the city.

Subsequently I sent my friends and the governors steaks of venison and slices of fresh pork; while at home I had the first roast meats that I had enjoyed for many months.

In a duck hunt shortly after this, which I had in another section of the country, I was not quite so fortunate in finding the people friendly. I did not know that the feeling against foreigners was so bitter there until I had rather dangerous proof of it. A small lake nestling among the hills had been a resort for thousands of wild ducks for a long time. The sound of a gun had never been heard there, for it was prohibited, and the people of the village near by caught the ducks now and then in nets. The day that I went there the governors gave the people permission to use their guns and hunt with me. They cast very savage looks at me, for they hated foreigners.

When I reached the lake small ambuscades had been constructed of bushes and boughs of trees along the shore, and the surface of the water was literally covered with ducks "so wild that they were tame." As the first volley of shot echoed among the hills a myriad of quacking creatures rose in a great cloud from the surface of the lake and wheeled over our heads in frightened confusion. The sky was darkened with the feathered fugitives, and the noise made by their wings was like a mighty rushing wind. Flock after flock swept in graceful curves through the air just above us, their white breasts flashing for a moment in the sun, and their wings in such rapid motion that they fanned our faces as they flew past and settled again slowly upon the surface of the water.

The lake had always been their quiet home, and they knew not whither to flee; besides, their enemies were completely hidden by the thick ambuscades. Another volley soon started them again, and they rose in the air leaving many of their dead and wounded companions upon the surface of the lake. Now their flight became swift and broken, and as they passed close above our heads we fired indiscriminately into their midst, causing the flocks to scatter in frightened confusion. Down they came at last upon the death-laden surface of the water, and so tired were they that they simply ducked their heads as shot after shot skipped along beside them. The firing continued the whole morning, until some of the flocks had retreated to a neighboring lake and the sportsmen were contented with the fruits of the slaughter.

At this juncture I was standing on the further margin of the lake leaning on my gun, my guard having left me for a few minutes, when I heard a peculiar whirr close to my head. Thinking it was a duck, I turned suddenly and saw the bullet had struck the bank beside me, spattering me with mud. On looking in the direction from which the shot came, I discovered a Japanese in full flight with his weapon trailing behind him. I knew that he had fired at me, for there were no ducks near at the time, and as the fellow was not yet out of range I raised my gun to reciprocate the compliment.

Shimojo, my interpreter, was near by, and I said to him, "Shall I shoot?" "Yes," he said, "for he fired at you; but we must not hope to escape, for they will kill us."

"Then discretion is the better part of valor," I replied; "for as he missed me, I think we had better not punish him."

I lowered my gun and went to the other part of the lake, where a dense grove skirted the shore. Here I stationed myself near a tree, when whirr! came another shot, skipping across the narrow arm of the lake and striking the ground near me; again another came, and I saw my guard lay down his gun and run to the water's edge. A boy who was standing near by had been shot in the calf of the leg, and though we washed the wound and sent him to the hospital at Shidzuoka, he died a day or two after.

In returning from the lake we happened into a perfect nest of small-pox, which I feared more than the Japanese swords or bullets; but fortunately none of us caught the contagion.

The people of Todo-mi, a province thirty miles south of my own, found a large hill with oil trickling down its side, and sent some of it to me for examination. I found it very good petroleum oil, and sent them several of its products obtained by distillation; they were very much pleased, and wanted to dig deep wells. The governors of the province requested me to come to the oil district and tell the people where to dig. Accordingly I started off at half-past four one morning, and tried to get on the journey before the heat of the day came on. Most of the distance we went in kangos, so that our progress was slow. It makes one feel like a monkey in a cage to be carried all over the country in one of these bamboo baskets slung upon a stick, and having people stare at you as if you belonged to a travelling menagerie. However, I soon became used to it.

We were delayed in crossing the rocky channel of a very wide river where the current was swift, and our flat-boat, propelled by bamboo poles, nearly upset us in the stream. The country through which we passed abounded in large snakes; they crossed our path repeatedly, and one black fellow, six feet long, coiled up on a foot-bridge and would not let the coolies pass. One of my bearers poked him gently with a stick, whereupon his snakeship moved slowly away into the marsh.

On arriving at the village I inspected the oil district carefully, and then selected the spot where I thought they ought to dig. Subsequently they sunk an artesian well, and struck oil in great abundance.

Before daybreak the next morning I was on my way back to Shidzuoka. Early as it was, the yaconims, or officials of the village, escorted us with gayly-painted lanterns to the end of their district, and then squatted on the ground, bowing their heads and heaving such deep sighs of respect that we almost regretted leaving them.

We were now passing along the sea-shore, and the early morning scene was perfectly enchanting. The gray mist still hung upon the face of the water, and the air was so peaceful that scarcely a wave rippled the surface of the ocean. Soon the sun rose. At first only a rim of light was to be seen slowly rising from the Pacific, then it began to glow into a great dome of fire, and finally the whole round orb was seen floating in the mist like a fairy world.

A few months afterwards a delegation of old men came to see me from the oil province, to thank me for going there, and to report that they were getting several hundred gallons of oil daily. These old men were dressed in the old-fashioned style, never having seen any foreign innovations, and I thought I would impress them with the wonders of the outer world by taking them into my laboratory. They looked in great astonishment at the performances of the electric machines, air-pump, steam-engine, and the model of a small saw-mill which I had just constructed; but what excited their interest more than any thing else was a small toy wagon wound up by clock-work, which had recently been sent to me from America as a present to a young Japanese. This wagon I wound up without their knowing it, and placed it under an inverted tub in the middle of the room;

then I asked one of the old men to lift up the tub. Away went the tin horses and wagon, prancing around the room before the astonished eyes of the old men, until, after making several complete circuits, and doing, apparently, whatever I told them, the tin horses stopped at my feet. The old men looked at each other in wondering silence a few minutes, and then said they didn't know " whether those painted horses were pulling the wagon, or the wagon was pushing the horses !"

They went home to dine with me, when their surprise was still more augmented at the strange things to eat ; and they returned to their province saying that it would take the rest of their lives to tell the wonders they had seen.

My scientific experiments were a constant source of delight to the Japanese, for they are fond of any thing practical ; and although my students understood the laws and principles concerned, the common people were bewildered and amazed.

I gave a series of experiments one day in my lecture-room before the governors of the province and a large number of people who came in from mere curiosity. I wanted to show the officials my model saw-mill, having a small circular saw run by a diminutive steam-engine. I told them it was a pity to see dozens of men and boys with long hand-saws sweltering and working the whole day in sawing boards from a single log, as I had seen them do in building my house, when a modern saw-mill could perform ten times the amount of work in half the time. They watched my little machine as it cut rapidly through small sticks of wood, and then said it was very wonderful; but, if they were to establish such a saw-mill in Shidzuoka, it would be mobbed or raise a riot among the workmen.

I never witnessed a more ludicrous sight than the effects produced upon the Japanese by some of my experiments. The innocent manner in which they stepped up to the various electric machines, and did whatever they were told, was only excelled by the dumb astonishment or the frantic yell with which they received the electric shock. No visible effect, however great, upon the first who wanted to take hold was sufficient to restrain the intense curiosity of those who wished to follow. They wanted to feel for themselves, and their ambition was usually satisfied after one trial.

Two of the governors took a "spark" from one of the machines, but the third was very dignified and would not deign to come up to the table, as it was contrary to strict etiquette. So I politely offered to bring him some electricity in a bottle. He doubted whether that could be done. In order to dispel his doubts, and also to bring him down to the level of ordinary mortals, I took a large Leyden jar, which I charged full of electricity, and brought it to him with good grace. He looked at the jar, and seeing nothing in it concluded to touch the brass knob at the top. The effect may be better imagined than described, only he didn't show any more dignity or touch any more jars that day!

There were a number of Samourai gentry on the back seats, who do not like foreigners very well, but who looked on very wisely, as though they understood every thing that was going on.

As they declined to come up to the table like the other people, or to touch any of the instruments, I thought I would close the entertainment by sending them a few electrical compliments.

At my request they all joined hands with great glee, thinking they were too far away to get hurt. I then connected my large Ruhmkorff's coil, which is a very powerful machine, with a battery hidden in the closet, and took the long wires to the Samourai gentlemen at either end of the line. They innocently took the wires, and the next moment I touched the key of the coil, and sent them an electric shock which tumbled the whole of them over among the benches!

The Japanese musicians of Shidzuoka favored me with several " concerts," which were as marvellous to me as some of my performances were to them. Their instruments were well made, but very curious. They were mostly stringed instruments, fifes, and drums.

Seating themselves upon the floor, the musicians would play together, making a chaos of sound beyond description.

It seemed like a chorus of wild animals suddenly let loose. I could not keep from laughing, although I wanted to appear polite. There was no "tune" to the music, and when they attempted to sing the effect was rather monotonous.

After the "concert" I gave the musicians a supper, which they enjoyed, showing their appreciation of the good things by filling their sleeves with them to take home to their families.

This is the Japanese custom, and they think it very proper.

The musicians were pleased with my melodeon; they wanted to know where the music came from, for they could not see any strings.

CHAPTER VI.

THE ASCENT OF FUJI-YAMA.

THE Japanese have an old legend, that their magnificent mountain Fuji-Yama rose from the earth in a single night, and at the same time a great depression formed in a distant province, which filled with water and became the beautiful Lake Biwa. The mountain has always been held in superstitious reverence, and the people perform pilgrimages of hundreds of miles that they may stand and worship upon the sacred summit.

Early in the spring, when the snow has melted on the mountain, the ascent is comparatively safe, and several days are usually allowed for the undertaking. Later in the year, as winter approaches, the mountain becomes well-nigh inaccessible. Its cone-shaped peak is shrouded in snow during ten months of the year, and fleecy clouds are continually chasing each other around the icy slope, or piling themselves in a peculiar pyramidal form on the mountain-top. Sometimes, when the sky is perfectly cloudless else-

FUJI YAMA.

where, a cap, curved like a dome, and formed from a single white cloud, will rest for hours upon the head of Fuji, crowning the sacred mountain with additional glory, and presenting a picture of surpassing beauty, as the snowy peak and the white cloud appear against the deep-blue background of the sky.

Fuji-Yama rises from the midst of an immense plain, and though smaller mountain ranges are seen on all sides, it stands absolutely alone in the grandeur of its proportions. Its summit is visible a hundred miles away, and the Japanese have constructed a large map of thirteen provinces, from each of which the top may be seen. The view presented in the accompanying picture is taken twenty miles from the mountain; in the foreground are a few farm hovels, and a small stream used in irrigating the rice-fields, which are always kept under water.

Since arriving in Japan it had been my constant ambition to make the ascent of the " Matchless Mountain;" but circumstances did not favor the attempt until the second year of my sojourn in Shidz-u-o-ka. Even then I was unable, owing to my duties, to select the proper season when pilgrimages are made, but was obliged to assail the mountain in the midst of storms, and under every possible disadvantage.

The first attempt was a failure, and I was forced to retreat after spending two days and nights in a terrible storm on the side of the mountain. The second attempt was successful, and I reached the summit and measured the height; but again I was caught in storms and again obliged to retreat. Both of these experiences, severe as they were, gave me a very satisfactory idea of the mountain and its surroundings. The first attempt was made on the north side, in company with my friend Rev. Mr. Ballagh, previous to his visit to my home in Shidz-u-o-ka; the second attempt was made on the south side.

Mr. Ballagh and I left Yokohama together, and travelled two days through an open region of country, leaving the usual route of the Tokaido, and crossing three mountain ranges; we then passed a broad lava plain which brought us to the base of Fuji-Yama.

The second day we rose by starlight, and started off, mounted upon a pair of Japanese packhorses. These pack-horses have huge contrivances fixed on their backs, which are grotesquely called saddles; upon these the baggage and sacks of food for the horse are placed, and firmly attached by ropes. You are then made to scramble to the top of it all as best you may be able; and it is much like being perched on the hump of a dromedary thus to ride on the back of a frisky Japanese horse, who only awaits his chance of upsetting you from your exalted position. A Japanese leads the horse by a loose rope halter; as your straw-shod animal picks his uneven way down some steep road or over some rocky mountain pass, you take your uncertain chance of either spinning over his head or sliding over his tail. If you happen to meet a few other quadrupeds of like persuasion, there immediately ensues a complimentary interchange of heels and hoofs and neighs, that in no wise improves the situation.

The Hakoné range of mountains was on our left, and before us stood the dark and clouded Oyama range, where a dread deity is said to reside; the highest peak of this range is visited by throngs of pilgrims, who worship at the shrine, and seek exemption from dreaded evils, which this frowning deity is wont to send upon mankind. Early in the morning, before daylight had dawned, we heard the tinkling bells and deep-toned gongs preceding the mournful worship on this mountain.

We crossed a river in the afternoon, where fine fish are caught by means of a *live* fish, which the Japanese put on the end of a line, and thereby entice other fish of the same kind and of gregarious disposition into nets prepared for their reception.

We took dinner at a wayside hotel, where we had good accommodations and an hour's rest, and on taking leave our host presented his bill to the fabulous extent of two cents and a half!

The districts through which we passed were given over to the cultivation of the tobacco plant, which thrives here well, and its broad leaves were spreading out in every direction. The sugar-cane fields were also very numerous, and looked like fields of corn twelve feet high.

Towards evening all vegetation was left behind, and we entered one of the most barren and desolate tracts of country I ever saw anywhere. It was nothing more nor less than one great series of lava-beds, and the soil was like packed coal-dust, without any object to direct us.

Before long we lost our way, and where to go or what to do we did not know. The night was as dark as pitch, and not a star could be seen, while dark and heavy clouds covered the sky. The earth on which we trod was blacker than the sky above us, and at every step the crispy lava crumbled under our feet. The only way in which we could pick our path through this trackless waste was by *watching for old straw shoes*, which had been left upon the wayside by pilgrims gone before.

Although the country was level, yet there was

absolutely nothing to be seen in any direction. Neither light nor lantern glimmered from afar, to guide us even to some lone hut or hovel, where a human being could be found to tell us where we were. Every thing was as still as death, and not a sound nor sight was there to show that we were in even remote proximity to a living thing. Not a cultivated spot did we meet for miles, and neither tree nor shrub was to be seen.

At last we came to a dead stop, for we had arrived on more elevated ground, and a small river was heard tumbling through a gully near us. The two Japs who were leading our horses knew as little about this part of the country as we did; however, they searched over the black fields with a little paper lantern, and ere long one of them struck upon a path. Following this, we passed through some low brushwood, and, turning the point of a dark knoll, suddenly found ourselves at the entrance of a village. This proved to be the place we were seeking, and, tired and hungry, we rode down through the long street, where the people must have taken us for ghosts: we had found it so cold on the lava plains that I had wrapped myself in two large sheets, they being the only available things I had with me, and consequently I looked like a mounted spectre come in from the wilderness.

When it was known that we were not ghosts, but foreigners, we were asked if we would like to put up at a temple ; and the offer was eagerly accepted, for both of us had once lived in temples, and we knew we should feel quite at home. So our horses were led into a secluded place among tall trees, where we dismounted, and tumbled in haste through the front door of the temple. We found things looking quite hospitable inside, and were delighted at the prospect of getting good rest and sleep.

The old idol was sitting in the middle of the place, in rather gloomy silence, as though he didn't like the idea of his sacred abode being made a wayside tavern for *Tojins*, or foreigners ; but we didn't mind what he thought about it, but passed along to the table and chairs which had been provided for us. Here we had steaming pea-soup soon placed before us, the savor of which must have been enough to rouse our bronze idol friend from his lethargy, had he been susceptible to any thing better than the incense usually burnt before him. The priests were very polite and accommodating, and supplied our wants as well as they could. After a good supper we stretched ourselves upon the clean straw mats, and were soon sound asleep.

Our sleep didn't last long, for at midnight I

was awakened by a general commotion at the door of the temple, and amid the glimmer of lanterns I saw a pair of foreign boots stride into the room, and heard a whistle of "Johnny comes marching home," and then a few loud orders given in plain Saxon that there was no mistaking. Half asleep as I was, I wondered if Mr. Ballagh had got up in a nightmare; but feeling around on the floor I soon found he was still asleep. My touch, however, awakened him, and we found that two other foreigners had arrived, and that they (with about a dozen coolies) were about to make themselves as comfortable as circumstances would permit.

We were in no very amiable mood at thus being roused from our sleep; and finding that we were not able to secure as quiet a night as we hoped, we arose and prepared ham and eggs for breakfast at three o'clock, with pineapple for dessert, and having ordered the horses we started off again in the dark.

The real ascent of Fuji-Yama now began, and passing a temple to the right—dedicated to the god of the mountain—we entered a broad avenue leading up the slope, and shut in on either side by a low and spare growth of sickly-looking pines. For nearly six miles there was little of interest to notice. The ground was easy to walk upon, being composed of the same black ashy deposit of lava which we met in the dismal plains below, and which reminded me of soft coal granulated to the size of large peas.

As the daylight came slowly on, we could see that the clouds were thickening about us, instead of diminishing, and that the mist and drizzle were changing to a regular storm of rain. However, we pushed on to the station, which we knew to be a little ahead, and just as the weather was getting the better of us we arrived at two old dilapidated straw shanties, where we set to work to make ourselves as much at home as possible.

As this was the station beyond which horses were not able to go, we had our goods unpacked and sent the horses away, retaining two coolies with us to carry things and make themselves generally useful. A small fire was burning on the floor of the shanty, and a forlorn-looking Jap had a scanty kettle of rice simmering over the embers. We piled on plenty of wood, and got ourselves well dried, and then spreading a straw mat and plenty of newspapers on the ground, we lay down and went to sleep. After a few hours we got up, and attempted to take observations on the situation ; but as we were still in the midst of clouds and mist, we could see nothing, and the rain continued to pour worse than ever.

At this juncture the two foreigners suddenly made their appearance, whom we had left snoozing some hours before at the base of the mountain. "Misery loves company;" so we greeted them in their wet garments, and put more sticks on the fire to give them a warm welcome. They were glad enough to avail themselves of the primitive hospitality offered, and after seating themselves on two empty wash-tubs, formally introduced themselves as "Mr. T——, of San Francisco," and "Doctor X——, of New Zealand." Before long we all held a council of war as to whether we were to attempt storming the heights of Fuji-Yama on that day or not. Some of us were in favor of pushing on, in hopes of rising *above* the clouds and out of reach of the storm. But one or two rain-soaked pilgrims, who came trotting down the mountain just then, reported heavy squalls of wind and rain near the summit, and we were forced to the unanimous conclusion that there was no mountain-climbing in store for us on that day at least.

We spent the day in reading, talking, and sleeping; and our English friend from New Zealand gave us no little information concerning the condition of affairs down there—where we usually consider things rather topsy-turvy, but where, judging from his account, they are decidedly right side up, progressive and hopeful. We were not lacking in canned provisions, so that we managed to get along quite comfortably, notwithstanding the limited accommodations for cooking.

Towards evening I explored the other shanty situated just below us, and though apparently intended for horses, I concluded it would serve a better purpose for our camping out over-night than the more fragile structure in which we were then stowed away. Its roof did not leak so badly, and it had a large fireplace on the ground, where we could keep up a rousing fire all night, and defy both wind, cold, and rain.

So we made the coolies collect large logs and piles of wood, and after making substantial seats to sleep upon, we took our traps and occupied our new quarters, leaving the coolies to get along as best they could in the other shanty. We also boarded up our new establishment on three sides, for it never had any walls, as it was merely a straw roof supported on wooden posts. Here we felt quite in luxury ; and as darkness came on and the storm increased we had a fire roaring and crackling away, which threatened at times to burn up our shanty and all that it contained.

But even in this elevated region our merciless foes, the fleas, did not cease from persecuting us ; and in order to be rid of them I climbed up on top of some long poles which were stretched across the garret part of the roof, and finding a bundle of straw reeds there, I unrolled it, got inside, and went to sleep. It was rather an uncertain roost to slumber upon, for the poles were a foot or so apart, and if I should unconsciously roll over or turn around lengthwise, I would surely go through.

Waking up now and then during the night, it was a curious scene to look down from my shaky perch to the spot where the camp-fire was burning brightly. There lay two or three sleepers stretched upon boards, and covered with all sorts of things imaginable; and once in a while a ghostly form would be seen moving stealthily around the fire poking the embers. The rain was driving in sheets against our frail habitation, and the wind howled mournfully about us. It was too cold to roost up on my pole berth for any length of time, even though the wind occasionally sent me a blast of hot air and smoke from the fire; so every half hour I took to the ladder and went down to warm myself, and to put on more wood.

We had a Robinson Crusoe experience of it that night, and in the morning the storm had not abated in the least, but the rain came down in torrents, as though the supply above was inexhaustible. We saw it was no use hoping any longer, and now whether to march down the mountain again, was the question. Two pilgrims, passing by in a sorry plight, reported a still more doleful condition of things above, so we gloomily wrapped ourselves up in large sheets of Jap oil-paper, and prepared to descend. I had half a dozen copies of *Harper's Weekly* bound tightly about my legs, which gave me quite a pictorial appearance ; and when fairly fixed, we started on a trot down the slope, leaving the coolies to follow with the baggage. The wind came in gusts that nearly took us off our feet, and the rain was blinding, so that we could scarcely see our way. But we made good time, and after an hour of thorough drenching we arrived at our temple hotel, wiser if not better men.

Not succeeding in getting *over* the mountain, we had to manage to get *around* it. So we soon started off again through the rain, some in kangos and some on horseback, and after six hours' travelling we arrived at a village on the Tokaido, from which the ascent of the southern side of the Hakoné Pass is made. When we came to the river Fusi-kawa, it was so swollen by the recent heavy rains as to be utterly impassable for boats. We therefore saw that we must experience another check, and settled down to our fate as best we could. However, it turned out better than we anticipated.

Just as we were starting out to look at the impetuous river, whom should we meet but my interpreter, whom I had previously sent ahead with provisions and supplies from Yokohama. He, too, had been stopped by the freshet, so that here we found all our boxes and baggage, and could afford to laugh at our empty lunch-basket and travel-soiled clothes; now we had provisions enough to stand a siege, and clean clothing enough to dress like daimios, or princes. So we made merry over our misfortune, and secured airy rooms in a quiet place, and fixed ourselves up for a sojourn over Sunday, expecting on the first of the week to start on our way again. Here at Yoshiwara, where we had to pass the Sabbath, Mr. Ballagh had two or three preachings during the day; and indeed everywhere we went, with inimitable tact and zeal, he scattered gospel truth. It was delightful to see how much good could be done on a simple jaunt of needed recreation, by one intent upon improving, or making, opportunities of speaking for the Master.

Although baffled in this first attempt to ascend Fuji-Yama, I by no means gave up, but kept watching from a distance, waiting to renew the effort whenever the clouds were fairly lifted.

But it was late in the season, and the rainy weather had set in, so that it was not till the middle of September that a real bright day made its appearance. However, on the sixteenth it was a glorious day, and a holiday at that, being the festival of the Mikado's divine descent, and also the day of my leaving Albany for Japan just two years before ; so off I started for Fuji-Yama, with the wild hope of finding myself at its summit within twenty-four hours of leaving Shidz-u-o-ka. This feat was really accomplished, but I never want to try it again !

I left home in the afternoon, reaching the river-crossing at Fusi-kawa about dusk. Passing over in a boat, I left the Tokaido, and struck across the country to Omiya, six miles distant. I had with me a guide and a Japanese student, whose pedestrian powers were not very promising. Arriving at the village, we put up at the house of the principal person of the place, who was a friend of ours and entertained us very kindly. I could not sleep though ; and having ordered three horses early, we started off again at precisely two o'clock, hoping to get well up the lower slope, or base, of the mountain before daylight. This early morning ride was one of the most charming I ever enjoyed ; and even the severe fatigue which succeeded it could not detract from its romance and beauty. The night was perfectly clear, and cool enough to make one's overcoat comfortable ; scarcely a cloud bigger than one's hand could be seen, and the new moon with its pale crescent was just rising as we set out. The dark outline of the mountain was before us, apparently so near that one might touch it ; yet we had to go just twelve miles before fairly reaching its base, and then ten miles more (as the Japanese call it) ere reaching the top.

After riding two hours we came to Mori-yama, the last habitable place to be met with. Here our road became a mere bridle-path, and entered a region entirely destitute of cultivation. Though this slope of country was not cultivated, owing to its elevation, yet it was far from presenting the dreary aspect of the section similarly situated on the northern side of the mountain, which I had traversed a few weeks before. Instead of black lava fields covering the earth like a pall, there was a broad stretch of land covered with long rank grass, presenting an appearance not unlike some of our Western prairies at home. As we came up higher, the surface became more undulating, and ridges had to be crossed. It felt home-like up in this region ; for the landscape at times had quite a New-England look, and was suggestive of many pleasant associations. As the sun rose, and threw its fresh morning glow over it all, the birds began to twitter and sing among the branches, while now and then a lark rose on the wing, and I could also hear the peculiar notes of the robin, which bird I have never before seen in Japan.

With the exception of the twittering of the birds, the silence of the place was unbroken; but once we were startled by a chorus of yells, which came from a lot of ragged grass-cutters, who live a wild kind of life up here, dwelling in huts, and carrying hay down to the neighboring villages. Soon after we heard the loud report of a gun, as these fellows sometimes shoot as well as mow; and the Japanese tell great stories about the deer, foxes, wolves, bears, and other animals to be met with in the woods.

At last we arrived at the place where the regular ascent of the mountain begins, and beyond which the horses could not go. So we sent the horses and coolies away, and prepared for the hard climb before us. We had anticipated finding a place suitable for taking a substantial breakfast to start upon. But in this we were disappointed; for though there was a dilapidated shanty, not a person was to be found, and there was nothing to be seen save desolation and disorder. After considerable difficulty we managed

THE ASCENT OF FUJI-YAMA.

to light a fire, and into it I threw a can of mutton and peas, for lack of any thing to cook them in. The two Japanese ate balls of rice, which they happened to have in their pockets, or rather sleeves, while I waited for the mutton and peas to get heated. But our cooking arrangements did not succeed, so we ate things half raw ; and after this scanty breakfast started on our way, light in stomach, if not in heart.

The route now lay through dense woods, and the path was very narrow, being a mere gully, with an abundance of rocks and roots to hinder the way. In every respect it was far inferior to the smooth path to be found on the other side of the mountain ; here and there huge trees lay across the way, completely blocking it, and broken branches and uptorn roots were scattered about, as the results of previous storms.

The woods became less inviting as we proceeded, and many of the trees were old and rotten, looking as though they could easily topple over on us. There was a great variety to be met with, and the Jap student was greatly surprised at seeing trees he had never heard of before. The birch-trees looked very curious to him; they were unusually large, and their white trunks rose up like mighty pillars on all sides. The maple was abundant, and the oak and various species of pine skirted the mountain for a long distance.

All the way up the mountain there are little huts or shanties, placed at intervals of half a mile or more, and during the pilgrim season these shanties are open and occupied by mountain-keepers, who make a considerable number of pennies by furnishing pilgrims with water and rice during the day, and a hard floor or mat to sleep upon at night. Glad would we have been to have had even such humble accommodations available to us; but as we passed one station after another we found the occupants gone, and every trace of them cleared out for the winter, so that not even a cup of water could we get for our thirsty lips. It seems the season usually closes about the 16th of September, and that the mountain-keepers had come down only the day before we went up. Consequently we found ourselves alone on the mountain, and we scarcely knew whether there was a single person within ten miles of us.

This was not very assuring, especially as we had nothing left to eat, except a small piece of bread and a little sugar. We kept on though, and as we reached the fifth shanty we crossed a ridge, which gave us an excellent view over the tree-tops; with the aid of the glass we could see an immense distance, the line of sea-coast stretching out before us like a chart. We also took a somewhat disheartened look towards the top of old Fuji, which now appeared almost in a perpendicular line over our heads. Something lively was evidently going on up there, for the clouds were sweeping wildly over the summit, as if to shroud it from all intrusion.

On leaving this station the real climbing fairly commenced, and for *five hours* we worked our way up that terrible steep. The pine-trees became very small and thinly scattered as we ascended, until at last there was nothing left but a low, shrub-like growth of fir. These stunted little trees, or bushes, were very curious, being scarcely a foot high, and showing in every tough, outspreading branch the effects of trying to grow in the region of hurricanes. Beyond the line of vegetation there is absolutely nothing but black, coke-like masses of lava and reddish scoriæ and loose fragments of stone, which roll and slip under your feet as you proceed, making it extremely difficult to walk.

Before emerging from the woods we were surprised at meeting a man coming down the mountain, for we supposed nobody to be nearer us than the people of the village we had passed early in the morning. But this man reported that a party of half a dozen pilgrims were in a hut a mile or so from the summit, waiting their chance to venture to the top. They had been there for two or three days, and were entirely out of food, and this man was on his way to the village to bring them rice. There were also two or three other persons at a place not so far up, where a shrine was situated dedicated to the god of the mountain. In front of the idols here was an immense pile of old straw shoes, thrown there by hundreds of pilgrims who had been there years before. One old man was purposely fasting up here, and had a vow not to speak for a certain time, thinking thereby to gain the favor of the gods. As we kept on up the ascent we heard the mournful sound of a deep-toned horn echoing through the woods; the guide said it was blown in supplication to the deities to remove the storm from the mountain-top, so that the pilgrims might go up and worship.

Finally we came to a low stone hut, where the half-dozen pilgrims were huddled together, waiting an opportunity to go to the summit. We managed to secure a little rice here, which we devoured eagerly; then I told my two companions to come along up the mountain. But the men had thoroughly frightened them out of the idea of venturing to the top, and they tried hard to back out. The roaring of the wind could be distinctly heard in the hut as it swept over the summit, and they said it was certain destruction to go up there; and that the stones were flying through the air by the force of the storm. The two Japs said they were already half dead, and for some time it was hard for me to overcome either their fatigue or fright, and induce them to resume the rocky ascent, which now became steeper at every step. At last we got a mile farther up, and had only three more stone huts to pass ere reaching the top. It was necessary to rest repeatedly, for one's strength failed every few rods.

The path could no longer be traced, and we had to clamber on hands and knees over the shapeless masses of black lava, and were well bruised if we happened to slip. It was hard to keep up sufficient courage to advance at all, but having fairly set out, not only was I determined to reach the top, but I was also anxious to obtain accurate measurement of the height of the mountain. For this purpose I had brought the proper instruments, which were in my Swiss knapsack, carried by the guide. I thought, if possible, I would gain the edge of the crater, then make the observations with the instruments, and hurry down again. So, pushing on in advance of the others, I waited now and then till they came in sight (for the gathering clouds hid us continually from each other), and then I would hurry on again.

Finally, I passed the last stone hut, and waited a few hundred feet above it, on a ridge of black boulders, till my companions reached the hut. I placed a small American flag (which had once waved in Sunday-school processions at home) upon the end of my long staff, and signalled my companions to come up where I stood. But they made great shouts, and beckoned me to come down ; I could not hear what they said, but supposed they would soon follow, so I passed out of sight over the ridge, and with great difficulty clambered towards the edge of the crater. The wind was now so furious, and I was so utterly exhausted, that I could not keep my feet, and was again and again blown over by the severe gusts. I had to nestle behind the big boulders, or in the crevices of the lava, to keep from being tumbled over the steep places. I managed to gain a comparatively sheltered place, in a gully near the crater, and here I sat down by a snow-bank, and ate snow, waiting for the guide to come up with the knapsack containing my instruments. The wind was still furious, and fragments of stone, with showers of scoriæ, whistled by my head, causing me to dodge behind a boulder at every fresh gust and fusillade. After waiting half an hour, I crawled over to the crumbled and broken edge of the crater, where the lava evidently had once poured itself out in a vast torrent down the steep declivity. A broad, deep gully marked its course, and the broken and jagged lips of the crater bore many traces of the severe convulsions which formerly had taken place there.

Not wishing to be blown over the edge, I made a careful retreat, and reached the snow-bank in safety. The temptation to eat snow was very great, as I could not stop my thirst; putting some in a handkerchief, I carried it down towards my companions. On approaching the stone hut where they were last seen I was unable to attract their attention; but supposing they were asleep I searched all about the hut. They were nowhere to be found, and the suspicion came over my mind that they had deserted me, and retreated down the mountain. I hardly knew what to do, for a storm was gathering below me, and the clouds were drifting up the slope into my face; there was no place of shelter, for even the little huts were blocked up securely with stones at their entrance, not to be opened till after the winter.

Cold and exhausted as I was, with the guide running away, and no visible path to follow, and darkness not far off, the prospect was not very cheerful; but what discomfited me more than all was the idea of having my instruments carried down the mountain, thus rendering all my plans of measuring the height futile, just at the moment when I had really gained the top!

After a great deal of severe tumbling I came in sight of the runaways, and made them halt; I restrained the lively inclination to roll them over the nearest precipice, and contented myself with scolding one in English and the other in Japanese. They made a multitude of excuses, but confessed they would have gone all the way down if they could. One said he spit so much blood that he was afraid to go higher, and the other said he could not give his life for my instruments. He was so faint for want of food, and so exhausted from the hardships he had endured, that he had fallen many times from weakness, and showed his blue and swollen limbs in proof of what he said. A friend of one of them had been lost the year before on the mountain, by being swept off by the wind. This, combined with the stories of other victims told them by the pilgrims below, frightened them from the attempt at getting any nearer the top.

It was now too late to reach the summit again, even if we had strength to do so; I therefore took the instruments and tried to content myself with

A TEA PLANTATION—FUJI-YAMA IN THE BACKGROUND.

THE ASCENT OF FUJI-YAMA.

measuring the height where I was. But we were now far down the mountain, and the barometer stood a little above 20.50 inches, which would give about 11,000 feet; the thermometer was fifty-five degrees in the shade (but it was very much colder than this at the top). I estimated the distance I had descended from the crater, and came to the conclusion that Fuji-Yama measured a little more than 11,560 feet in height. Subsequent observations, made with greater care, have proved that I was nearly right.

We hurried down the mountain, through the storm of rain which now poured up against us, until we arrived at Station No. 5. Here we tried to obtain something to eat, but did not succeed; so we broke the only piece of bread we had into three pieces, and after eating it continued down the mountain. Darkness was now coming on rapidly, and it was hastened by the heavy clouds which shut in upon us, and by the endless waste of woods through which we had to pass. The path was broken and rocky, and entangled with so many roots that it was very hard to traverse after all we had been through. But night was already upon us, and our lantern the guide had left at the station where we had sent away the horses in the morning; so we must push on, and that quickly, otherwise we would soon be hopelessly shut in for the night in that miserable forest, without shelter or covering. How we managed to get through I hardly know, for it was in total darkness and a drenching rain that we emerged at last from the woods and found our lantern, which was only a paper one. It was still six miles to the nearest village, and not a solitary house would we meet on the way; so as I stretched myself on the floor of the hut I felt inclined to stay there for the night. But one of the Japs was so afraid of the wolves (!) which frequented the neighborhood, that he would not listen to the proposal; besides, we could have no fire, no light, no food, and no covering, and even if we got through the night, we would find ourselves too stiff and faint in the morning to walk. There was no alternative, therefore, but to resume the journey; so we staggered along through the mud and clay, slipping and falling, and losing our light every few minutes by the wind and rain beating into our paper lantern. A weary time we had of it, but at last we arrived at the village, and were hospitably received at the temple. After a hot bath and a scanty supper I found myself stretched on the floor in a spacious room, with nothing to disturb me but the rats, and soon I was fast asleep.

We arrived here about eleven o'clock P.M.; and

as we had started out on the day's undertaking at precisely two o'clock in the morning, we had endured twenty-one hours of almost uninterrupted fatigue.

In returning from Fuji-Yama we passed through the rolling section of country described in my visit to the White-Rope Waterfall, where comical experiences and primitive bath-tubs awaited us at the old-fashioned farm-house.

In the lower levels of the country, and on the sunny hill-slopes facing to the south, we found the large tea districts for which this province is noted. A very large proportion of the tea exported from Japan to the United States comes from this Province of Suruga, in which I lived. I was therefore much interested in watching the cultivation of the tea-plant, and visited the fields frequently to see the leaf prepared.

The tea-bushes are not more than breast-high at full growth, and the young plants are quite small. When first set out they are allowed to grow three years before any of the leaves are taken; after that the leaves are freshly picked each season, yet the plant thrives, and lives about a man's lifetime.

The plant is never stripped entirely, but only the bright green leaves are plucked which appear on top of the bush in the spring and summer. If the older leaves are ever picked, it is simply to make a coarser and cheaper quality of tea. The very finest quality, and that which costs several dollars a pound, even in the province where it is produced, is made entirely of the delicate shoots found at the tip end of the stem, in early spring, just as the tiny leaf is in process of forming. These minute shoots are carefully picked first, and the leaves below them are gathered afterwards.

Upon approaching the tea-fields we find numbers of young girls and women scattered among the bushes, and busily engaged in filling their baskets with the fresh leaves. They are chatting merrily together, and to our Yankee eyes it seems like a good-sized huckleberrying party in New England; for the style of picking is the same, and the bushes are similar, only instead of yielding berries they bear nothing but leaves. The women, young and old, keep their tongues going as briskly during the tea-picking as their sisters of other climes are accustomed to do at their tea-drinking socials; so that the little leaf begins and ends in gossip.

When the baskets are full, they are taken to a long low house where several men are silently at work. Here they are boiled about three minutes to render them soft and tender, and after being pressed between mats and dried a little they are

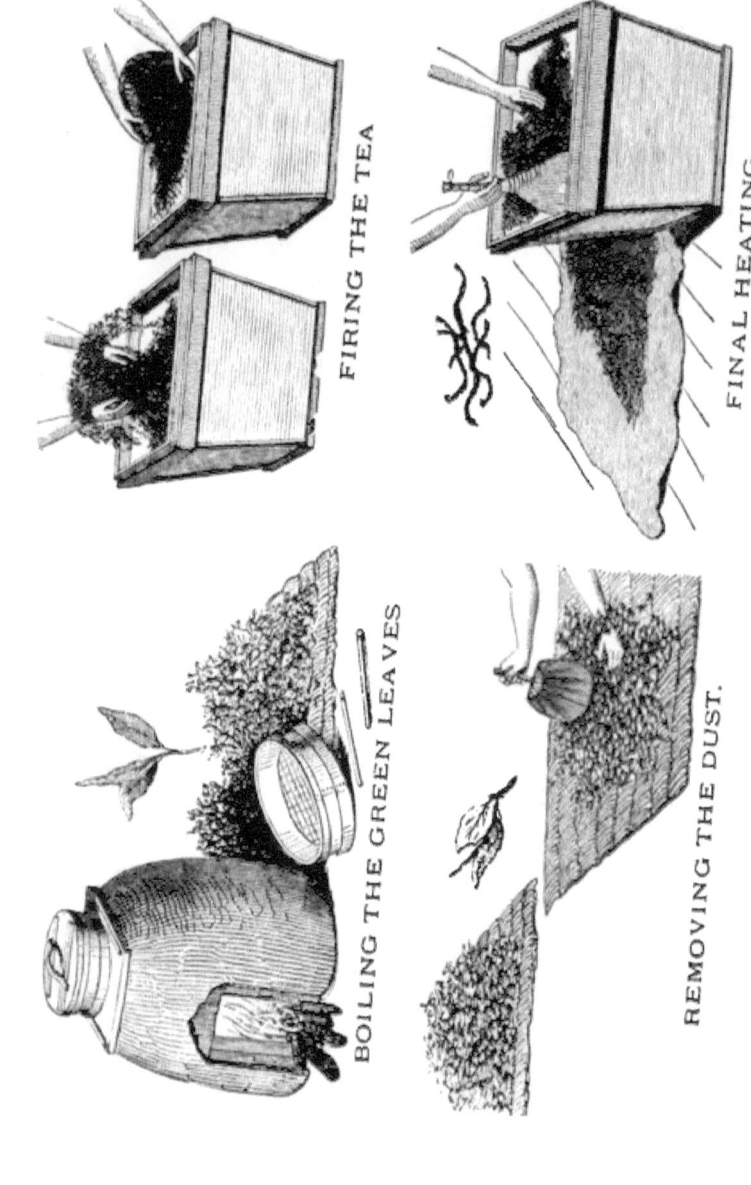

placed in small quantities upon a series of stout pasteboard trays or pans, set upon brick ovens containing smouldering embers of charcoal and straw.

These queer-looking pans are ranged in rows, and are maintained at various temperatures, some being so hot that you can barely put your hand on them. In front of each pan stands a Japanese, working and rolling the leaves between his hands and spreading them back and forth, to keep them equally heated throughout. The men are fine-looking fellows, but are naked as they were born, except the little sash around their loins, to which their pipe-cases and tobacco-boxes are attached.

It is here that the hard work of the tea-making process is seen. These men stand from morning until night over these slow fires, rubbing and rolling the leaves between their hands continually. The leaves are placed on the hottest pans first, when they are moist and green; but after being rolled and partially dried they are allowed to cool on straw mats, and then they are placed on a second pan, and rubbed and rolled again. This process is repeated twenty times or more, and is far more laborious than any one would suppose.

Gradually the leaves become drier and darker in color, and after the last rolling they are spread on moderately warm pans, and then placed in large baskets. On an average one man will roll and dry, in a whole day, as many leaves as would fill an ordinary tea-chest.

The next process consists in sifting and sorting the leaves; this is done in another house, where young girls are seated around low tables with piles of tea in front of them. Before sorting the tea, it is well shaken in sieves of various sizes, to rid it of dust and fine particles; then it is heaped upon the tables. Each girl takes her left hand full of the leaves, and throws them before her on the table, while with her right hand she picks out any stray stick, straw, or imperfect leaf, and then sweeps the rest to one side. This is done with great rapidity, and their fingers move in the same way as a hen uses her beak in pecking at corn.

The tea is sometimes still further sorted, when it is desirable to separate the fine, small leaves from the larger ones; the former always constitute the best qualities of tea, while the latter form the chief bulk of that exported to foreign countries. Of course the best tea remains in Japan and the poorest goes abroad; but as foreigners usually spoil the true flavor with milk and sugar, it does not make so much difference after all.

The exported tea has to be "re-fired" at Yokohama. This is done on an immense scale in

SIFTING AND SORTING THE TEA LEAVES.

large stone houses, where hundreds of men and women are employed in heating and stirring the leaves again, and putting a finishing touch on the whole process; this is absolutely essential to preserve the tea and render it fit for transportation. The fresh tea odors which greet one in passing the open windows of these tea-firing establishments would make some of our old lady friends smack their lips with delight. These were the pleasant odors that I noticed on first landing at Yokohama, and which were mentioned in the first chapter.

CHAPTER VII.

REMOVAL TO TOKIO.

THE long exile in Shidz-u-o-ka was drawing to a close. The Government had determined to centralize the educational interests at the capital, and the provincial schools were suffered temporarily to decline. The old feudal system was abolished, the Mikado had transferred his court to Tokio, which heretofore had been the capital of the military chief, or Tycoon. The latter had retired with his retainers to Shidz-u-o-ka, which became the St. Helena of Tycoonism. The men who formerly ruled Japan were therefore my associates and advisers in Shidz-u-o-ka. But their successors at the Mikado's capital found themselves unable to manage the affairs of government, hitherto left in the hands of the Tycoon. They had not the practical skill to guide the ship of state with steadiness through the troubled waters of political change.

Therefore they sent to Shidz-u-o-ka and called away my friends and my brightest students, assigning them important positions at the capital. Against this course I protested in a memorial to the "Mom-bu-sho," or Department of Education. The officials replied that Shidz-u-o-ka should feel complimented in being called upon to furnish young men for important positions in the capital. This was cold comfort, and I urged that the best students should be allowed to remain until the completion of their course. I also argued that no education was truly national which disregarded the interests of the interior.

The Educational Department admitted the truthfulness of the argument, of which they have since experienced the demonstration; yet my protests were unavailing, and the Government continued to call away my most valued friends and helpers. Katz and Okubo, who had been instrumental in bringing me to Japan, and had always been my best advisers, were called to the capital; the former resumed his old position as Admiral of the Navy, and the latter became Governor of Tokio. Nakamura, Shimojo, and all of my foremost students removed to the capital, saying that every thing was now changing in Japan, and that I should soon be called away also.

New governors were appointed over the province, who "knew not Joseph," and my old friends faded out, leaving me alone. My enthusiasm was dampened in seeing my cherished plans thwarted, and the labor of building up any permanent work appeared in vain.

I lived alone in the new house during the second year, and the sense of solitude became very oppressive. No one lived near me except the servants, who occupied the little Japanese building near the gate. At night, I sat in my room listening to the wind sighing through the pines that skirted the embankment of the moat. The screech of the night-owl could be heard, and the timid bark of the foxes who frequented the ruins of the castle. Now and then an earthquake would startle my reveries, sending me at a rapid pace out upon the balcony, where I had an out-door view of the phenomena. The ground shook and heaved, the moat trembled, the tree-tops swayed, the heavy house creaked and groaned, and the windows rattled as though they would break. The birds, frightened from their perches on the tree-tops, flew wildly around, uttering piteous cries ; the mountains looked as though they were ready to " skip like rams, and the little hills like lambs." But the stars twinkled silently, as though they never could shake, and soon all became quiet again.

During the long winter evenings the stars were my best companions ; I never wearied of studying them through my little telescope, and they were always found bright and cheerful.

The country people on the mountains near Shidz-u-o-ka sometimes set fire to the long dry grass of that desolate region at night. The whole mountain chain appeared at times in flames, and a fiery circle swept around the "peaceful hills," as the name Shidz-u-o-ka signifies. One could easily imagine that half a dozen volcanoes had broken out, and the first time I witnessed the startling scene I thought Fuji-Yama's volcanic fires were starting afresh, and that perhaps Shidz-u-o-ka would become another Pompeii. In the daytime the mountains looked blackened and bare, as though they had gone into deep mourning.

At the close of the second year at Shidz-u-o-ka an official order came, calling me to the Imperial College in Tokio.

I did not accept the new appointment very promptly, even though my loneliness and exile would be at an end, for I should have American and English society there. Finally, I submitted certain conditions to the Department of Education, which were accepted ; whereupon I prepared to remove to the capital.

The three conditions were afterwards fulfilled satisfactorily. The first condition was, that I should have the chair of chemistry only assigned to me at the Tokio College; secondly, that my philosophical apparatus should go with me; and thirdly, that a good house should be assigned me in place of the one I left at Shidz-u-o-ka.

Moving in Japan is not very easy work; but at last all my furniture was packed, and sent off to a seaport six miles distant, to be shipped on a Japanese junk. Every thing was done up in straw, making huge bundles and bales of every possible description. A long train of carts left the house one morning, loaded with my household effects. Each cart had a naked Jap pulling like a horse in front, while a woman pushed the cart behind, and children tugged at the wooden wheels, or pulled ahead with short ropes. The procession of carts made the most ridiculous freight-train I ever beheld; yet these poor people drew the cumbersome loads all the way to the seaport, for human labor is cheaper than that of horses, and each cart only cost half a dollar.

Six huge boxes containing philosophical apparatus, which could not be sent by sea, were subsequently carried on men's shoulders all the way to Tokio, over the Hakoné Mountains, a distance of one hundred miles!

The junk was obliged to pass around Cape Idzu, a bold promontory, which may be seen in the map. This cape is the dread of all the sailors of the region, and many a junk each year finds its tragic end among the rocky boulders and surging waves which encompass the cape. The French steamer Nil was lost here ; and one of Commodore Perry's steamers once grounded on the treacherous coast.

If even foreign ships were thus endangered, I had little hope for the safety of my dilapidated junk during a stormy winter voyage. The junk was only fifty feet long, and the goods were stowed away under a bamboo roof, in the middle of the boat ; the salt spray dashed over the junk, freezing the straw mats into icy coverings, while the boatmen shivered around a small fire kept burning in the hold.

Months passed without my hearing any thing of the junk, and I finally gave it up for lost, and bade farewell to my earthly possessions ; but at last it appeared, one frosty morning, among the crowded and forlorn-looking craft of Tokio, covered with ice and saturated with salt. I was delighted to see it, however, in any shape ; for it not only had my furniture and library on board, but hundreds of beautiful presents given in years past by the Japanese, which I should have been very sorry to lose.

My journey to Tokio was rapidly made, compared with the time first required in going over the same ground, when the yaconims met me at every town and village. The Tokaido had become an old story to me, for I had made the distance to Yokohama many times since my first journey, and every place on the long road was now familiar.

Once I took a flying trip to Yokohama in company with a jumping toothache, which quickened my progress considerably, so that the journey was made in a day and a half. But then I had the ex-Tycoon's horse and carriage, and rode to the foot of the Hakoné Pass. However, the poor horse gave up the ghost the next day, for Japanese horses cannot endure as much as the jinrikisha men, especially when the driver has a toothache!

After painful chloroform experiences in Yokohama, I returned to Shidz-u-o-ka on a steam-yacht, formally presented by Queen Victoria to the Tycoon; the United States consul was on board the yacht, together with a party of naval officers from the United States flag-ship Colorado. They paid me a very pleasant visit at my temple-home, where I entertained them as well as I could, though half of them had to sleep on the floor; afterwards they went off on a trip through the tea district. During their stay at Shidz-u-o-ka their bright uniforms greatly astonished the country people. They returned by the steam-yacht to Yokohama.

I made many trips on the Tokaido, and excursions into the neighboring provinces, of which there is not space for me to speak. But I cannot forbear mentioning the romantic feelings with which I finally returned to Yokohama, after being shut up so long in the interior of Japan. When I first landed in the country, and journeyed into the lonely isolation that awaited me so far away from friends, it appeared a strange dream, conducting my senses outside the world and all its familiar associations. But when I turned back again, leaving the pagan surroundings in which I had at last become so much at home, and re-entered the business life and social atmosphere of a civilized and Christian community, it seemed a greater dream than the other! Yokohama is to all intents a foreign city set down upon Japanese soil, and although it may look queer and quaint enough to all new-comers, from whatever land they hail, yet a Jap fresh from the provinces of the interior sees more to astonish his awestruck eyes than a verdant Vermont youth would experience in his first visit to New York City. The regular and paved streets, the substantial stone houses, the elegant shop windows, the fine equipages, the foreign style of dress, and the busy life of the people, all combine to produce an effect upon the bewildered senses of the country Jap, the like of which he never knew before.

And when he strolls along the water-quay and looks out towards those leviathan steamers which lie at anchor in the bay, or when, perhaps, he goes to the railroad depot and timidly asks for his ticket for the next train to Tokio, it begins to dawn on his mind that the nineteenth century is finding its way into his long-secluded country, and that the outside barbarians are not such offensive creatures after all.

On entering Yokohama after my long residence apart from foreign society, I looked upon the city with something of the wonder and curiosity of a veritable Japanese; and the first thing I proposed to my companions from Shidz-u-o-ka was a ride on the railroad just completed between Yokohama and Tokio.

We saw the locomotive and train coming as we turned down the hill towards the city, and the naked Japs who pulled our jinrikishas looked in astonishment at the smoking locomotive, wondering what kind of an animal it could be!

In journeying along the Tokaido, the newly constructed telegraph followed us the whole way from Shidz-u-o-ka, and the little wire seemed like a thread that bound me to civilization. The country people have a great deal of superstition about it, and dislike to have the wire cross their rice-fields; for they say the evil spirits prevent the crops from growing. At first the ignorant farmers used to cut the wire, and throw stones at the glass insulators on the poles; they would also watch the wire for hours to see the messages go by! What the crazy foreigners had stretched the wire across the country for, they could not imagine; but at last they ceased to trouble their heads about it, and left the telegraph alone.

But the railroad was far more wonderful; of *that* they could see the meaning, though the locomotive was entirely beyond their comprehension.

The road is only eighteen miles long, and there is a substantial stone depot at each terminus. The Yokohama station is very handsome, and all the arrangements are complete.

When I took my first ride on the railroad I was accompanied by a little boy who formerly lived with me, and who was now going to his father, the new Governor of Tokio. The little fellow had never heard of a railroad train, and when we were fairly seated in the car he looked around, wondering what kind of a little house we were in, with its curious doors and sliding windows. When the train began moving slowly out of the depot he grasped the seat with a look of terror, and glanced anxiously into my face to see if I was frightened also. But finding that I only laughed at his fears, he regained courage enough to look out of the window at the trees and houses which began to fly by us faster and faster. The first time the car stopped he ran out on the platform and peered under the wheels to see what was pushing it along; but when we passed one of the down trains he looked at the locomotive, and seemed at last to realize that this was the big black horse that was doing it all. In half an hour we arrived at Shin-a-ga-wa, a distance which it used to take more than half a day to journey over, and which brought us to the suburbs of Tokio. Here we took jinrikishas, with naked Japs, to draw us two miles more into the heart of the city.

On arriving at the capital, I reported myself at the Mombusho Department, where I had an interview with the Minister of Education. He received me very kindly, and stated that Mr. Hatakéyama, the newly appointed Director of the Imperial College, would confer with me there respecting my new duties in the institution.

Now it so happened that Hatakéyama was my warmest Japanese friend, whom I had known for several years in America, but who had changed his name on returning to his country, so that I did not at first recognize him. In the United States his name was Soo-gi-woo-ra; but this was an assumed title, and now he had resumed his family name.

He was one of the first students who left Japan to study in foreign countries, shortly after the bombardment of his native city, Kag-o-shi-ma, by the English war-ships. After remaining a year in England, he came to the United States, and eventually settled down to his studies at New Brunswick, N. J., where I first met him at Rutgers College. He was quite a lad when he left his native land, and his mother was very anxious about him, for she had heard strange stories about the barbarians who were reported as living in England and America. With a mother's solicitude she urged him to take a few bags of good wholesome rice with him, for she had been told that people in America lived on snakes, frogs, and lizards!

He became a Christian at New Brunswick, and joined the Second Reformed Church. When called to an account for this act by the government, he replied that he had come abroad to study into the true source of western civilization, and he found Christianity to be that source, therefore he had embraced it. The power of Christian countries did not consist in cannon-balls and gunpowder, as he had been led to believe when his native city was bombarded by the English; but there was a better principle underlying civilization, which had peace and love and religious life as its basis. His reason indorsed Christianity, and his whole heart accepted it.

Instead of the government calling him back to his own country and punishing him, as he had cause to fear—for Christianity was forbidden in Japan, and at one time was punishable with death—they placed more confidence in him than ever, and gave him the superintendence of the other students who were subsequently sent to pursue their studies in America.

At New Brunswick he was very earnest in his desire that I should go and help the cause of civilization in Japan, and before I started for that country he came up to see me in Albany. After spending a pleasant evening with some friends, we went to the depot near the Hudson River Bridge, and bade each other *Saionara*—good-by; and as the train moved off, Hatakéyama said, "You go westward while I go eastward, and we will meet around the world in Japan!"

I started from the same depot across the continent, and passed over the broad Pacific, while he sailed over the Atlantic; but owing to his

KAISEI GAKKO, OR IMPERIAL COLLEGE.

joining the Japanese Embassy, with which he travelled through all the countries and courts of Europe, he did not reach Japan until two years later, at the time I was called from Shidz-u-o-ka to Tokio. My surprise and pleasure may therefore be imagined when the Minister of Education informed me that Hatakéyama was now the new director of the college, and that he would consult with me concerning the duties and details which heretofore were contested with yaconims and petty officials.

Accordingly I went gladly to the reception-room of the Kai-sei Gak-ko, or college building, and awaited the coming of him who was at once my old friend and my new yaconim! The officials sat around in dignified silence, when the door opened and the new Director stepped in. He was greeted by my attendants and others with profound bows; and as I approached unobserved behind, and spoke his familiar name, he turned about with the same joyous bound as of yore, grasping my hands with the grip of bygone days, and burst forth with such a gleeful warmth of welcome as made the solemn officials look at one another with mingled awe and wonder, that such a boisterous breach of etiquette should come from one who usually was so dignified and calm. We cared little what they thought, however, and enjoyed ourselves for some time as hilariously as we pleased.

Hatakéyama said he had "piles of things" to tell me about his strange experiences in the various courts of Europe, and he afterwards gave me the most vivid descriptions of all that he had seen and heard. His official connection with the embassy afforded him rare opportunities of meeting many of the greatest men and princes in Europe. He did not forget to bring me some pictures he had promised from my old home in Geneva, Switzerland ; and I also gave him some large photographs of Niagara, which he requested me to bring from the falls for his mother.

The new Director assigned me my duties and residence at the college, and I was soon settled amid the novel experiences of life at the capital. I took new courage, and began my labors afresh.

Shortly after, the Saga rebellion broke out in the southern provinces of Japan, and Hatakéyama was sent down there in company with the former prince of his province to try and conciliate the insurgents. The attempt was unsuccessful, and a short but bloody strife ensued, in which many noble lives were lost ; among others, my former student and friend Katski, who studied with me in Albany, was beheaded with eleven of the leaders of the rebellion. Katski was a fine young fellow, and his cruel death was a great shock to me ; I had endeavored to persuade him not to go back to his province, when the rebellion first broke out, but he would not heed the advice.

When Hatakéyama started for Saga I expressed some apprehensions respecting his safety. He only smiled, and said quietly, "My trust is in the Lord, and my true faith will sustain me."

I had a long interview with him at his house before he left for the south, concerning the re-establishment of my Bible-classes in Tokio, especially at the Imperial College. He expressed surprise that no Bible-classes had been established there before, but said that as the law against Christianity had not been revoked, he was not officially able to give the permission desired. Personally, however, he said that he wished the plan God-speed, and as Director he would appear blind to any attempt that I might see fit to make. He wished most heartily, he said, that the young men of Japan might study the Gospel and abide by it.

Accordingly I started three Bible-classes in Tokio. Two were held in my house near the college, and one at the house of my friend Nakamura, where my old friends and students from Shidz-u-o-ka were gathered together. The students of the college were only permitted to leave the grounds on Sunday, which had hitherto been simply their holiday; although I needed the Sabbath for rest, after the week's hard work, I appointed the Bible-class for students from the scientific department at eight o'clock in the morning, and the class for students from the legal department at seven in the evening.

The other Bible-class was held at Nakamura's, two miles from the college, at three o'clock in the afternoon. Here I was warmly welcomed by my Shidz-u-o-ka friends who had removed to Tokio, and I continued the class for many months, finally giving it over to a missionary from Canada, for whom Nakamura built a house.

Nakamura had a piece of ground at the top of a hill called "Christian Slope," where he said he wished to have a church built before very long. It will be remembered that he once petitioned the government to build a Christian church, so as to give the new religion a fair trial! This "Christian Slope," near his house, was so called from a Jesuit missionary who was confined there in prison more than two centuries ago, for attempting to teach Christianity. The government would not permit the people to go near him, but still he succeeded in converting his jailer.

Soon after arriving in Tokio I attended a New Year's reception held at the educational depart-

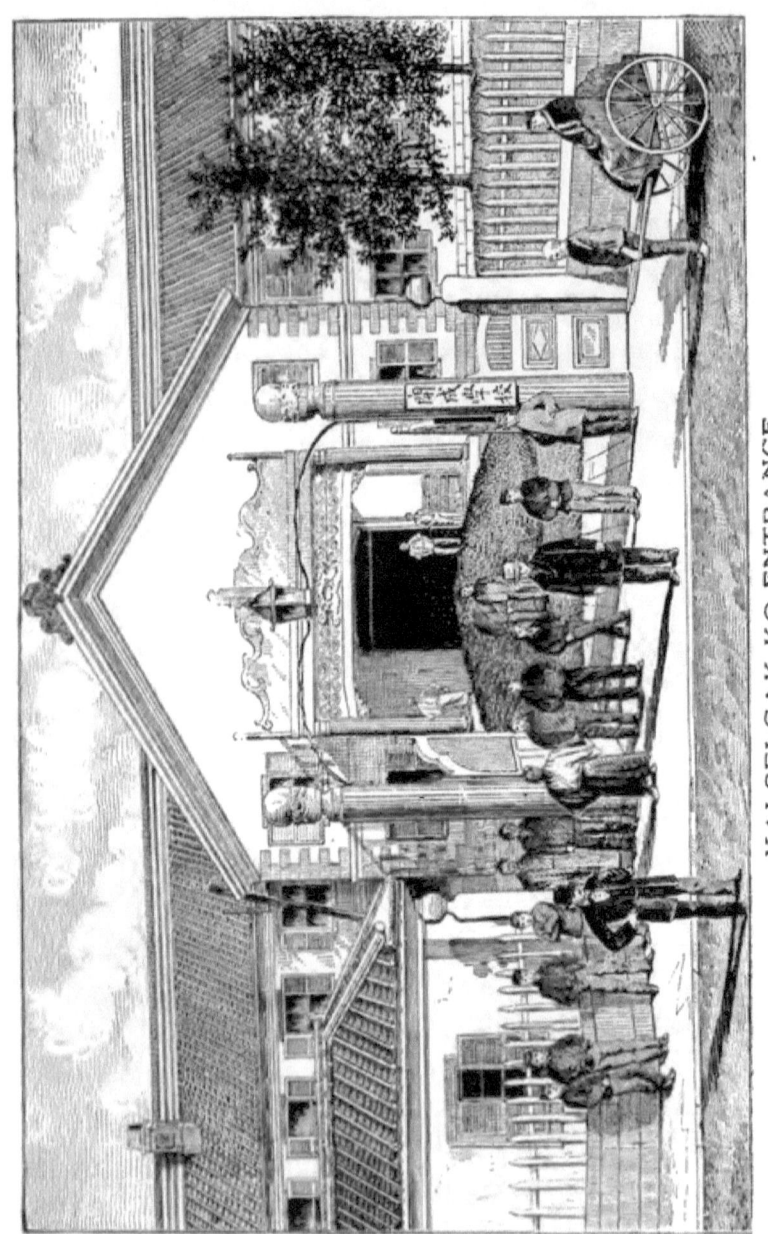

KAI-SEI GAK-KO ENTRANCE.

ment, at which all the foreign professors of the Imperial College were present. The body of instructors assembled were the most cultured and gentlemanly company I had met in Japan, and it was a pleasure to see the progressive interests of the country intrusted to such competent hands.

The new building of the Kaisei Gakko, or Imperial College, was opened with imposing ceremonies by the Mikado shortly before I came to Tokio. It was decorated with flags of every nationality, and presented a beautiful appearance. The building covers several acres, and has three long wings extending 192 feet to the rear. Behind these are the gymnasium, dining-hall, and storehouses. The first floor of the main building contains the library, laboratories, and lecture-rooms. The English department occupied the central wing, and the French and German departments the right and left wings. The second story throughout the building was used as a dormitory, for most of the students lived here.

In front of the main entrance was a grassy mound and high gateway; the latter is shown wide open in the picture. In passing this gate every student was obliged to leave a wooden ticket marked with his name. This was returned to him when he came back to the college. The rules and regulations governing the students were very strict.

In the picture of the gateway the name "Kaisei Gakko" is seen on the right pillar, in Chinese characters; my friend Dr. Veeder, the professor of physics, is standing in the centre of the picture with a few of his students around him; some of them are in regulation dress, and others in native costume.

The other view which is given of the Kaisei Gakko presents the front of the building as it appeared the day that the Mikado visited and opened the institution.

CHAPTER VIII.

RAMBLES ABOUT THE CAPITAL.

LIFE in Tokio was more varied than that at Shidz-u-o-ka. Something was always going on, and pleasant society was not wanting, whenever one felt the need of it. Evening parties and entertainments were frequent among the foreign residents, and the elegance and style seen on such occasions reminded one more of fashionable life at home than of residence in a pagan city.

The capital itself is not beautiful. There are no elegant boulevards or splendid buildings, such as those seen in European countries. Tokio is simply a vast wilderness of houses, containing nearly a million souls, but lacking all the evidences of comfort and luxury to be found in the capitals of western lands. The houses are built of wood, and a general view of the city presents an endless succession of tiled and shingled roofs, with here and there a fire-proof storehouse, having walls of white cement.

Yet there are places of great interest to visit,

notwithstanding the sameness and shabbiness of the city. Let us stand for a moment on the highest wall of the Tokio castle, built by the same great chieftain who constructed the castle at Shidz-u-o-ka. Close beside us is a large cannon, which is fired every day precisely at noon. All about us are the deep moats, massive walls, and colossal gateways of the castle, encircling a space of nearly a mile in extent, and forming a wilderness of walls, embankments, public buildings, and shady promenades, right in the heart of the city. At each angle of the castle wall there used to be a square tower, built of stone and covered with white cement ; the tower had narrow windows, from which arrows could be discharged, and the roof was made of heavy stone tiles, stamped with the crest of the Tycoon. Only a few of these towers now remain, the rest having been removed by order of the Mikado's government.

The picture represents a portion of the castle moat and wall, where the three-storied towers are still standing. The moat is filled with water.

There are also numerous canals which intersect the city in every direction, so that merchandise can be transported from one point to another. Boats of every description are poled or sculled through the canals.

I had a little canoe carrying but one person,

TOWER AND MOAT OF TOKIO CASTLE.

and propelled swiftly by a single paddle. In this canoe I cruised around the canals and moats of the capital, studying many phases of life among the boatmen and fishermen, which could not otherwise be observed. Frequently I would venture out upon the bay, but the canoe (which I called "The Rob Roy of Tokio," and which only drew two inches of water) would dance on the waves like a duck, while the salt spray washed over the thin deck, threatening to upset me. But it never did.

Sometimes I drew in my spoon-like paddle and raised an umbrella to the wind. The canoe would scud across the bay, greatly to the astonishment of the Japanese fishermen, who had never seen such a tiny craft before.

A large river emptied into the Bay of Yedo on the eastern side of the city, which may be seen in the small map of Tokio and vicinity. Near the mouth of the river was the small "concession," where foreign merchants and missionaries resided. Here were the foreign consulates, stores, schools, and chapels. Foreigners in the service of the Japanese Government alone were allowed to reside outside the limits of the "concession" at the capital; for Japan was not yet free to foreign trade, excepting five open ports.

The most beautiful and interesting places in

Tokio, and those which I most frequently visited, were the large temples of Shiba, Uyéno, and Asakusa. The two former were the burial-places of the Tycoons for several centuries, and their sacred groves, richly ornamented shrines, and spacious halls for worship were the most beautiful works of art of ancient Japan. Both temples are situated in the suburbs of Tokio, on opposite sides of the city, and their broad avenues and overarching trees afford splendid promenades for the people. The temple grounds serve the purpose of parks. At Uyéno, the large buildings were burned during a battle fought there in 1868, between the forces of the Mikado and the retainers of the Tycoon. The gateway leading to the grounds is still riddled with musket balls, and the trees are scarred by bullets. Only the tombs and a few smaller temples remain.

But at Shiba the temples are well preserved, and the carvings and gildings are very elegant. The eaves, pillars, and portals of the temples display figures of every possible variety, from the hideous scales and claws of the frightful dragon to the soft white plumage of the sacred crane. Massive bronze lanterns, six feet high, are ranged in rows in the court-yard, and covered corridors lead up the hillside to the tombs of the Tycoons.

There are six of these tombs, similar to the one

TOMB OF THE FIRST TYCOON.

built for the first Tycoon at the Temple of Kuno, near Shidz-u-o-ka. The picture gives an excellent idea of this tomb, with the Tycoon's crest upon it.

The tomb consists of a hollow cylinder of stone, placed upon a granite pedestal, and surmounted by an immense capstone weighing several tons. The dead body of the Tycoon is deposited in the tomb in a square casket, or sometimes in a large earthen jar; for the Japanese are buried in a sitting posture, and occupy but little space. The tomb is closed by a bronze door, upon which a large crest of the Tycoon is seen. This crest resembles three outspread clover leaves, turned inward upon each other. It is found stamped upon every thing throughout the temple grounds, even upon the stone tiles of the massive temple roofs.

Although the first Tycoon was buried nearly three hundred years ago at the Temple of Kuno, which he built for himself on a high cliff overlooking the sea, near Shidz-u-o-ka, yet all of his successors were buried at Tokio. The most beautiful building at Kuno was a five-storied pagoda (like the one seen in Chapter III.), which towered above the tall cypress-trees. This pagoda was taken down by order of the government, because it was characteristic of Buddhism, and they wished to make Kuno a Shinto shrine, in accordance with the ancient Japanese religion. From the ruins of the beautiful pagoda I obtained a large golden crest of the Tycoon, which had long glistened in the sunlight across the Pacific.

When the government attempted to change the largest temple at Shiba into a Shinto shrine also, the devout Buddhists were so enraged that they set fire to the beautiful temple, and burned it to the ground. It made a magnificent bonfire; and the copper sheets on the roof, and the metal ornaments, gave a green and crimson tinge to the flames.

The Japanese in Tokio are accustomed to large fires, however; sometimes I have seen half a mile of the city in flames at once. The people cannot put out the fire, but they tear down the wooden buildings around it, and thus stay its terrible course.

The most populous part of the city is on the eastern side of the castle area, near a bridge from which all distances in Japan are said to be reckoned. A fearful conflagration swept through this district before I arrived in the city, and destroyed five thousand houses and hundreds of provincial *Yashikis*. The streets were afterwards widened and straightened, and the district rebuilt in foreign style—*i.e.*, with sidewalks, gas-lamps, and two-story houses, half foreign and half Japanese. The main street was called the To-ri. This is the Broadway of Tokio; it runs from the new railroad station to the old bridge of Nihon-Bashi. After crossing the bridge, houses of the Japanese style are seen again.

The street life in Tokio may be studied by strolling up and down the Tori; and I frequently rambled through this street, to indulge my curiosity in observing the strange characteristics of the Japanese people. The native shops were ranged on both sides of the street, their fronts being thrown open so that the passer-by could see all the display of wares at once. The shop-keeper squatted upon the straw-matted floor, in the midst of his goods, toasting his fingers over a brazier of live coals, and smoking his tiny pipe, which was refilled at every third puff. If you stopped to purchase any small article, he would bow politely, and figure up the price on a little frame with rows of beads running on parallel wires, like the *abacus* used in schools. Unless you were expert in mental arithmetic, he would calculate faster with his fingers than you could with your brains. His result was always right.

Many of the streets crossing the Tori were devoted exclusively to the sale of special articles. "Bamboo Street" looked as though a forest of long bamboo poles had sprung up through its entire length; and the "Dyers' Street," where deep vats and colored fabrics are exposed to the air, is filled with odors strong enough to knock a person over, even in passing. Some streets contain willow and basket ware; others exhibit long shelves of lacquer-ware and cabinets, ornamented with every conceivable design. Another street contains folding screens, inscribed with pictures and poetry; still others have paper lanterns, wooden-shoe shops, silk establishments, book-stores with European maps suspended in front; and some streets are devoted to the sale of foreign goods, such as lamps, candles, kerosene, soap, toilet articles, and bottles of beer. The Japanese seem to think that beer and champagne are the characteristic marks of modern civilization. Unfortunately, too many sad examples have been set them in this direction by foreigners from Christian countries.

The most interesting sights in the streets are the games and sports of the children. The Japanese believe in enjoying themselves, and the young folks are as bright and merry as the children of other climes. The girls play battledore and shuttlecock, and the boys fly kites and spin tops. The girls enjoy their game very much, and are usually dressed in their prettiest robes and bright-colored girdles; their faces are powdered with a little rice flour, their lips are tinted crimson, and their hair is done up in a most extraordinary fashion.

They play in the open street, sometimes forming a circle of half a dozen or more, and sending the flying shuttlecock from one to the other. They are very skilful, and rarely miss a stroke. The boys like a strong wind that their kites may soar high; but the girls sing a song that it may be calm, so that their shuttlecocks may go right.

The boys have wonderful kites, made of tough paper pasted on light bamboo frames, and decorated with dragons, warriors, and storm hobgoblins. Across the top of the kite is stretched a thin ribbon of whalebone, which vibrates in the wind, making a peculiar humming sound. When I first walked the streets of Tokio I could not imagine what the strange noises meant that seemed to proceed from the sky above me; the sound at times was shrill and sharp, and then low and musical. At last I discovered several kites in the air, and when the breeze freshened the sounds were greatly increased.

Sometimes the boys put glue on their kite-strings, near the top, and dip the strings into pounded glass. Then they fight with their kites, which they place in proper positions, and attempt to saw each other's strings with the pounded glass. When a string is severed, a kite falls, and is claimed by the victor. The boys also have play-fights with their tops.

Sometimes I met boys running a race on long stilts ; at other times they would have wrestling matches, in which little six-year-old youngsters would toss and tumble one another to the ground. Their bodies were stout and chubby, and their rosy cheeks showed signs of health and happiness. They were always good-natured, and never allowed themselves to get angry.

On the fifth day of the fifth month the boys have their Fourth of July, which they call the "Feast of Flags." They celebrate the day very peaceably, with games and toys. They have sets of figures, representing soldiers, heroes, and celebrated warriors ; with flags, daimio processions, and tournaments. Outside of the house a bamboo pole is erected by the gate, from the top of which a large paper fish is suspended. This fish is sometimes six feet long, and is hollow. When there is a breeze it fills with wind, and its tail and fins flap in the air as though it were trying to swim away. The fish is intended to show that there are boys in the family. It is the carp, which is found in Japanese waters, and swims against the stream, and leaps over water-falls.

RAMBLES ABOUT THE CAPITAL. 157

The boys must therefore learn from the fish to persevere against all difficulties, and surmount every obstacle in life. When hundreds of these huge fishes are seen swimming in the breeze, it presents a very curious appearance.

The girls have their "Feast of Dolls" on the third day of the third month. During the week preceding this holiday, the shops of Tokio are filled with dolls and richly dressed figures. This "Feast of Dolls" is a great gala-day for the girls. They bring out all their dolls and gorgeously dressed images, which are quite numerous in respectable families, having been kept from one generation to another; the images range from a few inches to a foot in height, and represent court nobles and ladies, with the Mikado and his household in full costume. They are all arranged on shelves, together with many other beautiful toys, and the girls present offerings of rice, fruit, and "saki" wine, and mimic all the routine of court life. The shops display large numbers of these images at this special season; after the holidays they suddenly disappear.

I once bought a large doll baby at one of the shops, to send home to my little sister; the doll was dressed in the ordinary way, having its head shaved in the style of most Japanese babies. It was so life-like that when propped up on a chair a person would easily suppose it to be a live baby.

In going along the Tori I would often see a group of children gathered around a street story-teller, listening with widening eyes and breathless attention to the ghost story or startling romance which he was narrating. Many old folks also gathered around, and the story-teller shouted and stamped on his elevated platform, attracting great attention, until, just as the most thrilling part of the story was reached, he suddenly stopped and took up a collection! He refused to go on unless the number of pennies received was sufficient to encourage the continuation of the story.

Street theatricals can also be seen, and travelling shows with monkeys, bears, and tumbling gymnasts, who greatly amuse the children. Sugar-candy and various kinds of sweetmeats are sold by pedlers, who are eagerly sought after by the little folks. Sometimes a man carries small kitchen utensils on the ends of a pole, and serves out tiny griddle-cakes to the children, who watch him cook the cakes, and smack their lips in anticipation of the feast.

A showman will put a piece of camphor on the tiny model of a duck which he floats on a shallow dish of water, and as the children look on in wonder the dissolving camphor gum sends the duck from side to side, as though it were alive.

The boys delight in fishing, and will sit for hours holding the line by the moats and canals, waiting for a bite. I have seen a dozen people watching a single person fish, when there would not be a bite once in the half hour.

There are few vehicles in Tokio, excepting the jinrikishas; and most of the people walk in the middle of the street. When riding on horseback it is impossible to go at a rapid rate without endangering the youngsters who sprawl around in the street. Chickens, dogs, and cats are also in the way; the latter animal has no tail in Japan.

The greatest play-ground in Tokio appears to be the garden and cluster of buildings known as the Temple of Asakusa. The temple stands near the river, at the further end of the city. Here the people congregate in large numbers for pleasure and worship; the Japanese combine religion and amusement, and their temple grounds are the places of resort on all festival occasions. There is a perpetual holiday at Asakusa. The main temple is approached by a long avenue, lined on both sides with booths, stalls, and shops, in which toys and all manner of things are sold. The last table is devoted to the sale of small beans, with which to feed the sacred doves that throng the eaves of the temple by hundreds. When I purchased a penny's worth of beans and threw them on the ground, the whole feathery tribe of doves descended in a fluttering cloud, and picked the beans up in an instant. At another table larger beans are purchased to feed the sacred white horse. The horse is very gentle, and stands with due dignity in his stall, receiving with meekness all favors conferred upon him; he seems to "know beans" very well. The gods are said to ride upon this horse, therefore it is a religious act to feed him; he is plump and fat, like the lazy priest who attends him.

Inside the temple, the altars and images are protected from the birds by wire screens. There is a small wooden image which has been rubbed by the people so that its face, hands, and feet have been literally worn off. Whosoever touches the image is said to have his diseases cured by touching the corresponding portion of his own body. It was very pitiable to see the blind, lame, and sickly coming up to this hideous wooden image, hoping to be cured thereby.

To the left of the temple is a beautiful garden, with flowers, dwarfed trees, and miniature lakes. Here also is a grand display of wax figures, illustrating Japanese legends and romance; these figures are similar to those once seen at Barnum's Museum, but are more finely executed. To see these figures you pass through corridors of some length, winding through a labyrinth of passages, and coming at each turn upon new sets of groups, representing every phase of Japanese life and costume, poetical and tragical, from the farmer plodding the field to the goddess descending from the skies. At one point a fairy nymph is charming the lonely passer-by with music from a stringed instrument, as she sits in a shady bower; at another place a freshly-severed head lies hideously on the floor, with eyes half closed and death pallor on the cheek, while a furious monster holds his sword aloft, as though ready to come at you as the next victim.

In the neighborhood of Asakusa is a place called Mékojima, celebrated for its cherry-blossoms. The cherry-trees line the roadside on the river bank for a distance of two miles. They overarch the road so as to form a continuous bower, and the blossoms are so thick and flaky that the trees appear as if covered with light snow. People throng the place by thousands, and take more pleasure in their admiration of these cherry-blossoms than in any other form of amusement. Tea-houses and gardens abound along the bank of the river, and mirth and music are heard on all sides. Though the trees have such beautiful blossoms, yet they bear no fruit.

My home in Tokio was near the second moat of the great castle, in the centre of the city; the house stood within a compound, or inclosure, adjoining the college buildings. Within this inclosure most of the foreign professors resided; their houses were nearly all of the same style as the one shown in the picture. The view of my house was taken in winter during a snow-storm, to show that we had at least a little snow in Tokio. In the foreground are two jinrikishas, or little carriages such as I used in riding around Tokio. The two little girls in one of the jinrikishas were great pets of mine; they were the daughters of a lady friend, who had charge of the Government Girls' School. Two servants are standing in the doorway, and considerable snow covers the roof. The smoke-pipe on the left of the entrance shows that the Japanese carpenter could not be prevailed upon to build a chimney. None of the houses in the compound had chimneys, and many fires have originated from the careless way in which these pipes were put up.

The photographic camera seen on the table at the left was the one employed in taking some of the pictures of this book. Near the doorstep is

THE HOME IN TOKIO.

another table, with a sword-rack and sword presented by the Governor of Tokio.

When I first came to Tokio I met with great pleasure my friend and former classmate, Mr. Griffis, who had once tramped with me through Switzerland, and who was now settled at the Tokio College, after living a year at Fukwi, on the western coast of Japan. In his journey to Tokio he passed through Shidz-u-o-ka, when I went out to meet him with a mounted escort, and entertained him at my old temple home. At Tokio we lived together in the same house for several months; but after his return to America I was left alone, as I had been at Shidz-u-o-ka. Mr. Griffis wrote a large and interesting work on Japan while living in this house, which has since been published; and if my young reader wishes a more complete history of Japan than I have space to give, I would refer him to Mr. Griffis's book, "The Mikado's Empire."

A few months after Mr. Griffis left for America I invited Hatakéyama, the Director of the Kaisei Gakko, to come and live with me. He wished to do so very much, as his own house was small and two miles away, whereas mine was large and close to the college, and very convenient. I petitioned the Minister of Education to allow

Hatakéyama to change his residence, but for some unaccountable reason the request was politely declined.

The scourge of small-pox visited Tokio while I was there; two of the professors died with it, and great alarm prevailed.

The natives died by hundreds; but the Japanese seemed used to it. One of my friends at this time was suffocated from charcoal fumes in bathing in a Japanese bath-tub; I helped embalm the poor fellow, so that his body might be sent home.

Quite a tragic affair occurred at the Kaisei Gakko one morning, which nearly resulted in the destruction of the whole building by fire. I was giving a lecture to my chemistry class, when suddenly great confusion was heard in the second story, and the court-yard was seen filled with smoke. Dismissing the class, and advising them to keep cool, I seized the Babcock fire-extinguisher which always stood on the table in my laboratory, and asked my two assistants to bring a pair of the same instruments which stood in the hall, and which I had newly charged the day before.

With the three Babcocks we went upstairs, but so great was the confusion that we could not at first find the whereabouts of the fire. Beds, books, and furniture were being tumbled out of the windows, and students were rushing around like maniacs. At last I discovered the fire in the roof of the French department. It had caught from the red-hot smoke-pipe seen projecting from the corner of the wing of the college building in the picture a little further on. The fire had smouldered for hours, and then broken out with terrible fury, sweeping along the rafters under the roof, and would soon have wrapped the whole wing in flames. A Japanese hand-pump had been brought into the room at the corner of the building; the firemen had broken a hole through the ceiling, and were waiting for water to be brought upstairs in buckets! I laughed at their clumsy machine, and mounted the ladder leading into the burning loft above. The sight that met my gaze was appalling, and startled me so that I burned and blackened my arms in trying to get through the hole with the heavy Babcock on my back. Broad sheets of flame leaped along the rafters, and the smoke was so suffocating I could scarcely breathe.

I attempted to head off the flames, knowing that if they gained much greater progress they would be beyond control, and the whole building would be sacrificed. Swinging from one rafter to another, I turned on the magic stream of the carbonic-acid gas extinguisher, and the effect was instantaneous. Wherever the stream touched the fire it swept it out like a broom, and by the time I had emptied the first Babcock forty feet of the flames had been subdued. Meanwhile I was nearly extinguished myself by the thick smoke, and crept cautiously towards the hole, where I allowed the Jap pump to play on my face and head.

Thus revived, I took the second extinguisher, and nearly subdued the rest of the flames. As the third and last instrument was passed up to me, I heard a great noise on the roof over my head, and soon shingles and stone tiles began to fall, showing that the firemen were breaking in the roof in true Japanese fashion. In vain I called to them to desist, and not to let in the air; and I sent a stream of acidulated water into their faces to drive them away. Still they persisted in breaking in the roof, and at the same time men with stout poles began breaking up the thin floor beneath me. With the ingress of fresh air the fire started up again in several places. The treacherous cross-beams were some distance apart, and it was difficult to step from one to the other with the heavy instrument on my back. One young fellow, who ventured up to help me, fell through the ceiling like a shot, and disap-

SU-RU-GA YASHIKI, AND COLLEGE BUILDING.

peared from the scene. I crouched in the corner and played on the burning rafters as best I could ; reflecting on the pleasant alternative of being roasted alive, or struck on the head by a tile from above, or poked by a pole from below. A burning stick fell on my back, and warmed the situation somewhat. The extinguishers were true to their name, however, and after the third one had been emptied the flames were so far subdued that a few buckets of water finished them.

As a touching sequel to the affair, I stayed in bed for two days afterward. This is the nearest I ever came to being cremated.

The picture presents a portion of the Kaisei Gakko grounds. This view was taken in winter after a slight fall of snow ; but the snow melted so fast that I could not catch much of it with the camera.

The small tower and building on the left belong to the Suruga Yashiki, or official headquarters of the province where I lived. In this yashiki I was received by Katz and Okubo, and other officials of Suruga, when I first came to Japan.

Here a grand dinner was prepared for me in foreign style, and a reception given fit for a daimio. But, alas ! I had dined heartily with my friend Dr. Veeder just before going to the Yashiki, not knowing of the culinary preparations made for me. Nevertheless the banquet must be served, and my post of honor had to be at the head of the table. Etiquette made it essential that I should begin eating before any body else could commence. In vain I excused myself in broken Japanese, saying that I had just risen from dinner. This was supposed to be polite affectation, showing that I had a delicate appetite. The more excuses I made the more I was pressed to eat. To decline was a lack of respect to my hosts, and a reflection upon the excellent cooking; besides, whenever I stopped every body else laid down their knives and forks, though I knew they had been waiting a long time and were very hungry. To go forward I could not, and to stop entirely I did not dare! Course after course came and went. The dinner was excellent, and served in splendid style, in dishes belonging to the Tycoon, which I afterwards used on similar occasions at Shidz-u-o-ka. Soup, fish, meats, and savory viands came in endless succession. I tasted each course and then stopped. Every body else did the same. I wished for an artificial stomach, such as Jack the Giant-Killer possessed when he ate more hasty-pudding than the giant, and made the monster perform *hara-kiri*. Finally the last dish disappeared from the table. My companions still felt hungry, and I felt like exploding!

Beautiful presents were then produced. The Tycoon sent me a superb gold lacquer lunch-box, with solid silver saki bottles. It was the most elegant box of the kind I ever saw, and was worth five or six hundred dollars. I presented a large picture of the Yosemite Valley to Katz, and a diagram of the new capitol at Albany to Okubo.

So ended the first banquet and reception at the Yashiki.

CHAPTER IX.

A PEEP INTO THE MIKADO'S PALACE.

FOR long ages the Mikado of Japan has had religious reverence paid him by his subjects as the "Son of Heaven." He sat behind a screen at his ancient capital Kio-to, and no one might dare approach him except a few court nobles. His very existence was shrouded in sacred mystery, and neither his face nor his form could be seen, but only the voluminous folds of his imperial skirts. The military chieftain, the Tycoon, managed all the affairs of state during this time at Yedo.

At last, after the revolution of 1868, the Mikado came forth from his seclusion and established his court at Yedo, which thereupon became Tokio, or Eastern Capital. The Tycoon retired with his retainers to Shidz-u-o-ka.

Since my arrival at the capital I had been intensely curious to see the Mikado, of whom I had so long heard. I even planned to gain access to the emperor's palace, and see the whole of the imperial court and household, and in this, before many months, I succeeded. The lever that I used to pry open the doors of stiff etiquette and princely exclusion was the stereopticon!

I first gave some brilliant exhibitions of pictures at the Naval College for Mr. Katz, the Minister of the Navy; and afterwards at the Kaisei Gakko for Mr. Hatakéyama. These entertainments were attended by hundreds of officials and students, who of course were wonderfully pleased with the splendid stereopticon pictures of Europe and America.

Soon the fame of the stereopticon reached the palace, just as I intended it should! The empress and ladies of the imperial court were exceedingly desirous of seeing the beautiful pictures of western countries. But of course the ladies could not leave the palace; so I sent word politely to the lord chamberlain, through Hatakéyama, saying that I would come to the palace and give the empress an entertainment, and that the Mikado might come to the exhibition if he saw fit.

The offer was a novel one, as no foreigner had ever been admitted to the palace in such a way before; but my proposition was gladly accepted. My gallant offer to the empress and her ladies was amended, however, by the lord chamberlain, who said that the exhibition should be given for the Mikado, and that the empress and ladies might come in if they wished.

At an appointed day I went to the palace with Hatakéyama, and selected the largest of the state apartments, as the most suitable in which to give the exhibition. I then asked the lord chamberlain to fix the most convenient date. He stepped out in the garden and consulted the Mikado, who was just about to take a walk. His majesty said that Tuesday of the next week would suit him ; but if any important state duties interfered he would let me know.

Accordingly, about eight o'clock on Tuesday evening I had my instruments set up in the palace, and the large curtain suspended from the top of the partition of the apartment. Two large screens were arranged around the instruments ; where the officers at first fixed them so as to shut off the seats intended for the emperor and his household from all the rest of us in the room. But as soon as they had retired to give notice that all was ready, I made a slight and quick change, and pulled the screens backward, so as to make the way clear for a larger picture on the curtain. I placed the Mikado's elegant chair in the little alcove, formed at the end of the zigzag screen, just to the left of my stereopticon, where he would have the finest possible view in the room.

THE "MIKADO" IN MODERN DRESS.

In front of his chair was a small table, covered with a rich gold-embroidered silk cloth; on his left was another table, and a seat for the empress; while in the rear were several lines of upholstered chairs, for the maids of honor and other members of the household.

A few days previous to the exhibition, I had requested Mr. Katz, of the Naval Department, to lend me one of the marine bands to give music for the occasion. On riding up to the gate of the palace that evening I met *two* bands instead of one marching up the hill; they formed in line in two companies, inside the gate, numbering sixty men in all, and began tuning their instruments for the exhibition.

After waiting some time for the foreign leader of the band (who was unfortunately detained by some misunderstanding respecting the passport of entrance to the imperial grounds), I placed the musicians in a side room near the large parlors, gave them directions to play the pieces appropriate to the foreign countries, the pictures of which would be shown in geographical order.

As soon as every thing was ready for the exhibition, notice was sent to the Mikado's apartments that all things were awaiting his majesty's pleasure. The emperor and empress were ushered into the room, followed by an impressive retinue, consisting chiefly of young ladies dressed in white, with their long, dark hair streaming behind, and broad red sashes encircling their waists ; the effect was very pretty, and quite unique, as this charming procession of fair ones entered, and quietly seated themselves behind his majesty, while the band struck up the "Mikado's Hymn," and the word "Welcome," with the wreath of flowers, was thrown by the brilliant light upon the curtain.

The chief officers of the Kunaisho, or Household Department, sat on the opposite side of the room from his majesty. Tokudaigi, the lord chamberlain, and several other high officers were in attendance on his majesty ; and every thing passed off in a very pleasant and social manner, there being nothing stiff or formal, though there was a subdued stillness in the room.

At the outset dissolving views were exhibited of Windsor Castle, Sandringham Hall, the Parliament Houses, and other English and Scottish places of interest, during which the band played "God save the Queen."

Then followed many American views of Niagara, the Yosemite, and the principal scenes in Washington, New York, and Boston. After this the magnesium stereopticon was started, and the magnificent views of Paris, Berlin, Switzerland,

and Northern Italy were presented in brilliant succession.

Hatakéyama (who had accompanied the embassy in all their European experiences) sat near his majesty, and explained all the views as they were announced ; designating, at the same time, the particular places visited by the embassy, and enlivening the occasion by little incidents of their experience.

The Mikado seemed exceedingly interested, and although every body else was quiet in his presence, he conversed freely and naturally, asking many questions upon places of particular importance.

After a hundred of the various well - known scenes in Europe and America had been shown, interspersed with curious revolving chromatropes, and an ocean scene which was particularly impressive, a few comic figures were introduced, which created considerable merriment among the fair ones of the white-robed retinue sitting to the left, though they were very subdued and dignified in their expressions of delight and amusement.

The two bands of music played splendidly at first, but later in the evening, when the lights were down low, they lost their discipline a little, in the absence of the band-master. Some of them had seen the pictures previously shown at the

Naval College, and told their companions how wonderful they were. The musicians were so curious to see the pictures that they could not stay in the room assigned them, but stole slyly behind the stereopticon to see the show. When I discovered them they pretended they had merely come to ask what piece to play next! There were so many drums, trumpets, and fifes that half the band could make all the noise needed, while the other half came in to see the fun ; and they performed very finely.

The exhibition lasted an hour and a half, yet the court wished it to continue longer.

At the conclusion I thought that my turn had come to secure the long-desired peep at the Mikado and the fair members of the imperial household. The room had hitherto been dark, so that I could not readily see the distinguished people about me. Only a broad cone of light fell upon the screen from the stereopticon. But when the signal was given for the Japanese servants to approach with their little paper lanterns, I knew the Tokudaigi had planned to remove the Mikado and his court from the room, without giving the foreigner time to have a satisfactory look at them.

Science came to my assistance, however. The punctilious lord chamberlain knew not the marvellous potency of the magnesium light. No

EMPRESS IN COURT COSTUME.

sooner had the fair retinue risen from their seats than I raised the magic clock-lamp from one of the instruments, and shot a broad beam of white light, dazzling as the sun, down the long corridor through which the procession must pass. In an instant the Japanese lanterns glimmered like fireflies, and the darkness of the corridor changed to daylight. The Mikado and empress passed out first, followed by the ladies of the court, who walked quietly, two by two, and hand in hand. Their dresses were similar to some of those I had seen in pictures of the ancient Kioto court. The fair young faces turned one by one towards the brilliant light, which their curiosity led them to look at, and I noticed the little dots placed upon their foreheads, which designated the highest rank of nobility. Some of the ladies were very pretty ; they wore their hair in thick tresses down the back, which style is only allowable for ladies of the court. Their eyes were slightly oblique.

The Mikado is a little taller than the average Japanese, with an open, fair countenance, having no decided expression except that of serenity. His profile is not very pleasing, but his forehead is high, and his eyes are manly and expressive. His dark hair curls a little at the temples. He steps with ease and carries his figure erect. On the whole, the Mikado is a sensible man and a good emperor, but as " a god " he is fast becoming a failure. His subjects cannot continue to worship one whom they see to be a man like unto themselves. In the picture (which does not do him justice) he is dressed in foreign costume, with gold-lace coat, broad epaulets, white pantaloons, military cap, and European sword. This dress designates him as commander-in-chief of the army, as well as emperor.

The Mikado issued an order that all the native officials and military men should henceforth present themselves at reviews and receptions uniformed in foreign style. Some of the Japanese ladies thought they would adopt European dresses also ; but the emperor issued another order, saying that Japanese ladies looked well enough as they were, and did not need to change their native costume. Wherein the emperor was right. The ladies still wear the ancient style of dress, as seen in the picture of the empress. Elegant fans are carried on full-dress occasions by both sexes.

After the stereopticon entertainment the officers of the Kunaisho Department expressed much pleasure at the result, and said I must be fatigued and in need of refreshment. Accordingly I was led, with Hatakéyama and my two Japanese assistants, into the room where the

Mikado's ministers are usually received. Here a table of refreshments awaited us. Cakes and confectionery, stamped with stars, leaves, flowers, and chrysanthemums, were piled upon the table, colored with all the tints of the rainbow. The confectionery was too artistic to eat, and I told the lord chamberlain that I would take it home to show my friends; he said certainly, that I might take it all, for this is the Japanese custom. I had frequently given dinners at which the invited guests carried away in their sleeves all the good things that were left! So there was no impropriety in my carrying away the sweetmeats from the Mikado's table.

The Tokudaigi said he had ordered one of the emperor's carriages to convey me back to the college, and that it would soon be in waiting. The carriage drove up to the gate of the palace in grand style, with two horses, two bettos well tattooed, and a coachman in full livery. It was evidently the barouche of the empress, and was luxurious within; my Japanese assistants enjoyed the ride exceedingly, for they had never seen such a carriage before.

We drove out of the Imperial Guard Gate, across a narrow causeway over a very deep moat, where Iwakura, the Mikado's minister, had been attacked by a dozen of the two-sworded Samourai, and nearly assassinated. He was badly cut, but saved himself by rolling down the steep embankment into the moat. The imperial guards were alarmed, and the would-be assassins were afterwards captured and beheaded. I subsequently dined at Iwakura's house, and found him able to walk with the aid of a crutch.

When our carriage arrived at the college compound it was nearly midnight, and the sleepy gatekeeper was inclined to grumble at being disturbed so late. But when his half-opened eyes caught sight of the Mikado's crest on the carriage, he fell on his face, and then flew to the bars and opened the gate quicker than he had ever done before!

The next morning all my instruments were sent to the college in the emperor's express wagon. A month after, a magnificent gold lacquer-box came to me with the compliments of the Mikado and the thanks of the ladies of the court. The latter said they felt as though the stereopticon had taken them on a journey through foreign countries, and that nothing in their seclusion at the palace had ever afforded them half so much pleasure. They would remember the occasion, they said, all their lives.

The present sent from the Mikado was quite as elegant as the one formerly received from the ex-

REPRESENTATIVE CLASSES OF SOCIETY.

Tycoon, and was doubly valuable from its associations. The first gift—from the ex-Tycoon—represented the declining feudal power of the past; and the second—from the Mikado—represented a new era in the progress and enlightenment of Japan.

It is appropriate just here to say a few words respecting the various classes of society which prevailed in Japan before the advent of foreigners, and of the distinctions which are now slowly passing away.

In ancient times society was divided into four classes. The first constituted the literary and military class, called the Samourai. The second, strange as it may seem, was the agricultural class, or common farmer. The third was the laboring class, or carpenter and artisan. The fourth was the trading or money-making class, the merchant. These were the chief classes that existed from 1604 until 1868.

The Samourai stood at the head of the social scale. He was the gentleman—the soldier in war and the scholar in peace. He could wield either the sword or the pen. Of the two, he rather preferred the sword. The sharp steel blades thrust in his belt were to him the symbol of rank and chivalry. He might walk the streets without a hat, but never without wearing his two swords.

In the picture representing the classes of society in Japan, the Samourai is seen standing on the left, with his long and short swords thrust in his belt.

In the middle of the picture, sitting upon the ground, is the carpenter, who carries a square rule.

The man with a book is a street story-teller; and the girl on the right, with a sickle, is a farmer's daughter, who cuts grass, and carries it in the basket on her back.

The girl sitting on the left, with a musical instrument, is playing on the *Samisen*, or three-stringed banjo, which is more popular than any other kind of music. The strings are struck with a piece of ivory.

The man with a brick-shaped hat on the right of the group is a Ku-Ge, or court noble. Sanjo, the Prime Minister of Japan, wore such a hat when I first met him in Tokio.

The central and highest figure is dressed in the style which once prevailed at the court of the Tycoon. But these ridiculous fashions are now nearly abolished.

The two ladies on either side of the highest figure are members of the Mikado's court; their hair is brushed back in the way I have already described in this chapter. Two dots upon their foreheads denote their high rank. All the other ladies have their hair dressed in the style of the middle classes of society.

The men have their heads shaved at the top, in the old-fashioned way. The Samourai have the family crests upon their clothing.

Class distinctions are slowly breaking down in Japan with the incoming of western civilization. The Samourai no longer monopolizes the military power, for the government have called the common people to be soldiers, and the proud Samourai have been forced to labor honestly with their own hands.

It was my good fortune to witness a mock battle in the presence of the Mikado, showing the skill and discipline of the sturdy soldiers who now compose the new army. The battle took place in the suburbs of Tokio, between fourteen thousand Japanese troops. It commemorated a peaceful victory in diplomacy, which Japan had recently gained over China, in the adjustment of the Formosa question, which had long threatened war.

On the day appointed for the battle the troops were drawn up in double columns at an early hour, and the two divisions were placed a mile or more apart. When the Mikado arrived upon the field, skirmishers were being thrown out by both parties; these gradually fell back as the two armies approached each other. The soldiers were all dressed in foreign uniforms, and armed with foreign Chassepot rifles.

The fighting soon became general. Double and triple lines of troops were ranged across the plain, and were completely enveloped in the clouds of smoke which rose from their ranks. After two hours and a half of heavy firing and cannonading, the climax of the battle was reached by the troops of both sides becoming closely massed in face of each other, in front of a wooded hill-slope, beyond which the retreat could not be carried. Nothing could be more warlike than the scene now presented. For a distance of two miles, the cultivated land was trodden down by thousands of feet, giving an appearance of sad desolation. Far away, a column of smoke was rising like a cloudy pillar, and the roar of cannon greeted the ear, like the sound of distant thunder. White wreaths of smoke overhung the woods, and the sharp rattle of musketry was deafening.

The last charge was like the grand tableau of a drama; and being in the midst of the smoke, and close upon the heels of the advancing line, I was favored with the beauty and excitement of a battle without the danger and sickening sights thereof.

Covered by the heavy fire of a friendly battery on a neighboring hill, regiment after regiment responded to the bugle-note, and lowered their weapons to the charge. On they went, sweeping across the plain, their long lines circling up from the right, and throwing volley after volley of bulletless smoke into the stubborn ranks of the enemy. The latter were massed at the foot of the hill, and unseen regiments were in the woods above ; these opened fire by companies, and light lines of smoke drifted from the woods and scattered among the trees, like snow whiffs on a windy day. The wooded slope threw back ten thousand echoes, as the two combating forces closed upon each other. There was a rattle and roar loud and prolonged, and never did I imagine that mere rifles could produce such a continuous roll of sound. The shouts of the men and the blasts of the bugles mingled with the din and confusion, and clouds of smoke enveloped all parties. So thick was the smoke at times, that naught could be seen save the glitter of steel, and the bright intermittent flashes of the guns.

At last the enemy succumbed. The clouds slowly lifted, and the cracking and roaring ceased. The line of battle on both sides broke up into various detachments, and wearily the troops trudged homeward.

CHAPTER X.

A TRIP TO KIOTO.

KIOTO is the "sacred city" of Japan. Until a few years ago it was considered the spiritual capital, where his Mysteriousness the Mikado resided, whose august person was solemnly veiled from even the gaze of his own subjects. The idea of a foreigner from the outside world ever gaining admittance to the sacred city would have horrified the good Japanese of the olden time; nevertheless, wonderful things are happening in our day, and changes have come to pass which would have paralyzed the ancient court; so that I really went to Kioto and sojourned among its most sacred temples as comfortably as though I were rusticating on the beautiful banks of the Hudson.

The trip was a long one, requiring several weeks. I went to the port of Ko-bé by sea—a distance of 430 miles, and returned to Tokio by the whole length of the Tokaido, on the overland route. The most interesting and historical portions of Japan were visited on the way, though I cannot do more than mention them here.

After some delay in receiving my passport from the Gaimusho, or Foreign Office, I left Yokohama on July 23d, in company with an American friend and a young Japanese who had recently returned from the United States. We sailed in the Pacific Mail steamer Oregonian, which we nicknamed the " Roll-igonian" before we had been out many hours. The voyage only occupied a day and a half, but it was the roughest piece of sailing we ever wish to experience. The rolling and pitching qualities of the steamer were of the most unpleasant character, and as we were running through a very heavy sea, and there was no wind to steady the ship, our condition was really deplorable. I spent most of the time sprawling on the cabin floor ; for no sooner would I crawl into my berth than I was unceremoniously pitched out of it again. My companions tried to sit on chairs ; but in an instant the chair-legs would go from under them, spilling them on deck and rolling them helplessly against the gunwale of the steamer.

The captain told me as we were coming into port that there must have been a typhoon to the south-east of us, which died away, leaving the sea in the dangerous condition in which we found it, with high waves and no wind.

The British steamer Bengal arrived at Kobé the day before us, and reported that she had never met such heavy seas, which were weathered with the greatest difficulty. A former Japanese friend named Nagai, who used to study at New Brunswick, and was now going to Ozaka on business for the Treasury Department, told me that he had crossed the Atlantic seven times, but had never suffered from sea-sickness so much as on this short trip.

But even bad things have an end, and towards evening we came in sight of land, and steamed around a broad cape into the calm and sheltered waters of Ozaka Bay. All night we sailed quietly along the shore, watching the lights of the fishermen's boats glimmering across the bay.

The sun was just rising as we rode at our iron buoy in front of Kobé, and fired the signal gun, which echoed and re-echoed through the neighboring hills, telling the inhabitants that their mail had arrived.

We were anxious to reach the shore as speedily as possible after our misery on the "Rolligonian;" *terra firma* never felt so good as when we placed our feet once more on land. It was early yet, and few people were stirring. So we started off and visited a renowned water-fall in a cleft of the hills behind the town. After a steep climb we reached the fall, which tumbled from a height of sixty feet, making the rocky gorge reverberate with the noise and shock of its descent.

Kobé is very picturesquely situated between the mountains and the sea, and some of the foreign houses are very handsome. The town is merely the port and commercial outlet of Ozaka, and is connected with the latter city by a new railroad.

We took the 11.30 train for Ozaka, reaching the spacious depot on the suburbs of the city in just one hour. The cars are more elegant and comfortable than those on the Yokohama Railroad, and the locomotives are larger; both roads were built by English engineers, and the cars are small, in the English style. The Japanese conductors evince pardonable pride in the novel dignity placed upon them in collecting tickets and conveying passengers. They are very polite and competent however.

Ozaka is the second city in size in the Japanese Empire. It contains a population of over 500,000, and is more compactly built than Tokio. The streets are narrow and very crowded, but comparatively clean. So many large canals intersect the city that it might be called the Venice of Japan. Our hotel was conveniently located on one of these canals, and we made excursions from this point in every direction, exploring the sights of the great city. The shops were the finest I had seen, and were stocked with a great variety of goods; for Ozaka is the commercial centre of the country.

The three points of interest which we first visited were the imperial mint, the great castle, and the pagoda; from the latter a fine general view of the city may be obtained. The imperial mint was more extensive than the United States mint at Philadelphia, and quite as well conducted in every respect. We were politely shown throughout the whole establishment, and witnessed the money-making process on a scale we had never seen before. The mint is a granite building, and stands on the margin of the river; close beside it is a sulphuric acid manufactory, with a solitary brick chimney 150 feet in height.

We first passed through the rooms for melting gold and silver; here were small furnaces, containing red-hot crucibles. The melted metal is poured into moulds, and cools in the form of long bars several inches thick. These bars are rolled in another room between heavy cylinders moved by machinery. It appeared strange to see the workmen forcing these bars between the rollers, as if they were only sticks of wood. They come out flat and bow-shaped, and are dark and discolored ; the friction of the heavy rolling also makes them quite hot. Without thinking of this, and not noticing that the workmen had their hands protected by thick gloves, I attempted to pick up one of the bars from a freshly rolled cartful as we passed by. I dropped it quicker than I picked it up, somewhat to the amusement of those standing near, and concluded that money was sometimes a hot thing to handle !

The machines in the various rooms were very complicated and delicate : some were for punching the gold, silver, and copper coins, from the flat strips of these metals. Others were for rounding them off nicely, and turning up the edges ; and finally the coins were placed in piles, and run through grooves to the stamping machines, which closed upon each one of them with a "bite," impressing the "dragon" and the value upon one side, and the "rising sun" and imperial crest upon the other.

We watched for some time the continuous streams of gold and silver pieces which rattled from the mouths of the various machines : at one point it would be a silver shower of dollars or fifty *sen* pieces : at another it would be a golden rain of five, ten, or twenty *yen* coins, bright and shining as the sun stamped upon them.

The new pennies, which had recently been put in circulation to replace the old *tempo* cash, were being produced at a rate that would have made the little boys' eyes dance; they flew out of the hopper like chaff from a winnowing machine, and looked so bright that one would think them something more than copper.

The most beautiful instruments were those in the weighing-room, and the finest machine here was constructed by the Japanese. Each gold coin must be weighed to see that it is of the exact weight required by the standard. In the weighing-room there are six tables of apparatus, brass levers, armatures, and scale-pans, all enclosed in glass cases, and all moved by delicate band adjustments, connecting them with the same power that moves the ponderous machines in the other rooms. The gold coins are pushed forward one by one, by feeders, to the delicate scale-pan, which acts automatically and almost with intelligence. If the coin is too heavy, it drops to one side; if it is a little too light, it turns off to another box; but if it is just right, it goes straight ahead to a kind of contribution-box, which is usually better supplied than those for missionary purposes.

After visiting the mint, I was very much interested in inspecting the acid works. My companions could see nothing very poetical in leaden chambers and suffocating sulphur furnaces, even though they admired the big chimney, which is said to be the highest in Asia ; and, in this chimneyless country it is at least a consolation to know that the Japs have *one* chimney that even beats the average ! I told them the consumption of sulphuric acid was the true standard of a nation's commercial prosperity, for it is used in all the processes of manufacture ; and the acid works, with all their sulphurous fumes and furnaces, were a more reliable index of Japan's commercial condition than the glittering showers of gold through which we had just passed in the mint.

We did not forget to visit the great castle, which also stood near the river, and is remarkable for its high walls and deep moats, that once rendered it well-nigh impregnable. But the towers and buildings were totally destroyed by fire during the fighting which took place here some years ago between the forces of the Mikado and the Tycoon. The walls and foundations are still standing, and here may be seen the largest blocks of stone ever quarried in Japan. They are quite as wonderful as those I afterwards saw at the Pyramids ; but how the Japanese, with almost a total lack of mechanical appliances, could ever have transported these blocks and placed them in their present position, I cannot tell.

While waiting at the guard gate for permission to enter, I measured one or two of the stones in the side of the wall. The first one contained over 500 cubic feet, and the others varied from twenty-five to thirty feet in length, with a breadth of fifteen or eighteen feet. There are no quarries near Ozaka from which these massive blocks could have been taken, and it is supposed they were floated up the inland sea, on great rafts, from the province of Hizen. Near the top of the castle we found stone blocks still larger, and a well 120 feet deep, from which we drew the purest and coolest water, with an interminably long rope. The view from this point is very fine; and near the castle was a cannon foundry, and the government barracks, where 10,000 infantry and 3,000 artillery were quartered.

On our return to the hotel we visited the new State House, built in foreign style, with Corinthian columns, spacious halls, and the whole surmounted with a dome! This imposing building was in strange contrast to the squalor and architectural poverty which surrounded it. The interior is also a ludicrous mingling of the old and the new. In passing along the corridors

I peeped into the compartments set aside for the various branches of government. Here were dozens of yaconims seated around tables, with piles of paper and bulky documents in front of them, while they smoked their tiny pipes and jabbered as lively as ever; they looked intensely Japanese, and yet all this was in a modern republican-looking State-house!

The last evening in Ozaka we took tea with Rev. Mr. Gulick and his family. Here we met Mr. Gulick's aged father, who had spent many years as a missionary in the Sandwich Islands, and had now come to spend his declining years with his devoted missionary son in Japan. The old gentleman welcomed me with special warmth, saying that he had read a great many of my letters from Shidz-u-o-ka, which were published in the New York *Evangelist*.

We attended the quiet Sabbath service which Mr. Gulick and one or two other missionaries held, in a private house, our last Sunday in Ozaka, and were very much touched by the interest manifested by the few natives who came together to study Christian truth.

There is a river flowing from the vicinity of Kioto and Lake Biwa which empties into the bay at Ozaka. It is customary to go up the river by night, rather than jolt all the way to Kioto in a

JAPANESE GONDOLA.

jinrikisha. The canals of the city connect with the river, and as our hotel was located near the main canal we determined to take a moonlight trip to Kioto.

Accordingly we chartered a Japanese gondola, such as the natives used at Ozaka, and transferred our baggage to it, adding a supply of provisions for the long journey which we had in prospect after we should leave Kioto. The sun had just set as our boat pushed off and quickly made its way up the canal; a soft haze slowly settled over the city, and as the full moon came out it gave almost an enchantment to the scene, and to the weird dwellings on the banks, which in sober daylight are none of the prettiest.

Continuing on a mile, we passed numerous bow-shaped bridges, the extravagantly high arches of which were more convenient for the mast of our boat than for the muscular ease of the jinrikisha coolies, who are obliged to draw their passengers over them. The bridges are quite a feature in this city of canals, and add not a little to the quaintness of the views.

The night had fairly set in as we reached the low but picturesque craft, which I have styled a gondola; it was waiting in the stream for us, and having transferred ourselves and baggage to the cabin-like place which had been prepared for us, the boat moved up the river. There was plenty of space inside, though the cabin roof was scarcely four feet high; and stretching ourselves on the floor, to make up in length what we lacked in height, we looked out of the windows at the curious sights by the way. The evening was warm and pleasant, and thousands of people had gathered on the river in boats, to enjoy the cool breeze, in preference to promenading the narrow and sultry streets of the city. The surface of the water for a mile or more was covered with small crafts of every description. Some had old folks, smoking their pipes and taking their ease; others had family groups sipping their tea together; others again had numbers of merry young people who were evidently out for a frolic, and enlivened the air with laughter, music, and talk. Each boat carried two or three lanterns, and some were decked with whole strings of light, with various colors. So numerous were the gay crafts that it looked like a moving constellation as they passed backwards and forwards. Now and then the small skiff of a fruit-seller would be seen darting in and out between the large boats, and the tempting array of melons and peaches, illuminated by a paper lantern, would be offered to the various occupants, who were already enjoying their tea and other refreshments. A few fireworks were let off on the river-bank by the juveniles, and these combined with the reflection of the hundreds of lights on the water gave a brilliant effect to the scene.

But the sight on our own craft was by no means the least interesting part of the entertainment, for scarcely were we comfortably settled, than the boat began moving up stream at a wonderfully rapid rate; and the mode of its propulsion was among the most novel and characteristic things we had seen in Japan. Eight men armed with stout poles, twelve or sixteen feet long, would start together at the bow of the boat, each with his pole braced against his shoulder; and then, with a yell, they would plunge their poles against the shallow river-bed, and rush together towards the stern, making the boat fairly jump on its course. On both sides of the boat the raised gunwale of stout timber was cut with broad notches to fit the feet of the men, and, as they kept step with each other their nimble motions from one end of the boat to the other had all the effect of a machine. It was ludicrous to us who sat within to see this continuous procession of naked legs passing to and fro, for our windows being low, we could see the biped extremities of the human propellers with the least possible clothing.

However, they had a right to keep as cool as possible, for never did mortals work harder; and notwithstanding the difficulties of the current, and the shallowness of the stream, they tugged at their poles with a vigor and perseverance we have never seen equalled.

We continued up stream until nothing was in view but low meadows of long rank grass skirting the river bank. Our men toiled on, pushing their poles with as much vigor as at the outset, until coming to a place where the bank was low and level they suddenly ran the boat close to the shore and jumped off; and while we were wondering what it meant to see all the nimble legs disappear at once, we felt ourselves impelled by a new form of motion.

We went on top of the little cabin to take a view of the situation, and found the men about forty yards ahead of us, tugging away at a long rope attached to a short mast near the centre of the boat. This rope could be lengthened or shortened by a crank turned by the steersman, who with one hand guided the boat well out into the stream, and with the other accommodated the rope to the distance from the shore. It was a novel sight, from our perch on top of the cabin, to watch the men appear and disappear as they rushed along the path behind the tall grass and cane-brakes; sometimes we would sight another gondola, and then there would be a scramble and race to get ahead of it. There were some queer fouls in these races, but our boat always came out ahead. Boats from the opposite direction kept in the middle of the river, and were carried down by the current.

The night was still and clear, and the moon shone full and bright; the cool of the evening was in pleasant contrast to the heat of the preceding day, and as we sailed quietly along, the scene was like a picturesque panorama. At midnight we went below and crawled in the cabin window, where I stretched myself on the floor and was soon fast asleep.

I awoke at sun-rising, and saw the poor donkey-men still shouting and tugging far ahead. The river was now quite shallow, and sand-bars were on all sides. Though the boat was flat, it was difficult to make the few miles that remained. But the men worked well, either pushing at the poles, pulling at the ropes, scrambling through the grass and bushes, or jumping into the water, as emergency might require. I have never seen human beings labor more persistently than did these eight men through this long night's toil, stopping neither to rest nor to eat.

At last we arrived at Fushimi, the suburb of

Kioto, where we disembarked, and took jinrikishas; it was still early as we rode within the limits of the Mikado's old and mysterious capital.

We spent a week in Kioto, at a beautiful summer resort on the hillside overlooking the city; we visited all the points of interest, and enjoyed our stay exceedingly.

Kioto, above all other places in Japan, is the city of temples, and to mention half of them would be out of the question. Most of them are large, and their grounds are laid out on a magnificent scale; many have noted historical associations.

The ancient palace of the Mikado, which has always given the chief sacredness to the city, is located within a large enclosure near the upper end of Kioto; the grounds are in the form of a parallelogram, and contain a number of buildings with peculiarly-shaped roofs. No other buildings in the empire are allowed to have this style of roof, except the shrines and temples of the Shinto sect. The Mikado was worshipped as the Tenno, or Son of Heaven; his head must therefore be protected by a Shinto roof, and his very residence became sacred. No paint was ever used about the royal dwellings, but the wood-work was of fine grain, and kept clean and polished. Sometimes the ends of the rafters were tipped with white, but this was the only color permitted, and gave a pretty checkered effect when used on the dark beams of the gateway and roofs.

Behind the palace proper is a large square garden or park also enclosed by walls, containing spacious dwellings; here his Mysteriousness might retire if he chose, and live a peaceful prisoner, after giving up his duties of state to his successor.

All the interest connected with Kioto, as being the royal residence of the Tenno, has of course departed since the removal of the Mikado's person and his capital to Tokio.

Kioto contains nearly 300,000 inhabitants; its streets are laid out at right angles, and are as regular as those of Philadelphia.

Of the hundreds of temples visited, I will only mention that of "Kiyo-Midzu," or clear-water. This temple is splendidly situated; it was built about A.D. 798, and is considered among the most sacred spots in this neighborhood. It is approached by long slopes of stone steps. At the entrance of the temple is a pagoda, and along the edge of the buildings are high balconies or stages which overlook the slope. The priests and people were at worship while we were there, and the beating of drums made a continuous din. The high stages are partially protected by projecting rails, as they overlook a depth varying from 100 to 200 feet.

Within recent times it was customary for eccentric individuals, who did not want to go to war, to come and throw themselves off this precipice, preferring to die before the temple of their deity, rather than be killed in battle.

Descending by a winding path from the stages, we came to the waterfall of the " Clear-water," which is divided into three streams by stone troughs projecting from the edge. Underneath is a small shrine in the rock, and hither pilgrims come to worship, and bathe in the sacred waters.

We took a bath there ourselves, but it was with difficulty that either of us could stand more than a few seconds under one of those solid streams of very cold water, which fell upon one like a liquid hammer. And yet, soon after coming out, we saw three men stand for eight or ten minutes, each with his head bowed forward towards the shrine, and the stream of water falling upon his neck and back, while he devoutly counted his beads, a string of which he held between his hands, and repeated prayers either for his own purification or for the healing of some sick friend. Sometimes persons will stand underneath this fall for a long time, as a kind of penance for sin; and even in winter persons will kneel there, praying for sick relatives, till they are almost benumbed. The priests pretend that cures have been wrought through the efficacy of these waters.

The largest bell we have ever seen in Japan was suspended near one of the temples adjoining our quiet hotel. The bell was made of fine bronze, and was more than ten feet high and nearly five feet in diameter; it was immovable, as all Japanese bells are, but was struck on the side by a suspended beam of wood, pulled back and forth by a dozen men. No sound can be more pleasant to the ear than the deep booming tones of one of these bells; I do not wonder that the people love to listen to the solemn note, that may be heard on a still night for a circumference of many miles.

Our last evening in Kioto was passed in watching the merry scenes along the shallow river-flats, where the people congregate in large numbers to spend the warm summer evenings. The river-bed is mostly a dry gravelly waste, with streamlets flowing here and there through narrow channels. A fresh breeze may always be found here during the sultry evenings, and numbers of small platforms or stout tables are placed in the shallow portions of the river, upon which the people sit and enjoy themselves. The tables are connected with innumerable restaurants which line the river bank, and busy waiters bring fish, soups, tea, and saki down the sloping walks to the guests.

The delicacy always in the greatest demand consists of fried eels, which are consumed by the dozen. I walked into some of the noisy kitchens where business appeared rather brisk; fires were blazing and kettles were steaming, while baskets of live eels were brought in and skinned, cooked, and served piping hot in an incredibly short time. The jolly multitude appeared to enjoy their eel-feast exceedingly; and saki bottles were also emptied and replenished with marvellous rapidity, the boisterousness and merriment increasing in due proportion. It was the first noisy crowd I had yet come across in Japan.

But the scene was really brilliant, as we stood on the substantial brick-paved bridge which is the Nihon-Bashi of Kioto, and which marks the beginning of the Tokaido. As far as the eye can reach, thousands of lights flicker and sparkle along the shallow river flats, and thousands of well-dressed people are trying to enjoy themselves. Each light or lantern is the centre of a little group, and each group occupies its own little table, so that the great concourse is but a multiplication of social circles of every description.

Here sit half a dozen old men smoking their wee pipes around a brazier, and discussing the business items of the day. Here a cheerful family group are seated, the father chatting with his neighbors of the nearest table, and the mother (busy as usual) mending some small fabric; the boys toss tempos, and the baby sprawls on the floor after an orange. Near at hand may be seen young fellows having a merry time with their "musumé" companions.

The fashionable young Japanese is quite a feature in his way. He sits with loose flowing dress, and sleeves tucked up at the shoulders, with long-hilted sword in the background, gossiping merrily with the pretty lasses who look on him admiringly. The young "musumé" who sits gracefully on the table beside him is sweet and pretty, but not loth to flirt a little by waving her long silken sleeve. She is one of the belles of Kioto; is considered very handsome, and knows it. Her hands are quite small and white, and never did any thing more arduous than play the "koto" or "samisen." Her feet are clad in bewitching little socks cloven at the toe, and ready to slip into the bright lacquer shoes which stand on the stepping-stone. Her "obi," or sash, is of broad blue silk, fringed with golden lace, and streaming down behind in true court style. Her little wallet is embroidered in rich fantastic figures, and her paper parasol is light and fragile as a reed. Her hair is done up in the most approved Kioto fashion, which differs from that of the rest of Japan in being brushed up straight over the forehead, and after being held in place by sundry gold and tortoise-shell pins, projects several inches behind, over the freshly powdered neck. The face is fair and smooth, the lips brightly tinted, the eyes dark and slightly sad, and the teeth so beautifully white as to make the idea of blackening them seem horrible—as the married women often do.

Leaving this constellation of lights which twinkle like myriads of stars all the way up the riverbed until far into the night, we wend our way homeward across the bridge, and through streets which are decorated with flags and lanterns.

The neighborhood of our hotel abounded in tea-houses, mineral baths, and places of amusement. Music and laughter could be heard on all sides, and as we retired to sleep the merry prattle still went on about us. We were wafted off to dream-land, lulled by the plaintive melodies of old Japan.

We left Kioto in the morning amid the bows and regrets of our kindly Japanese host and his pleasant family, and walked seven miles over the hills to the beautiful Lake Biwa.

I placed the young Japanese who was with me in a "kango," as he was a little fellow, and might have been fatigued by the long walk. His name was Isami Kawamura, and he was but fourteen years of age; he had studied at Ann Arbor, Michigan, and only returned from America two months before. He had evidently been a great pet with his schoolmates at Ann Arbor; and I do not wonder they fell in love with him, for he was the brightest and prettiest Japanese boy I ever met. He was full of fun, and it was quite an amusement to me and my American friend to get Sammy, as we called him, to entertain us in talking about the nice things he had left at Ann Arbor, for which he evidently felt homesick. He was full of the schoolboy spirit of frolic. He spoke English perfectly, and used so many droll expressions and American idioms, which I had not heard since leaving home, that his tongue kept us in continual good-humor.

As we journeyed over the hills he made us merry telling of his experiences with the boys and girls in America, and he said it was very hard for him to come back to Japanese customs, food, and mode of living, after being used to such a comfortable American home as he had at Ann Arbor.

The stout coolies who carried him in the kango listened to his lively conversation, and wondered what it all meant. He would joke them in Japanese occasionally, which only increased their curiosity.

On top of the kango in the picture is the flat straw hat sometimes worn by the coolies. These men are very muscular, and will carry the kango for hours without fatigue.

On arriving at the town of Otsu, at the southern extremity of Lake Biwa, we put up at a pleasant house overlooking the lake, and spent a quiet Sabbath here.

Monday morning we started up the lake in a tiny steamer built and managed by the Japanese; the boilers of these little boats sometimes explode, but fortunately did not do so on this occasion.

Lake Biwa is nearly fifty miles in length, and is by far the largest lake in Japan. It is also the most beautiful. After sailing forty miles, we landed at Hikoni, a picturesque village at the upper end of the lake. Here we spent several days, making excursions around the lake and among the mountains; the view from the high castle of Hikoni is one of the finest in Japan.

The journey from Lake Biwa to the base of Fuji-Yama and the Hakoné mountain pass occu-

RIDING IN A "KAN-GO."

pied one week, during which we travelled 350 miles in jinrikishas. It was a most interesting trip, but we encountered three days of severe rain-storms on the way, and crossed many small rivers. The longest journey was that which we attempted on the first day : we left Hikoni by moonlight, at two o'clock in the morning, and continued travelling until ten o'clock at night, arriving at the city of Nagoya, at the head of a large bay, which may be seen in the outline map. The distance traversed on this day was seventy-five miles ; and that too on muddy roads, in jinrikishas pulled by men ! Of course we sometimes changed the men.

Nagoya is a flourishing city containing 120,000 inhabitants, and noted for its manfacture of china-ware, and elegant cloisonné enamel-ware, so much admired in America. Beautiful silk embroideries are also produced here, and artistic fans. The Nagoya castle is very large. On two of the towers there used to be immense fishes made of copper, and covered with plates of gold. One stormy night a robber attempted in a gale of wind to mount into the air by means of an immense kite, and steal the gold scales from one of the fishes ! He was caught, condemned, and boiled to death in oil ; the raising of large kites was afterwards prohibited. One of the fishes was subsequently taken down and sent to the Vienna Exhibition ; the other I saw at the Japanese Exhibition in Tokio. It was more than six feet high, with its golden tail upright.

Nagoya may be seen on the map, nearly ninety miles west of Shidz-u-o-ka, on the line marking 35 degrees of latitude. Kioto and Lake Biwa may also be found near the same line some distance further west. (In reading and travelling, it is always well to consult the map of the country studied.)

We passed through Shidz-u-o-ka, wet and wearied, after four days of drenching rains and muddy roads, and a great many experiences I have not time to narrate.

Beyond Shidz-u-o-ka, the rivers which I had crossed many times before were now swollen with the flood, and utterly impassable. So we chartered a Japanese junk and sailed across Suruga Bay. The junk had two masts and four sailors. A strong breeze was blowing, and we were soon scudding along at a rapid rate, under full sail. At first it was glorious ; but ere long the big waves came rolling in from beyond the stormy Cape Idzu, and we rocked helplessly in the bottom of the boat ! Wind and tide had no respect for our feelings, and the farther we receded from land the more the breeze freshened.

We ploughed through the water, scattering the spray in all directions, while at regular intervals a huge wave larger than usual would strike us fairly on the beam, and for the moment we thought we were going to the bottom. Jap boats are not very strong, and ours would shake and shiver as though ready to come to pieces; while ever and anon a shower of salt water would dash over the side to cool the situation.

More hideous than the noise of the waves were the shouts of the Jap sailors; the more the wind blew the louder they yelled, until they seemed like demons in the storm.

Finally we came into smooth water, having made thirty miles in three hours. The scene was really romantic as our boat struck the beach on the upper end of the bay, and we jumped ashore. High and gloomy peaks surrounded us on three sides, and on the south was the sea, breaking along the rocky beach in low, dull swells. Dark and threatening clouds hung on the adjacent mountains, and night was slowly creeping on us; here and there lights could be seen in the fishermen's huts.

An hour's climbing along the rocky cliffs, with the waves murmuring below us, and our narrow path lit by a single lantern, brought us to the open road leading to the city of Numadz. I was known and welcomed here; but it was eleven o'clock before we reached our hotel, and were fairly asleep. The next day we reached the familiar Hakoné mountain pass, where we found many friends from Yokohama.

Hakoné village had become quite a summer resort for the foreigners, and we remained here some time, enjoying the pleasant society and delightful excursions on the lake.

When we entered the village after our long trip we were surprised to see American ladies coming up the shaded avenue of pines, dressed in summer costume and wearing bewitching sunbonnets; they were the first foreign ladies we had seen for some time, and we looked at them with delight.

The streets of the village were swarming with children as usual, and mothers carrying their babies on their backs stared at us with the vacant expression peculiar to the common people. Sometimes the babies had little red caps on their heads (as I have before mentioned), which I once mistook for "liberty caps," but which I found to mean small-pox!

The accompanying picture shows the mode of carrying the baby.

MODE OF CARRYING THE BABY.

CHAPTER XI.

THE MISSIONARY OUTLOOK.

A FEW years ago, in journeying along the highways of Japan, the traveller would see at the entrance of every village and near the cross-roads a wooden edict-board hanging where every passer-by might read it, upon which was written in large characters, "The evil sect called Christian is strictly prohibited." This law No. 3 was suspended by the side of other laws against stealing, murder, and insurrection, and, like them, was formerly punishable with imprisonment and even death.

Why should the Japanese consider Christianity a criminal offence, worthy of punishment, when *we* believe it to be a blessing, and see in it the highest joy, love, and salvation? The answer is simply this:

In the sixteenth century, when Europeans first came to Japan, the Jesuit missionaries accompanied the traders, and succeeded in converting the southern provinces to the Roman Catholic faith. So successful were they, that a little later they entered into a conspiracy with some of the disaffected daimios, and attempted to overthrow the government of the Tycoon, and make Christianity the state religion. The conspiracy was discovered, and hundreds of Jesuits and Roman Catholic priests were banished from the country; a terrible persecution of the native converts also followed, in which tens of thousands perished by fire, sword, and crucifixion.

Christianity, so called, was swept from the land; its very name was written in blood, and children were taught to trample upon the cross. The edict-board which I have mentioned was written at that time, and placarded throughout the empire. Foreigners were expelled, and "the foreign religion" prohibited. The Japanese of later days looked back upon that bloody chapter in his country's history, and learned to associate the "Yesu followers" with ideas of intrigue, rebellion, and things worthy of contempt. He held Christianity accountable for the evil actions of the men who professed it; and he regarded the edict-board which daily met his eye as a righteous barrier against the dangerous sect.

Three centuries rolled away, when at last Commodore Perry's ships appeared and again opened Japan to foreign intercourse. As in former years, the missionary accompanied the merchant and trader; but this time the light of the pure Gospel of peace began to break upon the darkened pagan empire. American missionaries settled at Nagasaki, and afterwards at Yokohama and other ports; they did not bring the altars, candles, and crucifixes of the Jesuits, but proclaimed the simple story of the Scriptures.

Great prejudices had to be overcome, however; the name of Jesus had long been misunderstood, and the ominous edict-board still prohibited the "evil sect." Little progress was made at first, for the people were afraid, or openly opposed to the new doctrines. Even as late as the year 1872, Japanese who attended my Bible-class in Shidz-u-o-ka said they were astonished to find Christianity such a good thing, and so pure and exalted in its teachings, for they had been taught from childhood that it was evil and corrupt. They were so glad, they said, to learn that it was the true religion, of peace and charity, rather than evil.

Long and patient labor was required before this popular prejudice could be even partially removed. In the progress of events, however, the odious law against Christianity was taken down from the public highways, by order of the government, never again to be replaced.

So great was the feeling of thankfulness and Christian exultation at this result, among foreign missionaries and others, that I obtained possession of the original edict-board which had so long hung up in my own Province of Suruga, and sent it home as a trophy and relic, to show friends in America the last vestige of religious persecution.

This weather-beaten board travelled eight thousand miles, by itself, and is perhaps the only one which ever left the country. After it had gone the local governor who had given it to me tried to get it back again; but I replied that Japan had no further use for the law, and that I had sent it to America for safe preservation!

The missionary work, which was slow and difficult at the outset, has received a new impulse within the past few years, and much good has been accomplished at the five open ports, and in some districts of the interior which Christian men have been able to reach. As the provinces have not yet been freely opened to foreign intercourse, however, most of the missionary interests still centre about Yokohama, and here many of the missionaries reside.

In March, 1872, Rev. Mr. Ballagh organized the first Protestant Christian church in Japan. The church edifice, now completed, stands in Yokohama, on a portion of the ground where Commodore Perry made his treaty in 1854; and the first thousand dollars given towards the erection of the church was sent by the Christian converts of the Sandwich Islands!

The following year, in 1873, a Christian church was organized in Tokio, on the same basis as the Yokohama church.

Converts gathered by the missionaries of various denominations made up the membership of these "union" churches; and the Japanese wisely adopted their own method of church government, adapting their Christian polity to the necessities and circumstances of their own country. This independent course, which is the reasonable one, will be followed by other churches yet to be established.

Native pastors and evangelists are at present being trained in a Union Theological School just started in Tokio. The only hope of completely evangelizing a country is by means of a native ministry who can preach the Word of God to their own people and in their native tongue. Foreign missionaries must lay the foundations, however, and may implant spiritual influences which will widen and strengthen in coming years.

The most interesting and successful missionary work I found at Yokohama is that of the "American Mission Home," situated on "the bluff" overlooking the beautiful bay and harbor. The "Home" was established by three ladies sent out by the Woman's Union Missionary Society, and aims to educate and train Japanese girls in Christian truth, teaching them the religion of Jesus, which elevates woman to a position she has never been permitted to attain in the pagan countries of the East.

I often visited the Mission Home and enjoyed its kind hospitality; bright faces and a warm welcome were sure to greet the stranger at the door. It was a pleasure to see all the comforts and refinement of a truly Christian home placed on Japanese soil, and to meet groups of little Japanese girls, bright and happy, enjoying all the privileges and instruction which love and Christian care could afford.

In the accompanying picture the grounds and main building of the Mission Home are given. The three ladies above mentioned are seen in the garden. Mrs. Pruyn, of Albany, is seated on the left of the grass plot; Miss. Crosby, from Poughkeepsie, is in the carriage; and Mrs. Pierson, of Chicago, is seated at the side of the house.

Opposite this building is a new school-house, not seen in the picture, in which the first Sunday-school in Japan was established. The week-day school was also held here, which always opened in the morning with religious exercises. It was a very pretty sight to see the children gathering

AMERICAN MISSION HOME.

with their books and slates for school, and hear them sing the opening hymn in English, and then in Japanese. Mrs. Pierson accompanied them on the cabinet organ. The scholars were very smart at their studies, and compared favorably with Japanese youth of the sterner sex. Sometimes I brought down my chemical apparatus from Tokio and showed them experiments, greatly to their delight. On questioning them afterwards, I found they always remembered the principles explained.

Adjoining the school-house is another building of two stories, recently completed; here the smaller children and orphans are cared for by Miss Guthrie, formerly of the Calcutta Mission.

At the extreme left of the picture Rev. Dr. Brown's house is seen, with a broad, sloping roof. Dr. Brown has been over eighteen years in Japan as a faithful missionary, and is at present associated with Dr. Hepburn and others in the translation of the Scriptures.

The noblest life-work of Dr. Hepburn has been the preparation of the Japanese-English dictionary, which is an invaluable aid to students and missionaries in acquiring a knowledge of the two languages.

The missionary field in Japan is in many respects pleasanter that in other countries of the far East, such as China and India. The Japanese are more sympathetic and cordial than the majority of Asiatic people, and the climate of the country is one of the finest in the world. The mission cause is in its infancy, however, and many laborers must yet be sent to sow the seed of future spiritual harvests. Noble men have labored here in the past, in the midst of danger and discouragement; and the record of modern missions in Japan, though brief, is filled with honest Christian endeavor and unselfish zeal.

A stranger might say, "What is the use of converting the Japanese people to Christianity?" It is often argued that they are well enough off in their present condition. As a people, they certainly excel us in politeness, gentleness, obedience to parents and superiors, and in social manners are our peers. They have also a culture and native refinement that surprises the foreigner; and their sense of honor is at least equal to that of the average American. Some of our customs, to them, are far from being desirable traits of civilization. The common people of Japan, with their simple wants and frugal ways of living, are at least as happy and contented as the corresponding class of society among us. Buddhism teaches them various virtues, restrains them from excesses, costs them little trouble or expense, and seems to meet their present religious necessities. Why, therefore, press Christianity upon their acceptance, causing them to relinquish all the sacred legends of the past?

Our reply is, that whatever culture may be possessed by the higher classes of the Japanese people, even their lives on earth would be better, their hopes brighter, and their passive existence elevated and quickened, by the incoming of Christianity. The religion we present to them is not a mere myth like Shinto, or a bewildering form of worship like Buddhism, nor yet a callous moral code like Confucianism. It is the very life of the soul; it breathes into men a new being, and warms the heart with a new glow of love to God the Father of all. In the face of Jesus Christ, it solves the baffling mystery of life, points to hope and happiness beyond the grave, comforts the sorrow-stricken and discouraged soul, and gives peace and even joy, in the midst of sufferings that all mankind are called upon to bear.

Above all, Christianity brings salvation. Leaving out of view the benefits and blessings derived from it in this world, it means deliverance from eternal death. This life is a very small thing, when compared with the life beyond; and the possibilities and privileges of that life for us, all centre in the person and work of Christ.

The Japanese belong to the same sinful, tempted, sorrowing race, as ourselves, and they stand in need of the same Redeemer. "And how shall they believe in him of whom they have not heard?" Or how shall they hear, unless the missionary be sent to proclaim the glad tidings? Christ's own command is, to carry the Gospel to every creature; and *he* well knew that every people on the earth had *need* of it.

We know not God's mysterious plan concerning the pagan millions who yearly pass into eternity, nor how far divine mercy and infinite compassion may be exercised in their behalf; but we *do* know that God's word commands us to carry the Gospel to every member of our guilty race, and that the divine presence is promised in so doing.

In glancing over a letter written when about commencing my bible-classes in Tokio, and when unusual difficulties appeared in the way, I find this statement concerning my students: "I confess that when the feeling floods upon me, that *these* are souls for whom Christ died, and *mine* is the privilege to make the fact known unto them, it breaks through all bounds of mere expediency, and forces me to speak the truth at all risks. . . . There is a solemnity beyond expression, in the attempt to bring before these young men the words of eternal life."

The very avidity with which the story of the cross was received by some, and the self-righteous air with which it was rejected by others, both served to show that at least grace and the Gospel were *needed*.

In Japan, as in every other country, some hear the word gladly, and believe; others listen with utter indifference, or openly refuse the way of salvation. At one moment the heart of the instructor would be gladdened by the words, "Sir, please teach us to pray by ourselves;" or, "Sir, these are golden truths, and we thank you for them." At the next moment, a curling lip, and a skeptical remark from another source, would show that seed was being sown on stony ground.

Light and shadow blend together in the missionary's experience, but still his duty is to "preach the word." I once saw this illustrated on a long trip with Rev. Mr. Ballagh, in our first attempt to ascend Fuji-yama. We were passing through a village near Oyana mountain, where a dread deity is said to reside. Here we encountered a procession of people dragging a huge cart with long ropes. Upon the cart was a pagoda-shaped tower, decorated with flags and streamers, in which were dancing men wearing hideous masks of foxes, demons, and ghosts.

Drums were loudly beaten, and the people shouted to drive away the evil spirits.

As the people caught sight of the two foreigners the procession halted and the drums ceased, for we were great curiosities in this out of the way region, and even the dancing foxes looked slyly at us.

Mr. Ballagh was always ready to seize an opportunity for sounding the gospel trumpet ; so, jumping upon a low balcony, he asked the people in a pleasant way what this all meant. They said it was the day set apart to propitiate the evil deity of the mountain, who sent all the woes and suffering upon the people, and little foxes to destroy their rice crops. This deity sometimes assumed the form of a great serpent, and naught could be expected from it but evil.

The missionary listened to their explanations, and then raising his voice said : " There is a serpent that brought evil into the world, and suffering upon the human race ; but he does not live in yonder mountain, nor can his cruel power be broken by noisy processions or the beating of drums." Then with great skill Mr. Ballagh told the story of the serpent in the Garden of Eden, and the temptation and fall of man, closing with the solemn question, " Is there no deliverance or salvation from the power of this evil one ?"

The people could not answer. Then he explained to them with great tenderness the wonderful plan of redemption; saying, that God had given a promise in Eden, which was fulfilled in Jesus Christ, and that now, all who believed on Him might be saved.

Immediately there was a division in the multitude; some were deeply moved, and wished to hear more, but the others beat their drums and called upon the people to take hold of their ropes and drag the cart and dancing foxes. The priests pulled the people away from the preacher, and the noisy but diminished procession went on its way, dragging with difficulty the heavy cart. A few remained and listened to the word with increasing interest, until I reminded Mr. Ballagh of the lateness of the hour, and we continued the journey.

A few days subsequent to this, I saw the same missionary go up to the open door of a temple, and by his winning eloquence, and fluency in Japanese, turn the assembly of Buddhist worshippers away from their idols. The next Sabbath the priests of this temple came to our hotel, and listened for two hours to an earnest presentation of Christian truth!

It would be a pleasure to give a lengthened sketch of missions in Japan, but I have not space to do so in this little work. I will, therefore, close this chapter with a few explanations of the accompanying plate, of the Lord's prayer in Japanese.

It is a fac-simile of Matt. vi : 9–13, in the gospel recently issued by the Translation Committee at Yokohama. The orginal of this plate was prepared in New York, by the American Bible Society ; and it is the fairest specimen of printing in Japanese that I have seen produced outside of Dai-Nippon.

In reading the prayer, a person should commence at the right-hand column and read downwards. Some of the characters are seen to be square and more compact than the rest. These are Chinese words, which are introduced into the writings of Japan in the same way that Latin terms are frequently used in English. In this case, each Chinese word is explained by a few simple Japanese characters, written in small type on the right margin. This is necessary to enable the common reader to properly understand the meaning.

The Chinese literature has been studied as a classic for many centuries in Japan ; but only the Samourai, or two-sworded men, were permitted to become scholars, also the priests. The common people could only read the simpler forms of pure Japanese, which language remained quite unde-

主の祈禱　馬太傳第六章九節より十三節にいづる

天にましませるわれらが父よねがはくは御名たふとまれさせたまへ御國きたらせたまへ聖旨の天になるごとく地にもなさせたまへ我らの日用の食を今日もあたへ給へ我らに罪ををかすものをわれらがゆるすごとくわれらのつみをもゆるしたまへ我らを惡におとしいれずそれよりすくひいだしたまへ國と權能と榮光は爾のものなることかぎりなく有りたまふものなればなり アーメン

veloped. In publishing the Scriptures, therefore, to the people, a difficulty arises from the lack of a suitable language, which may be equally well understood by all. If the missionaries translate the Bible with the frequent use of Chinese characters, it places it entirely beyond the use of the masses; though its literary merit is elevated in the eye of the Samourai, so that it claims scholarly respect. If it is translated in the purely Japanese dialect, it becomes simple and apparently childish, and has little merit with the higher class; in fact, it is impossible to properly express spirtual truth in a language so immature, and so filled with crude mythological terms as the pure Japanese.

The translators are forced, therefore to strike a balance between the literary or classic language, and this simple but insufficient Japanese vernacular. This is accomplished by using as few Chinese terms as possible, and then explaining them in the margin so that common people may understand. Hence the use of the small letters to which I have referred.

I wish this Lord's prayer could be circulated in the country by thousands of copies, for it is a gospel in itself, and no tract more appropriate could be issued. Nothing appears less understood to a Japanese mind than the nature and meaning of prayer. This "talking to God" is a great mystery, and I was frequently called upon in my Bible-classes to explain, or attempt to explain, how we could reasonably and hopefully look to the Invisible One and say, "Our Father which art in heaven."

Some of my students once asked me to please write a prayer for them ; and what could better meet their wants in this respect, than that which came in response to the humble request of the early disciples, "Lord, teach us to pray."

CHAPTER XII.

FAREWELL TO JAPAN.

Shortly after returning from the trip to Kioto, I was called upon to bury my faithful servant Sam Patch.

It was somewhat remarkable that he died exactly three years from the day I first engaged him, and that *my* contract with the Japanese Government expired about the same date.

Though an associate of humble capacity, Sam was faithful in his own little sphere, and he was the only individual who remained uninterruptedly with me during my sojourn in the country. He had been unwell before I started on the Kioto trip, and I sent him to the Tokio hospital, where he had good care. But he was imprudent in leaving the hospital too soon, so as to have my house in good order on my return.

I sent him back to the hospital, and visited him one evening, and took to him the sad news that he must shortly die; for his diease—the "kaki," a kind of dropsy peculiar to the Japanese, was approaching his heart. The poor fellow was never very brave, and he cried a little ; for he thought he was getting better. I tried to comfort him with his Christian hope, and then bade him good night. The next day he was dead, and when I came to the house where he had been removed, he was already placed in the Japanese coffin !

To give some idea of the Japanese mode of treating the dead, I will briefly state how Sam's remains were disposed of ; but his case differs from others, in that I gave him a Christian form of burial, becoming his former Christian profession and the simple trust in Christ which he seemed to have to the last.

Immediately after death, and before the body became rigid, he was placed in the ordinary square coffin, with head bowed and knees doubled up and crossed in front, causing him to occupy a space so small as would appear incredible. When I first went into the room it was nearly midnight, and I had a flickering candle in my hand. Seeing a box scarcely three feet square in the corner of the room, I was told that it contained all that remained of poor Sam. Raising the lid, I glanced in and saw what appeared a shapeless bundle, with hand or foot projecting here and there; and this was the comfortless manner in which the Japanese usually bury their dead.

Sam's face, when raised, was calm and natural, and in his hand was a Testament which I had given him the year before, and which his wife had placed there to be buried with him, though whether at his request or not I do not know.

The little funeral occurred the following day, and I telegraphed Rev. Mr. Ballagh to attend; but as he was out of town, Rev. Mr. Thompson officiated, using the Japanese language. At the conclusion of the service, the hearse, which is a temple-shaped cart, five feet high, backed up to the door, and the sides and roof being taken off, the square box was pushed inside. The hearse was then put together again by piecemeal, and two old men drew it off, amid the sobs of some and the smiles of others.

Then came the queerest funeral procession in which I ever participated. Sam's wife and another woman were placed in a jinrikisha behind the bier; and then came my friends, Mr. and Mrs. Arthur, who had been very kind to Sam during his sickness, and finally Nakamura and myself brought up the rear in a third jinrikisha. Slowly this droll procession moved up the main street or Tori of Tokio, attracting great attention, from the fact that no foreigners had ever been seen with such a curious structure as that on the cart, and the people were at a loss to know what such a funeral-train meant.

The place of burial was two miles and a half distant, and I tried to hurry the old men who drew the temple-cart. But they were either too lazy or too dignified to run, and the big cart was very heavy, owing to its large roof. At last we moved on at a jolting rate, that nearly shook the hearse and its contents to pieces. The road seemed interminably long, and it was dark when we reached the ground of the large temple in the suburbs of the city, where I had secured a plot, and caused a grave to be dug that morning.

I had intended burying Sam beside my interpreter Shimojo, who had died the year previous, and whose tomb was not far from this spot. But strict regulations had recently been issued respecting the burial of persons within the city limits. Therefore I accepted Nakamura's offer to bury Sam beside the tomb of Nakamura's ancestors at the temple just mentioned, situated beyond *Khristien zaka*, or "Christian slope."

Arriving at the temple, I stopped the hearse at the main gate, and hurried forward to see if the grave had been dug as I directed. Fumbling my way through the compact rows of ancient monuments and head-stones, in the gathering darkness, I stumbled on the freshly turned earth, and found the deep square hole prepared as had been promised.

Coming back I met Mr. Arthur who found that the grave-yard was so cold and damp that it would be imprudent in his state of health to remain longer. So I thanked him and his good and amiable wife, and advised them to return, saying that it was too chilly for them, and I would bury poor Sam alone. (My good friend Mr. Arthur died of consumption only a year or two after this.)

Bidding them good night, I turned towards the temple, and was surprised to find it illuminated, and to hear a Buddhist service going on within. Stepping up to the porch and entering, I found a tastefully decorated apartment with mats and polished floors, and solemn-looking labyrinths beyond the dark line of pillars. Two finely robed priests sat upon a raised dais before the altar, intoning their prayers in a rapid and measured way, which struck me as being a funeral dirge; they took no notice of me as I stood in the shadow of the hall, looking on. The altar was a beautiful object, ablaze with tapers and shining with the gilt idols and golden leaves of the lotus lilies. Incense was burning before it in a bronze brazier, and the pleasant fragrance slowly filled the temple. But what attracted my attention was the white covered square box, placed directly in front of the altar, with a tall stick or tablet standing against it, having a name written upon it in Chinese, which I could not understand. Of course I knew that this box contained a dead person, but *who* it was I did not at the moment imagine.

I was simply awaiting the removal of my own box from the hearse, and certainly intended no heathen rites to supplement the Christian service already held. But getting suspicious finally that "something was up," I stole by the priests and went silently up to the altar.

There, sure enough, was *my* box, with Sam's body in it, for it had the same bunch of flowers and bamboo reed upon it, which had been placed on the lid. My first impulse was to stop the service; for, without my knowing it, they had brought the body in, while I was in the graveyard, and had commenced their heathen rites as usual. As I afterwards learned, the *sinjo*, or present of money, which I had previously given the priests, made them polite and particularly anxious to do the thing up well.

As I looked at the priests, and then at Sam's wife and the other woman kneeling on the floor, who seemed to be taking great comfort in the ceremony, I thought I would let it continue, especially as we were the only persons in the temple. I sat upon a mat under the shadow of a pillar, and for once the Buddhist service seemed solemn to me. The priests intoned finely and earnestly, the little bells chimed in harmoniously, and now and then a deep-toned drum broke the strain of the continual repetition of " Na-mi-ho Ho-ren-gi-ko."

I knew that Sam would not have highly indorsed this service himself, neither was it exactly compatible with the doctrines of the Testament within the coffin which stood before the heathen altar. Nevertheless, there was a novel interest in the scene, and as the service was soon completed, the chief priest bowed, and led the way to the cemetery, still repeating strange sounds, and wearing his silken robes. The bearers followed with the square box, which was safely lowered into the grave. The cemetery was lit up by the glare of the torches and lanterns ; and as the priest retired I leaned upon a gravestone, and waited to see the grave properly filled.

A man was still in the hole, and I saw him striking the box with his shovel. On being asked what he was doing, he replied that it was sometimes the custom to break in the head of the coffin and fill it with earth ! I told him he might dispense with that operation this time, and fill up the grave immediately, which he did.

Thus ended poor Sam's earthly career. His widow sent me a request for money to buy incense to burn before the tomb.

Over Sam's remains I caused a stone cross to be raised, upon which were inscribed the simple words, SAM PATCH.

My engagement with the Japanese Government was twice renewed at shorter intervals of several months, but as I did not feel that my life-work was to be in Japan, I made preparations toward the spring of the year to start homeward.

I arranged to leave in March, as I supposed I could then accomplish my long-desired tour through India before the hot season fairly commenced in that country. In this latter respect I was mistaken, however, for I fell into the very hottest season of the tropics.

On March 7th I met many of the students of the Kaisei Gakko, at a farewell gathering held in Dr. Veeder's house, as my own house was now in disorder with packing-boxes and trunks, and we all spent a pleasant evening together.

At the close I made the students a little speech, expressing my sorrow at parting, and giving them encouragement and hope for the future. I urged them to continue diligent both in their scientific and their religious studies, and to attend the Bible-class which Dr. Veeder had now opened for them, and which would continue the work of Sabbath-evening instruction.

They all seemed to feel deeply in reference to my departure, and also manifested no little awe at the formidable journey before me. One student, who was a most regular attendant upon my Bible-classes, but who formerly opposed Christianity, said to me, "Sir, we shall never meet again in this world, but .I trust we shall meet in heaven." He then asked me to write my name and his own in a Bible and hymn-book which I had given him. Another student said, "Sir, you have taught us great and beautiful things, both in science and in religion; and we are very thankful, and will never forget your kindness." Others said, "We wish you a happy time in your long voyage, and we know not where we may ever see you, but we hope *somewhere*."

Such expressions as these were heart-warming, and showed that the Japanese students were still as kindly affectionate and grateful as I had ever found them during nearly four years' intercourse and instruction.

At the close of the evening a short prayer was offered, and the students sung a hymn.

The next day, my American friends General and Mrs. Williams gave me a farewell dinner, at their elegant residence near the Treasury Department. I then paid my parting respects at the American Legation, and started for the railroad station.

At the Tokio depot quite a little ovation was given to me, which was at once a surprise and a delight. Over one hundred students walked two miles to the station to bid me good-by; they were accompanied by the second officer of the Kaisei Gakko, who made me a pleasant little speech. I told some of the students of the first scientific class that I should expect to meet a few of them in New York when I arrived there from Europe. The prophecy seemed like a dream to them, but it was fulfilled a year later, and they were really studying in the Columbia School of Mines when I arrived in New York.

It was a moment not to be forgotten when the space was cleared between myself and the cars, and I passed through the line of students and jumped upon the train. After bidding them a final "saionara," the whistle sounded, and half an hour later I found myself in Yokohama.

The day following, Hatakéyama, the director of the college, came down from Tokio, and gave me another farewell dinner at the Grand Hotel. He was very kind, and as affectionate as ever. I spent the last hour on shore in talking over "old times" with him, and in making plans for the future. He said that he would meet me the second time around the world at the Centennial Exhibition in Philadelphia, and that he would come *viâ* San Francisco.

He subsequently fulfilled his promise in coming to America, but I missed him by just one day in New York, and afterwards failed in seeing him at the Centennial. He was very sick at the time, of consumption, and started homeward shortly afterwards, *viâ* Panama. But he died on the Pacific, a few days before the steamer reached his native land; and though he was a member of the Christian church, he was buried in a Shinto cemetery in Tokio, with the most imposing pagan honors!

Thus one after another of my Japanese friends have been taken away by death.

The steamer Behar sailed from Yokohama at four o'clock. I was accompanied on my journey by Mr. and Mrs. Ballagh, and Mrs. Pruyn, of the Mission Home, who were going as far as Nagasaki to see me off. I also gave my chemistry assistant a trip to Kobé, and then sent him to Kioto.

The voyage to Kobé was not so rough as the one previously described, and the sail through the inland sea of Japan was delightful. The passage of the inland sea occupied a little more than twenty-six hours, and was fully as varied and beautiful as we anticipated. It contained all the panoramic effect of river scenery with the vastness and solemnity of the sea. At one point it broadens into bays and gulfs, stretching away as far as the eye can reach; and at another it tapers down to such narrow limits that there scarcely seems room enough to pass. As one island after another was left behind it still revealed an open stretch of sea beyond, and each bay and inlet had so many branches, that it appeared an unlimited archipelago, combining the beauties of the country with the wildness and majesty of the ocean.

The provinces bordering the inland sea have always been populous, and in old feudal times many strong castles towered in defiance along these shores. Some of their white walls and deserted parapets could still be seen, glistening through the dark-green foliage. Usually a large town or village would be seen nestled on the shore near the castle.

The eastern entrance of the inland sea is opposite the Ozaka Bay, and is simply a narrow strait not a mile in width. The western or lower entrance is situated at the Straits of Shimonoseki, which may be seen on the outline map, opposite Corea. Our steamer stopped at the town of Shimonoseki some hours, and we all went ashore and rambled over the hills. But the place is of no particular importance, except that it was here that the old Japanese forts were located which fired upon certain foreign ships a few years ago, and thus gave rise to the "Japanese indemnity." No great harm was done, however, and our government had no right to force Japan to pay $700,000 into the U. S. Treasury.

In olden times a very important naval battle was fought near this point by Japanese junks filled with armed men.

South of Shimonoseki, the city of Saga will be seen on the map, where the insurrection quelled by Okubo occurred, and where he beheaded my young friend Katski. This minister Okubo has himself since been assassinated in Tokio, and buried at the same Shinto cemetery as Hataké-yama.

At the south-western extremity of Japan is the city of Nagasaki, which has been open to foreign intercourse longer than any other point. To reach this place from Shimonoseki we passed through the straits into the open sea, rounding a bleak and rocky coast, until we came in sight of the coal islands of Taka-Shima, which stand near the entrance of Nagasaki Harbor. On sailing up the narrow and cliff-girt harbor we passed close beside the rocky islet of Papenburgh, from whose steep heights the persecuted Christians were once thrown into the sea. The harbor is a narrow arm of the sea, stretching eight miles inland, and not more than a mile in breadth. It is completely enclosed by broken ranges of hills, diversified at the upper portion of the harbor by cultivated fields, shrubbery and trees, native houses and huts, foreign residences, myriads of junks, and all that characterizes a native and foreign settlement. Long lines of shipping usually lie at anchor here, including steamers and men-of-war. The city contains about 33,000 inhabitants.

I only had a few hours to spare at Nagasaki, for here I was to bid farewell to my companions. The afternoon was rainy, and I spent it in tramping around with my friend Rev. Mr. Stout, a missionary of the Reformed Church. We both wore rubber coats and boots, and with such an excellent guide I soon visited the chief points of interest. We explored "Dezima," or made-land, a square enclosure of three acres at the water's edge, where the Dutch traders lived during the two hundred years in which they alone were allowed commercial intercourse with Japan. It was decidedly suggestive of the olden times to walk around these Dutch-looking buildings, and the stone warehouses which line the water front, and think of the sober, old-fashioned Hollanders who used to pace back and forth here at eventide,

JAPANESE SUMMER-HOUSE AND GARDEN.

smoking their pipes, and watching for their ships from Holland.

In the suburbs of Nagasaki we visited some very pretty gardens and summer residences, where I purchased a few pictures, while Mr. Stout talked pleasantly with the people. The grounds were laid out in the ordinary Japanese style, with gold-fish ponds, foot-bridges, dwarfed trees, and airy pavilions, like that seen in the accompanying illustration.

Behind the native quarter of the city there is a temple with groves and immense camphor-trees. The trunk of one of these trees measured thirty-five feet in circumference. Here are buried five hundred and eighty soldiers, or nearly all of those who perished in the recent Formosa expedition. Most of them died in sickness, and only a few in battle. Their graves are ranged in rows of twenties and forties, and the regular lines of tombstones, divided off into sections or companies, present a sad and impressive appearance.

The last place visited was the Roman Catholic chapel, located half-way up the hill-slope, and facing the valley of Ura-Kami, where so many Christian converts were persecuted. The interior of the chapel is dim and solemn, and well calculated to impress the Japanese converts with awe. Near the altar were two colossal paintings, representing scenes of martyrdom at the time of the severe persecutions at Nagasaki. One of these pictures in vivid colors the crucifixion of some two hundred converts at once, upon the mountain of *Campeera*, "God of the sea," a bold bluff overlooking Nagasaki Harbor. Beyond this mountain there are boiling sulphur springs, called by the natives "Little Hell." Into a large open pool, boiling and steaming like a natural cauldron, it is said that Christians used to be cast who refused to give up their faith. With these horrible vats, and the rugged precipice of Papenburgh at command, the persecutors did not lack in natural facilities for torture.

But the hour for my departure drew near as evening came on. I took tea at Mr. Stout's, and spent the early part of the evening with my friends. Mr. Ballagh and other missionaries kindly gave me a "general epistle," commending me to the various missionary brethren I might meet on the long journey before me. Then I was committed to the watchful care of Providence, and amid mingled feelings of regret and hopeful anticipation I bade my friends farewell.

As I reached the steamer, all was quiet on board, and the rain-drops were pattering on the slippery deck. The night was dark, and the wind whistled mournfully through the rigging as I went below. At early dawn the steamer was sailing down the harbor, bound for Shanghai, China. The Japanese sun-flag floated at the stern, for the vessel belonged to the new Japanese line of the "Mitsu-Bishi" Company.

I looked out of the cabin window at the murky waters of the Yellow Sea, and realized at last that I was face to face with all the dread uncertainties of a long and lonely journey around the world.

www.ingramcontent.com/pod-product-compliance
Lightning Source LLC
Chambersburg PA
CBHW022053230426
43672CB00008B/1155